PRAISE FOR

Borderline Personality Disorder Demystified

"Dr. Friedel offers a scholarly, compassionate, and wise book that will enlighten people with borderline personality disorder and those who love them. Drawing from his longstanding commitment to their care and inspired by his life-long devotion to his deceased sister, Friedel's perspective on borderline patients is uniquely well-informed and heartfelt. Readers will find it reassuring to learn that, contrary to what many people believe, this disorder is both understandable and treatable."

—John Gunderson, MD

"Every page of *Borderline Personality Disorder Demystified* flows with compassion and hope for clinically diagnosed borderline patients and their family members. The author's cogent summarization and analysis of the latest research-based information is critically needed in this time of increasing public awareness. Even more importantly, Dr. Friedel's willingness to share his own heartfelt personal story will help give a sympathetic face to this much misunderstood disorder that causes untold suffering for millions of people."

—Randi Kreger, coauthor of *Stop Walking on Eggshells* and the *Stop Walking on Eggshells Workbook* and owner of BPDCentral.com

"Dr. Friedel provides a concise and nicely organized compendium of the latest, up-to-date information on everything you need to know about the medical causes and treatment of borderline personality disorder. This book is easy to read and filled with useful information and engaging vignettes."

—Larry J. Siever, MD, professor of Psychiatry and director of the Mood and Personality Disorders Research Program at Mt. Sinai Medical School

"Dr. Friedel has personally cared for patients with BPD, conducted significant pharmacological research with patients with the disorder, and organized numerous national symposia to teach others about this illness. As readers will discern as they move through this volume, Dr. Friedel has 'lived' with the problem and brings it clearly to light."

—S. Charles Schultz, MD, Professor and head of the Department of Psychiatry, University of Minnesota

"Help at last! People with borderline personality disorder, their families and friends can now easily understand this perplexing medical-neurobiological condition and how to find help for it. Dr. Friedel has condensed decades of research and clinical experience into this information-packed book. Readers will be delighted with chapters on diagnosis, possible causes, disturbed neural circuits, medications, psychotherapy, and a hopeful future."

—Bernard D. Beitman, MD, professor and chairman of the Department of Psychiatry, University of Missouri at Columbia

"This book should be required reading for everyone with borderline personality disorder and for the families, spouses, friends, and mental health professionals who are involved with them."

—Kenneth R. Silk, MD, professor and associate chair, Clinical and Administrative Affairs, Department of Psychiatry, University of Michigan Medical School

"Dr. Friedel's book uniquely demystifies the challenging clinical puzzle that is borderline personality disorder, resulting in a much-needed message for patients and their loved ones—there is hope—and the scientific data is emerging to back it up!"

—Warren T. Jackson, PhD, ABPP, Borderline Personality Disorder Program, Department of Psychiatry and Behavioral Neurobiology, University of Alabama at Birmingham

"This is a clinically rich and honest description of borderline personality disorder that allows us to experience the devastating effects of this illness on the lives of the people who have it as well as their families. It will help those with borderline personality disorder understand not only their illness, but themselves."

—Steven Secunda, MD

"Truly, as Dr. Friedel states, in dealing with this condition, 'knowledge is the edge.' And knowledge is precisely what he has provided so well in this book."

—Don R. Schulte, MD

"Borderline is a complex and heterogeneous disorder, but Dr. Friedel succeeds in weaving a coherent story that demystifies the disorder for the reader."

—Hagop S. Akiskal, MD, Professor of Psychiatry and director of the International Mood Center, the University of California, at San Diego

"This book is a great guide for patients and the people close to them. It will also help professionals working with these patients improve their knowledge of and therapeutic interventions for the disorder."

—Sabine Herpertz, MD, Aachen Technical University, Germany

ROBERT O. FRIEDEL, MD, is Distinguished Clinical Professor of Psychiatry at Virginia Commonwealth University (MCV/VCU) and professor emeritus at the University of Alabama at Birmingham (UAB). He received his undergraduate and medical degrees from Duke University, and completed a medical internship and residency in psychiatry at Duke, with an intermittent two-year period engaged in research at the National Institute of Mental Health in Bethesda, Maryland.

Most recently, Dr. Friedel was the Heman E. Drummond Professor and chair of the Department of Psychiatry and Behavioral Neurobiology at UAB. He has also served as vice chair of the Department of Psychiatry at the University of Washington, chair of the departments of psychiatry at Virginia Commonwealth University and the University of Michigan, executive director of the Mental Health Research Institute at the University of Michigan, and senior vice president and director of Research, and a member of the Board of Directors at Charter Medical Corporation.

Dr. Friedel has founded Borderline Personality Disorder Clinics at UAB and at MCV/VCU. He now directs the MCV/VCU Clinic. His research interests have focused, in part, on the biological basis of borderline personality disorder, and on developing effective pharmacological treatments for patients with this disorder.

In 1999, Dr. Friedel was appointed founding editor-in-chief of the journal *Current Psychiatry Reports,* and in 2003 the cofounding editor-in-chief of *Current Psychosis and Therapeutics Reports.* He serves on the Scientific Advisory Board of the National Education Alliance for Borderline Personality Disorder, the editorial board of the *Journal of Clinical Psychopharmacology,* and is a member of a number of professional and scientific organizations. Dr. Friedel has published over 100 scientific articles, book chapters, and books.

Borderline Personality Disorder Demystified

AN ESSENTIAL GUIDE FOR
UNDERSTANDING AND
LIVING WITH BPD

Robert O. Friedel, MD

*Foreword by Perry D. Hoffman, PhD,
Dixianne Penney, DrPH, and
Patricia Woodward, MAT*

MARLOWE & COMPANY ■ NEW YORK

BORDERLINE PERSONALITY DISORDER DEMYSTIFIED: *The Essential Guide to Understanding and Living with BPD*

Published by
Marlowe & Company
An Imprint of Avalon Publishing Group, Incorporated
245 West 17th Street • 11th floor
New York, NY 10011

AVALON
publishing group incorporated

Library of Congress Control Number: 2004108703

ISBN 1-56924-456-1
ISBN 13: 978-1-56924-456-2
9   8

Designed by Pauline Neuwirth, Neuwirth and Associates, Inc.

Printed in the United States of America
Distributed by Publishers Group West

In memory of Denise

∞

CONTENTS

FOREWORD

I T IS OFTEN difficult for people with borderline personality disorder to receive an accurate and timely diagnosis, and to find an effective treatment program staffed by clinicians knowledgeable about the disorder. It has also been difficult to find supportive psychoeducational programs that provide patients and their families help and guidance in understanding the symptoms and treatments of the disorder, and in establishing a well-informed support network. Finally, it has been difficult to find authoritative and comprehensive information written specifically for lay people on the disorder.

Indeed, it was this lack of services and information that led to the organization of the National Education Alliance for Borderline Personality Disorder (NEA-BPD) by an experienced professional and by family members and consumers whose lives had, often after many painful years, reached the point where they could commit to helping others. Founding members came together to formulate a mission "to raise public awareness, provide education, promote research on BPD, and enhance the quality of life of those affected by this serious mental illness."

We believe the attitudes of patients with borderline personality disorder, their families, and their clinicians make a significant difference in the quality of life of all involved. Knowledge of the disorder, its symptoms, nature, causes, and treatments, can help people make well-informed and highly effective decisions and plans. *Borderline Personality*

Disorder Demystified provides a broad spectrum of such information to individuals with BPD, their families, and their mental health clinicians.

As Dr. Friedel notes in the Introduction, this book began life as a handout for his patients with borderline personality disorder, and for their families. It gradually expanded in detail and depth over the years, often as the result of reader input. We believe an important feature of the book is that the text is written so that lay people can readily understand and absorb the information, even in times of crisis.

The information in *Borderline Personality Disorder Demystified* has been of help to the patients who have entrusted Dr. Friedel with their care and who participated in his research, and to their families. We at the National Education Alliance for Borderline Personality Disorder join him in the hope that by offering the book to a wider public, others will find this information a basic building block in their quest to better understand borderline disorder.

The NEA-BPD has enjoyed the privilege of helping to ready *Borderline Personality Disorder Demystified* for publication. Those who attend Dr. Friedel's Borderline Personality Disorder Clinic, and their families, have had the benefit for many years of having the information in this book available to them, and we have been pleased to play a part in widening its readership.

Perry D. Hoffman, PhD
Dixianne Penney, DrPH
Patricia Woodward, MAT
National Education Alliance for Borderline Personality Disorder

INTRODUCTION

I T'S UNFORTUNATE THAT information about borderline personality disorder is not more widely distributed and commonly known. There's much more information available about medical disorders such as cystic fibrosis, muscular dystrophy, and multiple sclerosis, diseases that are far less prevalent than borderline personality disorder. People who suffer from these diseases benefit greatly from the information that is available to them. This knowledge helps them see that they have a well-defined illness and that others share their condition. It also enables them to understand the nature and causes of their illness, and to realize that physicians have well-researched and effective treatments for their illness. It's reassuring to know that scientists are conducting research to better understand the causes and to develop more effective treatments, and even cures, for these diseases.

Until recently, this has not been the case for borderline personality disorder. It's estimated that approximately 2 percent of the general population suffers from this condition. That amounts to approximately six million people in the United States. Although recent research has raised some questions about this number, it's still safe to say that women are three times more likely to develop borderline personality disorder than men. That means about one out of every thirty-three women may suffer from the disorder. Many people with borderline personality disorder don't realize that their symptoms and problems are the result of a real medical condition, rather than a lack of willpower or personal frailties. Many physicians and other health workers are not as aware of this disorder as they are of less-common diseases, so the diagnosis of borderline personality disorder is often missed and the person is deprived of effective treatment.

An unfair stigma has developed about borderline personality disorder, even among mental health professionals, which adds to the mystery and perception of the illness. This stigma is based on several different myths about the disorder:

- **Many people believe that the symptoms and behaviors of people with borderline personality disorder should be entirely under their control.** This is not the case. To a significant degree, borderline personality disorder is the result of disturbances in brain pathways that regulate emotion and impulse control. In other words, this is a true medical disorder and, basically, is no more under one's control than diabetes or hypertension.
- **There are some health professionals who don't believe in the validity of a borderline personality disorder diagnosis because of the wide variety of symptoms and the frequent overlap of symptoms with other disorders.** However, there is now a large body of research that indicates that borderline personality disorder is a valid psychiatric diagnosis.
- **There is a general sense of pessimism about the effectiveness of treatment.** This myth is prevalent because many health care workers do not know enough about the treatments that have been shown to be most effective. There is no denying the fact that treating someone with borderline personality disorder can, at times, stretch the clinical talents of even the most experienced and skilled psychiatrist. It can be a difficult disorder to treat, but the important thing to know is that it *is* treatable.

One unfortunate result of these myths is that there has been a lot less research devoted to borderline personality disorder compared to other medical illnesses of similar severity and importance to society. This situation is now improving with increased funding for research on the disorder from the National Institute of Mental Health and from private research foundations.

Despite the fact that these myths are not true, they persist. Therefore, a lot of people with borderline personality disorder believe that they are alone and, as the result of inaccurate diagnoses and ineffective treatments, they believe there is little that can be done to help them. Because of the chronic, recurrent, and episodic nature of their symptoms, and the additional problems they experience, they, their families, and their friends lose hope.

Why I Wrote This Book

I had many reasons to write *Borderline Personality Disorder Demystified*, but ultimately it came down to two. First, there is an urgent need for more factual information on borderline personality disorder for people with the disorder, for their families and friends, and for health care professionals who treat patients with the disorder. Second, one of my sisters suffered from borderline personality disorder, so I know both professionally and personally how devastating it can be. It's important to me to try to help.

Over the course of my clinical work and research in the area of borderline personality disorder, I've realized that very few people who suffer from the disorder understand very much about what's wrong with them, and what can be done to help them gain control over their lives. This is true even for people who have received many years of psychiatric care.

When I explain to my patients what borderline personality disorder is all about and what can be done to help them, they generally feel extremely relieved and become much more hopeful about their future. The same is true of their families, who have tried, usually with little success, to help and to cope with the affected family member. As a result of these experiences, I realized that there was simply not enough time during treatment sessions for me to personally explain to each of my patients with borderline personality disorder and to their families all of the information that would be useful to them, and that would answer many of their questions. So I decided to write a handout that provided much of the important information they typically asked of me. As my patients and their families read the handout, they made suggestions on how to add to and otherwise improve it, and it grew in length.

Several months ago, the leaders of the National Education Alliance for Borderline Personality Disorder, a prominent lay advocacy group and important educational resource (see Resources, p. 219), read a copy of the handout and suggested that I add some more material and make it available to a wider group of readers. They also made their own suggestions on how to improve the content. It struck me that turning the handout into a book would give me an opportunity to expand the information so it would include even more topics of interest for people affected by borderline personality disorder. Many people want to know the origins of the name and concept of "borderline personality disorder." Some ask about the evolving and rapidly expanding research on the disorder. Still others want to read more detailed accounts of people with borderline personality disorder, or need information on how and where to obtain professional help and other services.

Who This Book Is For

I wrote *Borderline Personality Disorder Demystified* primarily for people who have the disorder. The information in this book will give you a better understanding of the symptoms, causes, and nature of borderline personality disorder; the indications, effectiveness, and risks of various methods of treatment now available; some guidance on how to make critical decisions about your treatment program; how to locate resources for additional help; and much more.

This book is also intended to provide useful information to others who are affected by borderline personality disorder, especially family members, spouses, and friends of those who suffer from the condition. Finally, this book is meant to help mental health clinicians, and physicians in other medical specialties who encounter patients with borderline personality disorder in their practice.

The ultimate purpose of this book is to help restore hope to people with borderline personality disorder, and to their families and friends. There is good reason to be encouraged. More scientific articles have been written about borderline disorder over the past decade than in all previous decades combined. The new technologies of modern medical research are now being used to study the problem. Information from this research has shed new light on the causes, nature, symptoms, and treatments of borderline personality disorder. More physicians are becoming aware of borderline personality disorder and learning how to treat it effectively.

Don't Lose Hope

If you have borderline personality disorder, please do not lose hope. Be persistent in your efforts to find a psychiatrist, or another physician or mental health professional who understands and is trained to treat people with borderline personality disorder. Participate actively in the development of your treatment program, and then stick to it. If the treatment program doesn't seem to be effective, or if you are experiencing side-effects to medications, discuss these problems with your doctor. Ask for and accept the help and support of your family and friends. Work with them, because they are an important part of your life and can play a significant role in your continued improvement.

It takes great courage to struggle on with the symptoms of borderline personality disorder, but do so with the knowledge that others have persevered and have been rewarded by gaining much more control over their lives than they ever believed possible. You can too! I believe that the information in this book will help you in your quest to do so.

How This Book Is Organized

There is a considerable amount of information in this book, so I've organized it in such a way that you can read the chapter or section that is most important to you at any given time. Perhaps you want to start out slowly and concentrate only on the first few chapters. Or maybe you're most concerned right now with understanding the causes of borderline personality disorder, or about the different methods of treatment. If you're a family member of someone with borderline personality disorder, you'll probably refer most often to the chapter written specifically to help you. At other times, it may be the chapters on the biological nature of the disorder, or about scientific research in the field. In order for you to easily find what you're looking for at any time, you can refer to the following brief descriptions of each chapter.

From this point forward, I use the term "borderline disorder" instead of "borderline personality disorder" to refer to the condition. I do so because "borderline disorder" is a less cumbersome term, so it will help facilitate your reading, and also because I've had many patients tell me that the term "borderline disorder" is less offensive to them and helps them to accept the fact that they have this medical disorder.

Chapter 1: What Is Borderline Personality Disorder and How Is It Diagnosed?

Borderline disorder is characterized by four groups of symptoms: (1) poorly regulated emotions; (2) impulsivity; (3) impaired perceptions and thinking; and (4) disturbed relationships. This chapter describes in detail the specific symptoms and characteristics of borderline disorder.

Chapter 2: You Are Not Alone

When you have borderline disorder, it's often hard to believe that others also suffer from the same painful feelings and experiences that have plagued you. In this chapter, I tell the stories of two people with borderline disorder in order to help you feel less isolated and to help you better understand the disorder. The first story is about my younger sister Denise, who was the first person I knew with the disorder. The second story is about "Mrs. Davis," one of the first patients I treated with borderline disorder. Throughout the rest of the book, I comment on specific episodes of their stories and of those of other patients with borderline disorder, in order to illustrate and clarify important points.

Chapter 3:
The History of Borderline Personality Disorder

This chapter will give you a clear understanding of the origin and meaning of the term "borderline" and key historical landmarks in clinical and scientific thinking about the disorder.

Chapter 4: What Are the Causes?

There are a number of misconceptions about the causes of borderline disorder. This chapter clarifies some of these misconceptions and describes the biological and environmental factors that put people at risk for it.

Chapter 5: Tracing the Course of the Disorder

This chapter describes the symptoms of borderline disorder as they may emerge and evolve from adolescence to old age, and how these symptoms are affected by changing events and relationships throughout life.

Chapter 6:
Borderline Personality Disorder and the Brain

The brain is vastly more complex in every respect than other body organs. However, we now know enough about it to begin to describe the brain circuits and some of the chemical signal transmitters that seem to be affected in people suffering from borderline disorder. Some of this information is provided in this chapter.

Chapter 7: Common Co-occurring Disorders

Borderline disorder appears to make people with the disorder vulnerable to a number of other mental disorders. In some instances, it may be misdiagnosed as one of these disorders, and therefore not treated. In other cases, the diagnosis of other disorders may be mistaken for the symptoms of borderline disorder, and those disorders not treated properly. This chapter reviews the disorders most commonly associated with borderline disorder and their distinguishing features.

Chapter 8: The Key Elements of Treatment
Chapter 9: Medications
Chapter 10: The Psychotherapies

These three chapters describe the strategies involved in the effective treatment of borderline disorder. They include the selection of a primary clinician, the proper level of care during the treatment process, the use of medications if they are needed, and the choice of the most appropriate type of psychotherapy.

Chapter 11:
Borderline Personality Disorder in Children

Some controversy exists among experts in the field about the diagnosis and treatment of borderline disorder in children. In this chapter, I discuss the current thinking on this problem, and provide parents of children who may have borderline disorder with guidelines to help their child.

Chapter 12: When A Loved One Has Borderline Personality Disorder

This chapter is written for people who have a family member or spouse who suffers from borderline disorder. A family member with this condition can cause many serious problems and conflicts in the family. It's fortunate that there are now sources of help available to you so that you are better able to act effectively and supportively, both during times of major crises and during times of calm. Ten guidelines on how best to respond to specific situations are provided.

Chapter 13: Research: The Ultimate Reason for Hope

Much of what is known by the medical community about borderline disorder has been learned over the past two decades as the result of research. This chapter will describe some of the main advances in our knowledge and opportunities that are being explored, and will provide you with some suggestions on how you can help advance research on borderline disorder.

I've also included a resource section that has a comprehensive list of organizations and groups that offer information and support to patients, families, and friends with borderline disorder and related illnesses. The glossary lists medical terms used throughout the book that may not be familiar to you, but that are important to your understanding of this book and your condition. The first time these terms appear in the book, they will be in **boldface**. Finally, there are references to information about borderline disorder that I discuss in this book. References are organized by chapter and by section so that you can locate them easily.

ONE

What Is Borderline Personality Disorder and How Is It Diagnosed?

THE CAUSES OF borderline disorder often vary in type and degree from one person to another, so it makes sense that the symptoms also vary considerably in type and severity. Nonetheless, once the basic symptoms are understood, it usually becomes apparent to the individual and family that borderline disorder is present, and that it's a major contributor to the difficulties they are experiencing. Simply recognizing that you *have* borderline disorder is the critical first step in gaining control over your life.

From what we can gather, borderline disorder is the result of physiological and chemical disturbances in certain pathways in the brain that control specific brain functions. You may be born with these disturbances, or they may be amplified because of events that occur after birth. Estimates are that borderline disorder affects as many as 2 percent of the population. It appears to be more common than schizophrenia and bipolar (also known as manic–depressive) disorders. For reasons that are unclear, borderline disorder seems to occur more frequently in women than in men, by a ratio of 3 to 1. Therefore, about one of every 33 women and one of every 100 men suffer from the disorder.

The Symptoms

In order to be diagnosed with borderline disorder, you must experience and demonstrate a minimum of five of the nine symptoms listed in Table 1.2 on p. 19. These symptoms are separated into four different groups, or, as experts in the field of personality disorders refer to them, **behavioral dimensions**.

TABLE 1.1

The Four Groups of Behavioral Disturbances in Borderline Disorder

1. Poorly regulated emotions
2. Impulsivity
3. Impaired perception and reasoning
4. Markedly disturbed relationships

Most people with borderline disorder don't have all of the symptoms in each of the four groups of disturbed behaviors, but most do have at least one symptom from each group. Many of my patients find that the arrangement of the symptoms of the disorder into these four groups makes it easier for them to understand their symptoms and the consequences.

Group 1: Poorly Regulated Emotions

A number of experts in the field believe that difficulty in regulating emotions is the driving force behind many of the other symptoms of borderline disorder. If you have borderline disorder, your emotions may change quickly and you may find it difficult to accurately perceive and express your emotional responses, especially to unpleasant events. Most often, you may overreact emotionally. However, at other times your emotional responses may seem blander than the responses one would anticipate from the average person, only to be followed by hyperemotional reactions at a later time. Here are the major symptom indicators of poorly regulated emotions.

Mood Swings and Unstable Emotions

The emotions of people with borderline disorder are often very unstable and undergo rapid changes that they have difficulty controlling. This is referred to as **emotional lability**. These labile emotions can include negative feelings of anxiety, anger, fear, loneliness, sadness, and depression. Less often, these emotions can also include positive feelings such as happiness, joy, enthusiasm, and love. Your emotions may fluctuate quickly from feeling good to feeling bad, sometimes for reasons that are obvious to you, but at other times for causes that are not apparent. Because of these rapid fluctuations in mood, and because you are more likely to develop feelings of depression and episodes of *major depressive disorder* than people who do not have borderline disorder, at some point you may have been diagnosed as having bipolar disorder (previously referred to by psychiatrists as manic-depressive disorder).

Your feelings may also be **hyperreactive**, that is, you may seriously overreact emotionally to some situations. For example, you may become very upset over criticisms, separations, or disagreements that other people seem to take in their stride. Such events may cause a wave of anxiety, sadness, anger, and desperation. In addition, you may find that you have great difficulty calming down your emotions and soothing yourself by focusing on reassuring thoughts or by engaging in usually pleasant activities. During these periods of severe hyperemotionality, or "emotional storms," as they're called, you may feel so desperate that you turn to alcohol or drugs for relief, lash out in anger or rage, or engage in other destructive behaviors.

Recent research also suggests that people with borderline disorder have more difficulty in accurately identifying the emotional responses of other people and in balancing mixed feelings, and have more intense responses to the negative emotions of others than people who do not have the disorder. For example, you may find that you become very upset when something bad happens to someone else. You may even feel that it is almost happening to you. You may also react strongly to the plight of others, such as their living situation, their handicaps, or any other negative aspect about what's happening with them. One patient told me that at such times "it is like someone is putting a dagger in *my* heart." This person also told me that the situation did not even have to be happening to real people; it could occur if she were watching a movie or even a television commercial. She knew the situation was not real, but she felt as if it were and that it was happening to her. She added that at these times, the pain from her emotional involvement in these situations lasted for quite some time. This is another characteristic of poor emotional control in borderline disorder. Emotions do not return to their normal level as quickly as they do in people who don't have the disorder.

You may also be hypersensitive to the real or perceived negative behaviors of others toward you, always on the lookout for the slight frown, raised eyebrow, or minor change in a person's tone of voice that indicates that they are irritated or angry with you. When you believe you detect such critical reactions, not matter how subtle, your response may often be way out of proportion to the situation. You may feel anxiety, self-recrimination, and anger that are simply not warranted under the circumstances. You may be vaguely aware that you are overreacting, but the feelings are just too real and too strong to ignore.

Anxiety

Episodes of severe anxiety are common symptoms of borderline disorder. One of the first psychiatrists to write in detail about borderline disorder believed that "anxiety is the motor" that drives the other emotional symptoms of the disorder such as anger, and behavioral symptoms such as impulsivity. Anxiety can produce tension-related physical symptoms including migraine headaches, backaches, stomach pains, irritable bowel, rapid heartbeat, cold hands, hot flashes, and excessive sweating. Anxiety may even reach the level of the massive and disabling but fairly brief symptoms referred to as **panic attacks**. More often, the anxiety is more pervasive and may last for hours to days. Or the anxiety may quickly be replaced by anger, despair, and physical symptoms. You may also attempt to relieve the anxiety through impulsive behaviors I discuss below.

Inappropriate Intense Anger or Difficulty Controlling Anger

Poorly controlled anger is very common and causes significant problems in people with borderline disorder. You may feel irritable and angry much of the time, and often can be argumentative, quick-tempered, and sarcastic. You may even become furious, sometimes enraged, in circumstances that do not warrant such responses. The slightest event or exchange can result in an angry outburst. You may then say and do things that are very destructive, and later regret that you did so. Recent research has shown that people with borderline disorder have greater changes in anger and depression than other people, and that they may fluctuate between anger and anxiety more readily as well.

You may realize in the midst of your rages that you are overreacting, but seem unable to control the strong emotions that are sweeping over you. As one patient put it, "I know my husband does not deserve all the anger and abuse I heap upon him, but he's the one around most of the time. I don't seem to be able to control the anger. At the time, I think he deserves it—so he gets it." Your family, your spouse if you are married, and others close to you have learned that they must be very careful about what they say or do. Many say "It's like I'm walking on eggshells all the time. I never know what I will do to cause her (or him) to blow up." This apprehensiveness on the part of your family can result in a persistent low level of tension in your home. Since you may be very sensitive to the negative feelings of others, this can make an already tense living situation even worse.

Chronic Feelings of Emptiness

Another strong feeling you may experience is a sense of persistent emptiness. This sense of emptiness is often accompanied by feelings of boredom and loneliness. In turn, these feelings may lead to dissatisfaction with the people in your life, and with your life in general. Dissatisfied with your life, you may be prone to change friends and jobs frequently, and even to engage in brief affairs. For a time, these changes can feel very exciting and temporarily relieve the emptiness, loneliness, and boredom. However, the feelings return after a while, and the life patterns of inconstancy repeat themselves. One young patient told me recently, during our initial meeting, that these feelings of emptiness and boredom were so strong that she felt as if she had a big hole inside her that wouldn't go away. It did diminish when she was involved in a relationship with a young man, at least for a while, then would return in full force when they fought or when he left her. She added that, when severe, this feeling was so emotionally painful she would do almost anything to relieve it, even cut or burn herself, although the emotional pain always returned shortly thereafter.

Another patient, whom I describe in more detail in Chapter 2, told me early in her treatment that when she felt empty and bored for a long period, she would leave her husband without notice and travel to another city. There she would see a former teacher for a brief two- or three-day affair, then fly home again. Although she temporarily felt excited, desired, and satisfied by these escapades, ultimately she was plagued by guilt and remorse for her behavior, and she dreaded having to deal with her husband about her absences. Nonetheless, the pattern continued until she was able to understand the nature of the feelings and the life situations that triggered this behavior, then to take measures to gain control over it. Fortunately, her husband was able to tolerate the behavior until she was able to develop alternative and much more effective responses to the emptiness and boredom she often felt.

Group 2: Impulsivity

The tendency toward impulsive, self-damaging behavior is so common and so strong in people with borderline disorder that some experts in the field consider it the most important problem in the disorder. They believe it is more important than the symptoms of emotional instability and impaired reasoning, because impulsivity appears to be the best predictor of the long-term outcome of the disorder. Those people with borderline disorder who are very impulsive tend to have a much worse **prognosis** than those who are not as impulsive. Research suggests that impulsivity in people with borderline disorder is the result of an imbalance between those **neural** systems (nerve cell pathways that control specific behaviors) that regulate emotions, impulse control, and reasoning. Research has also shown that impulsive behavior is present to some degree in most people with borderline disorder. Following are the major groups of symptoms within the broad category of impulsivity.

Impulsive Behavior that Harms You

If you have borderline disorder, there are many ways that you could behave impulsively, such as binge eating and spending money recklessly on clothes or other items. You may also engage in other more serious impulsive acts like uncontrolled gambling, excessive drinking and drug abuse, sexual promiscuity, and violent, aggressive acts. You may also commit illegal acts such as speeding and shoplifting.

For example, when one of my patients felt especially anxious and empty inside, she would go shopping at expensive stores and steal clothing and other items, even though she could afford to buy them. Before these actions could be brought fully under her control, she was arrested for shoplifting and was convicted of a felony. When another patient felt particularly neglected and abandoned, or was criticized by her husband, she would go to bars, drink excessively, and strike up conversations with men in an attempt to feel better about herself and to "get even" with her husband. These episodes would occasionally lead to brief sexual indiscretions that were very destructive to her self-esteem and to her relationship with her husband. These episodes also exposed her to a considerable risk of being seriously harmed, as she knew little of the men she picked up, and she did not protect herself properly from sexually transmitted diseases.

There is a lot of research on the commonness and importance of impulsive behavior in people with borderline disorder. However, there is a scarcity of research on the events and warning signs that lead up to such behavior, and on why some people with borderline disorder are more impulsive than others. In general, impulsive behaviors often follow episodes of emotional storms and disruptions in close relationships, especially real or threatened abandonment. They also appear to be more common in people with borderline disorder who have been physically or sexually abused as children. In order to fit this particular diagnostic criterion, you need to exhibit impulsive behavior in at least two of the self-destructive ways I mentioned above.

Recurrent Suicidal Behavior, Gestures, Threats, or Self-Mutilating Behavior

This is a particularly striking group of impulsive symptoms that occurs among many, but by no means all, people with borderline disorder. They are referred to as **parasuicidal acts**. The severity of these behaviors ranges from very serious acts that may inadvertently be life-threatening, to threats that are often attempts to control a situation, gain attention, or seek help. You may physically hurt yourself by hitting yourself, cutting or scratching your wrists and arms or other parts of your body, burning yourself with cigarettes, or taking overdoses of medications. At times, you may do these things in the desperate desire to have others take care of you, or to "get even" with them, or to get your way. More often, you may hurt yourself in order to help reduce the emotional pain you frequently feel when it reaches an intolerable level. As one patient who frequently cut her thighs with a razor blade explained to me, "When I see the blood and feel the pain, somehow the pain and dead feelings inside go away for a while and I'm again back in control and in contact with the world."

This symptom of borderline disorder is very distressing to family members in particular. It's also such a striking type of behavior that it has been dramatized in movies. For example, the character played by Glenn Close in *Fatal Attraction* demonstrated this and most of the other symptoms of borderline disorder. She engaged in cutting behavior twice in the movie. In an early scene, she cut her wrists when the character played by Michael Douglas attempted to end their relationship. This persuaded him not to end the relationship then, and to make sure that she received the proper medical care. In the final scene of the movie, she absently poked at her leg with the point of a knife until it bled while she was talking with his wife before attacking her. For dramatic purposes, this movie presents the symptoms of borderline disorder in their most severe form. You should realize that by no means is this the typical behavior exhibited by most people with borderline disorder.

I often ask patients who engage in self-injurious behavior when they recall first doing so, from where did they get the idea to do it, and under what circumstances did it first occur. Their answers are frequently quite similar. The first event usually occurred when they were teenagers; it was often in response to a serious fight with parents or the threat of abandonment by a boyfriend or girlfriend. Surprisingly, most of my patients cannot account for what prompted them to commit such an unusual act; the idea just came to them. Once done, the immediate rewards of the decrease in emotional pain and the increase in attention were quickly realized. These two responses to their actions rapidly reinforced the behavior and made them increasingly likely to do it again in response to periods of high stress and emotional turmoil. I think it's remarkable that such behavior should occur spontaneously to a young person. I don't believe that the idea to hurt oneself in these ways and under these conditions spontaneously occurs to most individuals.

There is no single symptom of borderline disorder that indicates with certainty that a person has the disorder. But if you engage in self-injurious behavior of the types mentioned, I recommend that you see a psychiatrist who is well trained and experienced in borderline disorder in order to determine if you have the disorder.

Munchausen's Syndrome

A very striking and serious form of self-injurious behavior that may occur in people with borderline disorder is Munchausen's Syndrome, also known as a **factitious illness**. People with this disorder hurt themselves intentionally, but in a way that looks like a *bona fide* medical problem. For example, they may place a drop of blood in their urine to make it appear they are bleeding from their urinary tract, or create a serious skin infection and then seek medical help. Tests are then performed to determine the mysterious nature of the illness, often over a great length of time and at great expense. During these episodes, the person receives a considerable amount of medical care and attention.

Many people with Munchausen's Syndrome have some direct familiarity with the medical profession, and they are quite knowledgeable about the symptoms and signs of diseases that are especially difficult to diagnose. More dramatic cases involve severe self-injurious behavior such as injecting a vein with infected material, thus causing widespread infections of unknown origin throughout the body that require extensive medical evaluation and treatment. In the extreme, people with Munchausen's Syndrome that are highly knowledgeable about the practice of medicine are able to produce symptoms that result in multiple unnecessary operations.

Munchausen's by Proxy

A particularly severe sub-type of Munchausen's Syndrome is Munchausen's by Proxy. In this disorder, one parent of a child, usually the mother, will repeatedly inflict a medical illness on the child, and will then seek medical care and attention for the child. In this way, she will also receive attention, support, caring, and sympathy from medical professionals, family, and friends. Tragically, some of these children die before the correct cause of their illnesses is discovered. Again, I want to emphasize that Munchausen's Syndrome and Munchausen's by Proxy occur only in a small percentage of individuals with borderline disorder. However, when these serious conditions are recognized, it's essential that borderline disorder be considered as a strong contributory factor. Unfortunately, if the underlying problem of borderline disorder is missed and not treated, the behaviors will likely continue, regardless of the potential medical, legal, and personal consequences. However, if the diagnosis of borderline disorder is made and the person enters treatment, there is hope for recovery.

Suicide

The most extreme case of self-injurious behavior is suicide. It's important to understand that some people with borderline disorder *do* intend to commit suicide. If you have borderline disorder, you may have already thought of ending your life. You need to recognize the difference between hurting yourself for the reasons I discuss above and the presence of a significant risk of suicide. You can learn to determine early in the progression to suicide that you are at risk for doing it. The first stage in the process is having the thought that life is not worth living, that it's simply too painful. The next stage is thinking about suicide itself, at first occasionally, then more and more frequently. You may then find yourself planning how you would do it. This is a dangerous stage in the progression toward suicide, as the next stage is the final one, the suicide attempt itself.

Certain circumstances increase your risk of suicide. If you have borderline disorder and engage in highly impulsive acts, especially the abuse of alcohol or other substances, your risk of suicide, based on historical data, is between 4 and 9 percent. Whether or not you fall into this very high-risk category, if at any time you recognize the above symptoms of the suicide process, or you do not feel safe for any reason, you need to know how to get help quickly. I will discuss some ways for you to do so at greater length in Chapter 8.

> **IF YOU** believe you are at risk for attempting suicide, you should immediately contact your physician, if you have one. If not, or if you can't get through, call the closest hospital emergency room, or dial 911.

There are a number of other reasons why you may be at high risk for suicide. For example, major depressive disorder and bipolar disorder are very common in people with borderline disorder. They carry a high risk of suicide in any patient with the problem who is not treated for it. I discuss these disorders in detail, and how they relate to borderline disorder, in Chapter 7. In addition, those people with borderline disorder who abuse alcohol or drugs, who engage in self-injurious behavior, or who were physically or sexually abused as children or teenagers are more likely to commit suicide than those with the disorder who have not had these experiences. Not surprisingly, those who are most impulsive are most at risk.

Finally, when you go through many suicidal gestures and acts of self-injurious behavior to reduce emotional pain and to deal with difficult situations, it is very easy to overlook a real threat to safety. Remember *The Boy Who Cried Wolf?* There's a reason why that fable has endured for so many generations and in so many cultures. You need to realize that repeated parasuicidal acts may result in your physician and family mistaking your reports of a real suicidal situation for parasuicidal behavior, and not getting you the emergency help you need. So it's essential that you learn how to stop parasuicidal behaviors. (The specific treatments for parasuicidal behaviors are described in Chapters 9 and 10.) It's also important that the clinicians and families of patients with borderline disorder learn the *risk factors* for suicide in borderline disorder and take great care to remain constantly alert to the risk of suicide in patients with the disorder.

Group 3: Impaired Perception and Reasoning

People with borderline disorder often say that they have difficulty with their memory, especially under stress. You may also misperceive experiences, expecting the worst from others, even when nothing negative is intended. You may have difficulty with your concentration, and with organizing your thoughts and behaviors. You may not be able to think a complex problem through adequately and determine reasonable alternatives, and the consequences of these alternatives. These difficulties with the perception of important events, thinking, and reasoning may result in faulty decisions that could have highly detrimental consequences. Although these problems are not listed as such in the diagnostic criteria for borderline disorder, they have been shown to be present in people with the disorder through careful neuropsychological testing, and they constitute important features of the disorder.

For example, problems in remembering and reasoning seem to be related to the emotional state of most individuals, whether or not they have borderline disorder. Most of us have had moments when we're unable to clearly recall the details of an event when under great emotional stress, such as a house fire, a dangerous automobile accident, or an incident that provoked severe anger. We realize that our reasoning ability at these times is also impaired. When we are at the point where we panic or are very angry, we don't seem to be able make as rational and thoughtful decisions as we do otherwise. That's why professionals such as soldiers, physicians, policemen, and firemen, who are often exposed to life-threatening situations, are carefully selected and highly trained to remain calm and to carry out specific procedures under these conditions. At these times, they must not panic and engage in inappropriate responses. However, if you have borderline disorder, you may have difficulty with memory, thinking, and decision-making even in the face of only minimal stress. Your tolerance of stress is often much lower than it is for people without borderline disorder.

We have already discussed the difficulty that people with borderline disorder have in the area of emotional control. Therefore, it is not surprising that you may have difficulty in participating in reasonable conversations to solve problems when you are in a hyperemotional state, or to remember accurately the content of these situations afterward. In other words, the emotional hyperreactivity common in borderline disorder often gets in the way of normal reasoning in social or interpersonal situations. This difficulty in social reasoning seriously impairs your learning and developing the skills you need to have mature, successful, and sustained personal relationships. The section below on *impaired relationships* deals with this problem in more detail.

Brief Episodes of Paranoid Thinking

Research shows that people with borderline disorder are more likely to expect others to behave badly toward them than people who do not have the disorder. When exposed to severe stress (usually criticism), or imagined or real abandonment, when under the influence of alcohol or drugs, or when treated with certain classes of stimulants such as **amphetamine**, or with certain antidepressants, some people with borderline disorder become very suspicious and have difficulty thinking rationally. Brief episodes of **paranoid thinking** may occur, when they falsely believe that others are planning harm against them. These episodes may last from a few hours to several days, or even longer. Very rarely, people with borderline disorder may experience **hallucinations**, such as hearing strange voices, music, or other sounds.

Dissociative Symptoms

You may notice that there are periods of time during which you can't recall what you said or did. These are called **dissociative episodes**. At their extreme, dissociative episodes can be so severe that the person actually splits off part of their feelings, thinking, and behavior, and temporarily creates one or more separate personalities. When this occurs, it's referred to as multiple personality disorder. Multiple personality disorder is experienced by an unknown but probably small percentage of people with borderline disorder.

Magical Thinking

In addition, you may have odd thoughts, such as unrealistic and **magical thinking**. Magical thinking is the use of highly unrealistic thoughts and beliefs to solve the challenges and problems in your life. For example, you may believe that somehow you will become a lawyer or architect, although you barely succeeded in completing high school. You may believe you have a sixth sense or are even clairvoyant.

Depersonalization

You may have episodes of depersonalization during which you feel unreal, as if in a dream, and strangely detached from the world, or outside of your body. Or your body may feel numb or hollow. An unusual example of depersonalization was reported to me by a patient. She said that at times she has incorporated characters and situations from books or television into her thinking, as if these characters or incidents were real.

Unstable Self-Image or Sense of Self

You may frequently feel that you have little self-worth, and that your self-concept depends mainly on the attitudes and behaviors of people close to you. If they seem loving and attentive, you feel good about yourself. But their criticisms may cause you great anxiety, feelings of worthlessness, and despair. Regardless of what you have accomplished, it doesn't seem to counterbalance the opinions of others. In other words, you may feel as if you have little *self*-esteem, that your esteem is almost totally dependent on others.

You may often feel unsure of who you really are, what values you truly believe in, what career you should pursue, what causes you should support. You may have difficulty in feeling "centered," and in developing a constancy of purpose in your life that serves to stabilize and to give integrity and predictability to your peace of mind and behavior. As one patient put it, "I feel as if I too easily adopt the characteristics of the people I am with. I am desperate that they like me. I adopt their mannerisms, their way of speaking, and their attitudes, even the ones that I don't usually agree with. Other people's opinions of me are much more important to me than my own opinions and convictions. I feel as if I have an emptiness inside of me that only other people can fill."

This tendency at times to be overly flexible in one's values, attitudes, and preferences in order to please others may even extend to sexual relationships and result in multiple heterosexual and even homosexual encounters. Especially when under stress or the influence of alcohol or drugs, it may seem that your central beliefs do not hold, and your internal touchstones are not enough to guide you to the appropriate courses of action. I want to emphasize that the presence of these qualities is a characteristic of borderline disorder and *does not* mean that you are without morals or convictions. People with borderline disorder just don't seem to be able to withstand the very strong need for approval. However, there may be times when you swing to the other extreme. Then, you may be very critical, inflexible, and dogmatic about certain beliefs, to the point that you offend people around you. As a result of these difficulties, it's understandable that you may do better in stable, highly structured situations, especially with people whose behaviors and personal values are solid and stable.

Group 4: Markedly Disturbed Relationships

Given the three groups of symptoms of borderline disorder I've already described, it's not surprising that your life may be marked by tumultuous relationships. Usually, the closer the relationship you have, the greater the turmoil. During childhood and early adolescence, the major problems in relationships usually occur with parents, other family members, teachers, and friends. Later in adolescence, difficulties can also occur with boyfriends or girlfriends and, in adulthood, with spouses, children, co-workers, and employers.

A PATTERN OF UNSTABLE AND INTENSE PERSONAL RELATIONSHIPS

You may have noticed that you fluctuate dramatically and quickly in your feelings and attitudes toward those people who are very important to you. At times, you may perceive someone to be more wonderful than anyone could reasonably be; capable of making you feel happy, safe, important, and alive under any circumstance. In other words, you unrealistically overvalue and idealize this person who is so central to your sense of well-being. You may find that you cling, almost desperately, to these people and worry continually about their well-being. You may even call them often to reassure yourself that they're all right because you believe *your* well-being depends so much on them.

Of course, no one is able to live up to these unrealistic standards for very long. Then, disappointed that the relationship cannot stabilize your feelings and life, you may have an abrupt change in attitude that moves too far in the other direction. For example, after a small slight, you may perceive the other person to be uncaring, unsupportive, selfish, and even punitive, to a much greater degree than is actually the case. In doing so, you devalue the importance of that person, finding fault with them at every turn. You won't be able to tolerate this situation for very long, so you may abruptly swing back to the other extreme, only to find that the cycle repeats itself, over and over again.

A Black-and-White Life

Many people with borderline disorder report that they see themselves, other people, and the world in general as black or white, as good or bad, and they have great difficulty in dealing effectively with the gray areas of relationships. These gray areas, of course, constitute the vast majority of human interactions. You may have a hard time accurately weighing positive characteristics and behaviors against ones that you don't like, in part because you often over-respond emotionally to negative actions, and also because of your difficulty in social reasoning.

Consequently, it may be quite difficult for you to reach a well-balanced and reasonably integrated opinion about people, especially those important to you. This makes it difficult for you to deal with important relationships in positive ways that enable you to adapt well to the reasonable frailties of other people. It follows naturally that you may also find it very difficult to determine effective ways to have others adapt well to your own shortcomings. To some degree, this may be because, when you're symptomatic, you believe unrealistically that your difficulties are mainly the result of the behaviors of other people, not your own.

Frantic Efforts to Avoid Real or Imagined Abandonment

People with borderline disorder find themselves caught in a bewildering, frustrating, and stress-provoking dilemma. On the one hand, you may have a strong, often unrealistic and uncontrollable fear of being abandoned. Even brief separations from people who are important to you and on whom you are dependent are very traumatic and may result in a severe flare-up of your symptoms. On the other hand, you may have an equally strong fear at times of becoming too closely involved with another person, of losing your fragile sense of individuality and self-control, or of being hurt should the relationship go badly. You may feel as if you are going to fall apart or cease to exist if you become too close to other people.

For example, one patient complained to me frequently that her husband was away in class or studying much of the time, leaving her alone. When she felt he was away too much, she felt abandoned, anxious, and angry. At these times, she wouldn't go to work, which put her job in jeopardy, or she had brief encounters with another man, which placed her marriage at great risk. She spent months looking forward with great anticipation to a vacation she and her husband had planned where they would drive across the country together. By the third night of the trip, she felt so confined and trapped in this situation that, while her husband slept, she left their motel room in the middle of a rainstorm, dressed only in her nightclothes. After walking several miles along a deserted road, she came to a telephone booth and somehow managed to call me. Only after considerable discussion was she able to gather herself together and return to the motel and her husband, and to complete the trip. When they got home, she returned to feeling anxious, lonely, and angry much of the time because he was away from her so often.

For some people with borderline disorder, the issue of separation, abandonment, and aloneness can be even more complex than this example. As one patient explained to me, "Sometimes I have an impulsive desire to be alone, to move far away from everything and everyone I know. I don't think it's because I'm afraid of becoming too close to someone, or that I will lose my individuality. This impulse occurs when I have strong feelings of anger, hopelessness, or even regret and shame. I feel that I've messed up this life and want to start a brand-new one, in a place where I can't get into trouble again. Most of the time I realize that these very strong feelings and this impulse are unrealistic. I know my difficulties would simply go with me. But at the time, the feelings seem very real and escape seems the best solution."

TABLE 1.2

Diagnostic Criteria for Borderline Personality Disorder

THIS TABLE lists the symptoms of borderline disorder as described in the *Diagnostic and Statistical Manual of Mental Disorders* of the American Psychiatric Association. This is the official listing of mental disorders prepared by experts in each disorder under the auspices of the American Psychiatric Association. It includes the diagnostic criteria for each of these disorders and is considered the "gold standard" across most of the world. According to the definition of borderline disorder in this manual, people with the disorder have a broad spectrum of symptoms, listed below, but each individual does not necessarily have all of the symptoms listed.

A pervasive pattern of instability of interpersonal relationships, self-image, and affects, and marked impulsivity beginning by early adulthood and present in a variety of contexts, as indicated by five (or more) of the following:

1. Frantic efforts to avoid real or imagined abandonment. Note: Do not include suicidal or self-mutilating behavior covered in Criterion 5
2. A pattern of unstable and intense interpersonal relationships characterized by alternating between extremes of idealization and devaluation
3. Identity disturbance: markedly and persistently unstable self-image or sense of self
4. Impulsivity in at least two areas that are potentially self-damaging (e.g., spending, sex, substance abuse, reckless driving, binge eating). Note: Do not include suicidal or self-mutilating behavior covered in Criterion 5
5. Recurrent suicidal behavior, gestures, threats, or self-mutilating behavior
6. Affective instability due to a marked reactivity of mood (e.g., intense episodic dysphoria, irritability, or anxiety usually lasting a few hours and only rarely more than a few days)
7. Chronic feelings of emptiness

8. Inappropriate, intense anger or difficulty controlling anger (e.g., frequent displays of temper, constant anger, recurrent physical fights)

9. Transient, stress-related paranoid ideation or severe dissociative symptoms

Source: *Diagnostic and Statistical Manual of Mental Disorders,* Fourth Edition (Text Revision), American Psychiatric Association, Washington, DC, 2000.

TWO

You Are
Not Alone

OVER THE YEARS, many of my patients have told me that they realized there was something different about them, or something wrong with them, when they were very young. Regardless of the specific way in which they thought they were different, and how their lives eventually seemed to confirm these differences, the end result is the same. They feel that no one truly understands them and they feel painfully isolated. If you have borderline disorder, you may feel this way too, that you are alone and at the mercy of the symptoms that plague you, your emotional storms, your impulsive behaviors, your self-doubt, and your tumultuous relationships. You may believe that these problems separate you from everyone else. Even worse, you may believe that you have caused or deserve this condition.

In this chapter, you will read the stories of two people with borderline disorder. I hope that these stories will help you understand that you are not alone. These stories are very personal to me. One is of my sister Denise. The other story is of "Mrs. Davis," one of the first patients with borderline disorder who I treated. In order to maintain confidentiality, I have changed a few details in her story.

These details are unimportant to our purposes here, but they might serve to identify her. Of course, I have not used her real name.

Although you will see similarities in these stories, there are significant differences as well. Somewhere in these stories, I think you may recognize some features of your own life.

Denise

My sister Denise was born a year and a half after I was. I can't recall, with any clarity, specific memories of her as a child. Photos of her during this period, and stories told to me by my parents and relatives, seem to blur out personal recollections. But given the purpose of this story, it's probably more fitting anyway to begin with some of the memories of a central figure throughout Denise's life: our mother.

As I described in Chapter 1, pervasive feelings of emptiness and a negative self-image are among the main symptoms of borderline disorder. In the next chapter, I discuss the early opinions proposed by psychoanalysts that these symptoms are the result of poor nurturing by a mother incapable of providing warmth and affection to her children. It's difficult for me to reconcile that idea with the reality of my own mother. One of my most vivid memories of my mother was the way her face would light up whenever she saw one of the family. It made me feel good to my core to be caught in the radiance of her smile and the warmth of her embrace. I would watch her bestow the same love on every member of our family, down to the youngest great-grandchild, and watch them respond as I did. There was never any doubt: she loved us all deeply and unequivocally.

Everyone seemed to understand this except Denise, who often appeared uncomfortable with Mom. Of course, my mother knew this too. Later in her life, she tried to explain to me why she thought Denise was often so unhappy and had so many difficulties. She believed that the main cause of Denise's problems was that Mom had received a mild anesthetic during her delivery and that the medicine had affected Denise's brain. She had not been given an anesthetic during the delivery of my older brother or me, and she certainly refused any during the births of our sister and brother born after

Denise. When I asked her why she believed this so strongly, she said it was because Denise behaved differently than the rest of us from the day she was born. She went on to explain that, by comparison, she cried more, did not eat as well, was more easily upset by any change in routine, and was more difficult to soothe and comfort when she was upset.

In her early childhood, Denise clung to my mother when relatives or neighbors would visit. She frowned a lot and didn't smile warmly or often. I believe there is only one picture taken of Denise as a child when she was smiling. It was the only childhood picture of her that Mom would display. Years later, Denise told me that as a child she always felt that she was different from the rest of us, that she was more anxious and less happy. She also believed that Mom and Dad loved her less than they loved us, and she resented it.

Denise's difficulties became more apparent as she grew into adolescence. Her disposition and behavior worsened. Most obvious and most disruptive to the family were her outbursts of anger that could rapidly grow into full-blown episodes of destructive rage. When this occurred, nothing was safe. She would lash out verbally and physically at all of us, including Mom and Dad. My sister Beatrice, younger than Denise by two years, was a frequent target of her anger and abuse. Denise would also throw or break anything at hand, even pieces of Mom's fine china. Particularly disturbing was the fact that no amount of reasoning or appropriate threats of punishment, or even punishment itself, seemed to have any effect on these or future outbreaks. If anything, discipline seemed to make the situation worse. To the rest of us children, it appeared as if there were two standards of behavior in the family: one for us, and the more lenient standard for Denise.

Not surprisingly, the family thought Denise was simply willful, and we hoped that she would grow out of it. We were worried, though, because she also had episodes of anxiety accompanied by complaints of severe stomach cramps that kept her from school. When she was anxious, she would wring her hands and twist and pull strands of her hair to the point that she developed bare spots on her scalp. The doctor reassured my parents that Denise was just "high-strung."

When I think back on those years, I remember two incidents that changed my impression of, and my attitude toward, Denise. We were in our mid-teens when they occurred. At the time of the first, it was winter and there was snow on the ground. I was cleaning my golf clubs in preparation for the spring, but one was missing. I looked everywhere in the house—no club. Denise walked by, so I asked her if she had seen it. She calmly said yes, she had broken it in two and thrown the pieces into the snow behind the house. It seemed we had argued over something a few weeks earlier, and she had done it then. At first, I thought she was taunting me. She knew how hard I had worked and saved to buy those clubs. Surely no one would do such a thing, not even Denise. Then I remembered the broken china. Even though to me, at that age, there was little comparison between the value of a golf club and fine china, I knew how much my mother valued it. Later, when the snow melted and I found the broken club, I realized that something was truly different about Denise, and that it was probably best not to provoke her in any way, for any reason.

My impression that Denise had serious problems was reinforced a few months later. In the midst of a big argument with Mom, Denise impulsively announced that she was leaving home. This was a new threat, so Mom didn't know how to handle it. Not that it would have made any difference, because Denise was out the door in a few moments. When she didn't come home for dinner that night, my mother and father left in the car to find her. Given the drastic lengths to which she would go when angry, I did not think they would locate her until she was ready to return home. That turned out to be two days later. Denise had found a small church that remained open all night and she stayed there, existing only on water. She then came home, explained where she had been, and life went on as before. She was about fifteen years old at the time. After that, I don't recall ever having another serious argument with Denise. Over the years, we grew very close to one another.

One of the things that perplexed us about Denise was how well she seemed to do between her episodes. During these periods of relative calm, she would excel in school, be pleasant, caring, and even fun at home, get along with her friends, and make the high school cheerleading squad. Yet it all hung on a thread. Within moments, it could be gone. At her best, she was bright, creative, sensitive, beautiful, and intent on doing good things for others in this world. What a shame it was that she could not remain at that level consistently.

Denise tried many ways to hang on, to stabilize her life. After high school, she commuted with Dad to New York City to work for the same company as he did for about a year. That seemed to go fairly well for a while, but she then became bored and dissatisfied. Her demons were still plaguing her.

Ultimately, she decided she needed a quieter, more structured and disciplined life. So, at the age of nineteen, she entered a Catholic convent. For the first year, Mom and Dad received a letter from her each month, and visited her once a month. As I read these letters now, it strikes me that this may have been the most tranquil period of her life. After five months in the convent, Denise wrote:

It just doesn't seem possible that it's been that long since I left home and yet in other ways it seems to me that I've never known or could ever hope for any other life than this. Not that I haven't missed you either, on the contrary, it seems that I love, appreciate and feel much closer to you all now than I ever did at home. I've found so much peace and happiness here . . .

A year after she entered the convent, she sent the following note to Dad in a "Spiritual Bouquet."

Dear Daddy,

After living with you for approximately nineteen years it was only last summer, traveling back and forth with you (to and from work) and visiting you at odd moments during the day, that I came to really know and love you.

I've often told you since last September that I think of you and pray for you every day. Well, it's true, I do, and when I think of you I realize I love you so much because you're so like God in one of His most loving ways—His completely unselfish love of His children. And since He has promised that as you've done to the least of His brethren (your family) as do you also to Him, you can be assured Daddy of a place in Heaven very close to the heart of God.

Prayerfully, in the Sacred Hearts of Jesus and Mary, your loving daughter, Sister Denise

Three months later, the letters stopped in accordance with the regulation of the convent to limit outside communication during the second year of training. Though she remained in the convent another year, there is no record of what she was thinking or feeling during this period. Then, one year before taking her final vows, she decided that her life in the convent was too restricted, and she returned home.

At this point, she decided that she would like to be a teacher. In spite of her lack of formal education and training, she was appointed to a position in a Catholic grade school badly in need of teachers. She also dated, but she was not happy with herself or with her life for very long. She had a very close but troubled relationship with one young man of whom she was very fond. However, after about a year, he broke it off. Within six months, at the age of twenty-three, she decided to marry a man she had known since her mid-teens.

Her marriage and relationship with her husband seemed to provide Denise with some stability for several years, until their first child was born. Although she worked hard at being a good mother, over time the responsibilities and stresses were too great. The episodes of anger, anxiety, and depression returned. Arguments with her husband increased to the point that they separated soon after the birth of their second child. Denise took the two children and lived with our parents; but within a year, she returned to her husband, and they soon had a third child.

By this time, Denise was about thirty years old. I was in residency training in psychiatry at Duke University Medical Center, some five hundred miles away. The phone calls began during this period. Two sentences into the first of these calls, I realized that Denise was in serious trouble. Her voice was a low monotone, devoid of life or enthusiasm. On occasion, she had suffered from several days of depressed mood when something had gone badly for her, but this was different. She offered little information spontaneously. I had to ask questions to keep the conversation going.

After a few minutes, I noticed that she was slurring her words slightly, so I asked her if she had been drinking. She said she had had a few glasses of wine. She gradually revealed that she had become increasingly depressed over the prior few months, and was now suicidal. After much coaxing, and a talk with her husband, she agreed to be hospitalized. She seemed well enough to return home after about two weeks, though she was far from recovered.

From that time on, it was rare that a month passed that I did not receive a phone call similar to the one I just described. She began in psychotherapy, but the psychiatrist knew very little about borderline disorder and she made little improvement. The only antidepressants available at that time caused her to gain weight, which she hated. They also made her suspicious, and sometimes even paranoid, so she refused to take them. According to her husband, she was now drinking daily and beginning to neglect the children and the house, though up to then she had been a fastidious housekeeper and a loving mother. The situation was deteriorating so rapidly that I suggested to her and her husband that she come to visit with my family so that she might undergo an evaluation at Duke. She came.

One of the senior faculty in the department of psychiatry, a man whose clinical skills I admired greatly, saw her. He told her that she needed to stop drinking for several weeks so that he could examine her properly. She did so, but the depression did not improve. Because she had failed to respond to multiple antidepressants, he suggested a course of electroconvulsive therapy (ECT). ECT is most often used for patients who have severe depression or manic episodes who don't respond to medications, or for whom medications cause serious side-effects. It usually consists of a series of six or more individual treatments, typically administered every other day. During each treatment, patients are administered a quick-acting anesthetic, then a carefully controlled amount of electric current is applied to the head; this results in a seizure. The muscle contractions associated with the seizure are eliminated by the simultaneous use of a muscle relaxant. It's not known how ECT causes its therapeutic effect, but it may be compared to applying electric current to the chest of someone who has had a cardiac arrest in order to restore normal heart rhythm. After a course of ECT, Denise's depression improved considerably, and she seemed to be herself again, so she returned home.

Again, Denise appeared to do well. At the age of thirty-four, she and our younger sister Beatrice enrolled in a local community college to get nursing degrees. It was during this period that she wrote a number of poems, a few of which were published. The following one suggests she was still struggling each day.

IDENTITY

Because mother's she—I'm me.
Because father's he—I'm me.
Because of them, I am what I am,
In spite of them, I am me.

Because of my schooling—I'm me.
Because of church ruling—I'm me.
Because of the norm, obey and conform,
In spite of the norm, I am me.

Because of three wars—I'm me.
Because of bomb lore—I'm me.
Because of the fear, year after year,
In spite of the fear, I am me.

Because of the times—I'm me.
Because of the clime—I'm me.
Because of the pall, wrapped over this ball,
In spite of the pall, I am me.

Because there is caring—I'm me.
Because there is sharing—I'm me.
Because there is fate, indifference and hate,
In spite of my fate, I am me.

Accepting, rejecting the mold.
Accepting, rejecting don't fold.
Accepting, rejecting man and his earth.
Is this all I am, all I'm worth?

Within this sum total I see
A more basic awareness that's me
To be fought for each day, lest it wither away,
The true me—if I want to be free . . .

Denise graduated at the top of the class and gave the valedictory address. She worked as a nurse for a few years; but then the slow, relentless slide began.

When she was in her late thirties, I received a phone call similar to those of a decade before—same tone of voice, but the words were more slurred. We talked, and she promised to stop drinking, though she believed there was no point to it. She did stop drinking for a while, but even then she was barely holding on. Her husband and children were withdrawing from her and she felt increasingly abandoned.

At these times, she would contact my mother, who lived nearby and would do as much as she could, helping Denise clean her house and offering her encouragement. Denise would also contact Beatrice, who would also try to help as best she could. It was difficult to know what did help and what did not. She would have a few good weeks, maybe even one or two months; but overall, the slide continued. Although both her family and ours remained very concerned and upset, we had no idea of the horrors that awaited her and us.

About eleven o'clock on the night of Denise's forty-third birthday, I received a phone call from my mother. Dad had died some nine years earlier. Denise had been out to dinner with her husband and children, celebrating her birthday. She had been drinking since late afternoon. Midway though dinner, she choked on a piece of food. This is not an uncommon event in people who have had too much to drink, because alcohol inhibits the gag reflex. She hurriedly went to the ladies' room, indicating she was okay, but was found unconscious on the floor ten minutes later.

Denise was immediately taken to the closest hospital where she was found to have suffered massive brain damage as the result of lack of oxygen to her brain. She remained unconscious and was placed on all of the necessary life support systems. A team of neurologists evaluated her and gave her husband and the rest of the family the tragic news. She would never regain consciousness.

After months of round-the-clock care, Denise was weaned off the respirator and nourished through a feeding tube. She was moved to a long-term care facility where she had worked as a nurse, and the family's vigil continued. The entire family would visit regularly, but my mother would go to see Denise every day, bathe her, change her nightgown, and talk to her softly. The only indication that even the deepest survival systems of her brain functioned were the regular, autonomous beat of her heart, her breathing, and the occasional contortions of her muscles, including those of her face that made her appear to be smiling or grimacing in pain.

It was impossible to persuade Mom to take a day off. She spent a large part of each visit praying for Denise's recovery. Mom said that being with Denise was not a burden. Actually, she said, she was finally able to give Denise the love and care she had always tried to extend, but that Denise had resisted. Months passed with no positive change. Instead, her general condition deteriorated gradually but noticeably.

It's a measure of the agony experienced by the loved ones of people so afflicted that my brothers, sister, and I began to discuss our own thoughts and feelings about what should be done. Denise's family and most of our family lived in northern New Jersey at the time. The legal debates about the fate of Karen Ann Quinlan had recently concluded with the decision by the New Jersey Supreme Court to allow the removal of extraordinary life support systems from people who were brain-dead. Therefore, this alternative was fresh in our minds. During the period surrounding our father's death years before, Denise herself had mentioned that she would never want extraordinary measures taken to keep her alive if she were brain-dead.

Ultimately, we decided to speak with Denise's husband. He and the three children, now teenagers, were suffering terribly. I cannot imagine the toll it was taking on each of them. With great reluctance, he revealed that he thought Denise's feeding tube should be removed. He knew this would result in Denise's death, but he was increasingly concerned about the children. We told him we supported his belief and offered to approach our mother with him.

Mother prayed, spoke with the priest, and agonized over the issue. With great emotional pain, she agreed that it was cruel to the children and to Denise to allow her to die by inches in front of their eyes. We were now all agreed on what needed to be done, but we did not realize that the legal and moral problems were to be decided by others.

There were two major difficulties. First, Denise was under the care of a devout Catholic physician. He and the administration of the hospital both opposed our decision on moral grounds. We were forced to hire a lawyer in order to obtain relief from the court. Second, the Quinlan decision did not provide a crystal-clear precedent in cases such as ours.

The entire family testified in open court, and the newspapers carried the story. The judge even heard from the children. The family testified to Denise's wishes regarding not wanting any extraordinary measures to be being taken to keep her alive if she were brain-dead. Our plea to the court was unanimous: "Declare her incompetent and make her husband legal guardian. Allow this suffering to end." The judge granted the petition, but did not rule specifically on the removal of the feeding tube. Although asked to remove it by her husband, the doctor refused on moral grounds. Denise died seven months later at the age of forty-five. She was in a coma for one year and eight months, from the time of her accident to the time of her death.

I thought another perspective on Denise would be interesting, so I asked Beatrice to write some of her memories. Beatrice was closer to Denise in many ways than were we three brothers.

MY SISTER

DENISE WAS two and a half years older than I. In order to understand our relationship, you have to know my personality and my place in the family. I was fourth of five children, the second girl, and had two older brothers and one younger.

My parents and grandparents told me I was a happy and contented child from the moment I was born. Relatives and strangers gravitated toward me and I loved my parents and siblings.

In retrospect I now realize that on some level I was aware of the upheaval in the family caused by my sister's temper and that I always tried to make everyone laugh to ease the tensions of the moment. My personality became very accommodating because of Denise's flare-ups. I became the peacemaker.

I believe that my sister loved me deeply, but her feelings were conflicted as we grew up. During her "healthy" periods she was a loving, nurturing person who gave me great advice and would even iron my clothes for me when I wanted to go out. She was a joy during these times, a wonderful older sister for whom I would do anything.

However, I wasn't always aware of the changes taking place when her dark side would emerge. Sometimes I would borrow an article of clothing without asking first. She never said a word. But later I would discover that one of my favorite skirts or blouses had disappeared. I quickly learned not to cross her. As we grew older and entered high school we were not close. On weekends I would stay at one of my friend's homes, while Denise slept all day in our room with the shades drawn.

Later, when our children were young, we did have good years. We were as close as you could be with Denise, but she hated separations. If I were planning one for whatever reason, she would begin her own separation from me days or even weeks before I left.

Together we entered Nursing School, when I was thirty-two and she was thirty-four. She excelled and was a highly motivated, "A" student, while I was content with a B+ average and not nearly as dedicated or zealous. From 1972 to January 1975, we drove together in her car and spent four to eight hours at school where we developed a nice group of friends in labs and at lunch. Things appeared to be quite normal; but then in February 1975, just a short time before we were scheduled to graduate, without a word or phone call, she failed to pick me up one day. I finally got to class that day, only to find Denise sitting in her usual seat. She never looked up or acknowledged my arrival. After class, when I tried to approach her, she ignored me and walked out without a word. Calls to her home later went unanswered.

While I attended the "capping" ceremony held by the nursing school, I did not attend the graduation exercises where Denise gave the valedictorian's address. We both began working at the same hospital that fall, but never addressed what had happened at school. Before long we slipped back into our old sister routine—I gave of myself, Denise took what she wanted and rejected everything else. She became a highly respected nurse, specializing in geriatrics, and was loved by her patients.

As the years passed, Denise went from being a social drinker to one who drank more and more. She began to call me at all hours of the night and I would listen to her incoherent rantings until she hung up. Then she began to call to tell me she was going to commit suicide. I would rush over to her home to find her overdosed on drugs or, on several occasions, with her wrists slashed. She was hospitalized after these episodes, with little apparent improvement.

Just before her forty-third birthday she became very angry with our mother, refusing to see her or even talk to her. My mother was terribly hurt and I could hear the anguish in her voice when she called me. I realized how futile it would be to try to change Denise's mindset, but I called her anyway to tell her that if she could not give Mother the time she deserved, I would no longer have time for her. I told her not to call me again.

She never did. At dinner celebrating her birthday she choked on a sparerib. Rather than cause a scene in the restaurant, she went to the ladies room where she collapsed. Deprived of oxygen, she had a seizure and when she arrived at the hospital forty or so minutes later, she was declared to be brain-dead, and put on a respirator.

Denise had so much to give, and when able, she gave it with generosity of spirit. Although we were often anxious about her and angry with her, we knew she suffered greatly through her life and we loved her deeply. No one in our family emerged without emotional scars. She died much too young, and I still miss her terribly.

Mrs. Davis

Specialty training in psychiatry typically begins with clinical rotations on psychiatric inpatient units. Here, the **residents** (physicians engaged in a formal training program in a medical specialty) are responsible for much of the daily care of patients, under the supervision of a member of the faculty. In order to qualify for admission to the hospital, the patients must be very ill.

After spending a year and a half to two years training on a number of inpatient services specializing in different psychiatric disorders, psychiatry residents continue their education in the psychiatry outpatient clinics. It's in these clinics that residents learn to treat patients who are severely or chronically ill but don't require inpatient care. A very important part of this training is learning the skills of various types of psychotherapy. **Psychodynamic psychotherapy** involves learning and applying a body of knowledge about complex psychological processes and behaviors. To learn these skills, a resident must engage simultaneously in two tasks: first, a series of seminars and readings on the topic; and second, the treatment of patients using the knowledge they've acquired, all under the careful direction and supervision of a member of the faculty. Not all psychiatric patients are good candidates for psychodynamic psychotherapy. Therefore, residents have to carefully select a few patients they believe would benefit from this type of psychotherapy from among the patients assigned to them in the clinic.

I was a resident involved in this process when I first met Mrs. Davis. She came to the Duke Medical Center psychiatric resident clinic because she could not afford the regular fees of a fully trained therapist. When I first met her, she was a twenty-two-year-old medical technician and the wife of a first-year law student. She was a well-groomed, nicely dressed, and attractive young lady. During the initial interview, she told me that she was seeking help for frequent episodes of anxiety and occasional spells of depression.

Mrs. Davis said that she had experienced these problems off and on since high school, but that they had increased in frequency and severity since she and her husband had moved, three months earlier, from a city in the Midwest so that her husband could start law school. They had only been married for a few months prior to the move, and she had never been that far from her family for such an extended period. Mrs. Davis had just been hired at Duke Hospital, and she and her husband depended on the income in order to pay the bills. She had finished her training a few months before her marriage, and this was her first full-time job.

As I carefully took her medical history, I detected no indications of **psychotic episodes** or behaviors suggesting a lack of self-control. She was intent on finding out why she suffered from anxiety and depression, and on making whatever changes were necessary. In short, she seemed to be an ideal patient for psychodynamic psychotherapy. I reviewed my notes carefully with my faculty supervisor, who suggested that projective psychological tests might help determine if we were missing something important.

There are several categories of psychological tests that we use to evaluate an individual's psychological status. Projective tests are used to gain insight into a person's areas of concern and internal conflict, and to determine the types of psychological adaptations or "defenses" that they have available to deal with life's challenges. Some of these psychological coping patterns are more effective than others. In other words, some people can tolerate more psychological stress than others before developing symptoms such as anxiety, depression, and even more primitive symptoms such as paranoid thinking. The two most frequently used tests of this type are the Thematic Apperception Test (TAT) and the Rorschach. The TAT consists of a set of thirty pictures depicting one or more individuals. The patient is asked to make up a story based on each picture. The Rorschach is the well-known inkblot test.

Mrs. Davis readily agreed to the testing. Afterward, I met with the psychologist who had administered and interpreted these tests, a senior faculty member who had an excellent professional reputation. She reviewed the results with me and assured me that she could not determine any reason to not use psychodynamic psychotherapy in the treatment of Mrs. Davis.

With these assurances, I confidently instructed Mrs. Davis on the "ground rules" of therapy. I expected that she come to every fifty-minute session (to be held twice a week), that she come on time, and that, to the best of her ability, she talk about whatever came to her mind, no matter how painful or difficult and without editing her thoughts. She was also expected to pay my charges each month. I believe they were one dollar per session.

In turn, I told Mrs. Davis that my responsibilities in therapy were to be there on time for every session, and to listen to and record carefully what she had to say. Finally, I told her that we had a mutual responsibility, in the last ten or fifteen minutes of each session, to attempt to understand the meanings of what she had talked about that day. I indicated that early in treatment, I would probably make more interpretations of the information than she did, but that she would become more skilled in the process as treatment progressed.

Our work together began with our both slowly learning the process of psychotherapy. Each week I met with my supervisor and read to him every word she had said that I could write down, plus my rare comments and questions to Mrs. Davis during the session. I also reported our thoughts on the meaning of the material that we discussed at the end of each session. My supervisor would then try to help me better understand the different conscious and unconscious layers of meaning and the themes of the sessions.

Everything seemed to go well for about six weeks. Then, during a session that seemed initially no more remarkable than any other, Mrs. Davis became increasingly suspicious of her section head at work, of her husband, and of me. She claimed we were conspiring against her, and that I had broken my pledge to her of total confidentiality. No amount of reassurance that I offered that I had not spoken with either person made any difference. Mrs. Davis was becoming paranoid and increasingly agitated right before my eyes. There had been no warning signs that I could detect with my limited knowledge and skills. I recall vividly being surprised, confused, and more than a little anxious. What had caused this response?

I quickly tried to divert Mrs. Davis's attention from her paranoid thoughts to routine issues at work and at home. Remarkably, within about five minutes, she calmed down and became much less suspicious.

By the end of the session, she seemed no different than when the session began. She assured me she was fine. After careful consideration, I thought it safe for her to leave.

Fortunately, I was scheduled to meet with my supervisor later that day. He listened carefully to my report, asked me several questions, then sat back in his chair and reflected on what had occurred. A few minutes later, he leaned toward me and gently said "Welcome to the mysterious world of borderline personality disorder." He went on to tell me about the characteristics of the disorder, as well as they were known in the late 1960s. I don't recall having heard of the diagnosis before then, in spite of my many rotations on the inpatient services. He told me to go to the medical school library to do some serious and extensive reading on borderline disorder before my next therapy session with Mrs. Davis.

This reading assignment was not an easy chore. The usual sources of information were of little help. Most of the leading psychiatric textbooks at that time contained little useful information about borderline disorder. The *Diagnostic and Statistical Manual* of the American Psychiatric Association, then in its second edition (DSM-II), did not even include the disorder. I was left with the time–consuming prospect of performing a literature search from primary sources, that is, original articles in scientific journals and the few books written on the disorder.

My initial readings of this material left me confused about the diagnosis of borderline disorder and somewhat discouraged about the prognosis for Mrs. Davis. There was no clear agreement among a number of authors about what symptoms defined borderline disorder. A few even referred to the disorder as "a wastebasket diagnosis for patients who do not meet criteria for any other disorder," which may have been why the DSM-II didn't even include borderline disorder. As confusing as this was, there was even less clarity about the specific treatments for borderline disorder, other than **psychoanalysis**, which was considered to be ineffective by most authors and harmful by some.

I returned to report my findings to my supervisor and to ask, actually plead, for help before my next visit with Mrs. Davis. From what

I had read, I knew that her brief break with reality in our therapy session was a common occurrence in patients with borderline disorder treated with psychodynamic psychotherapy or psychoanalysis. Indeed, it was one of the hallmarks of the disorder. Clearly, a change in my therapeutic approach was necessary. My supervisor instructed me to reduce the number of our therapy visits to one a week and to change to supportive psychotherapy. He also suggested that I be careful about the use of medications, as they were rarely helpful for patients with borderline disorder, and might make her worse.

And so our work together began again. First, I had to speak with Mrs. Davis about her potential new diagnosis and our change in treatment strategy. I was uncertain how to raise the issue of diagnosis, as I was concerned it would make her anxious, especially because I was unable to describe clearly the confusing problem to her. However, I thought it best to tell her what I had learned and deal with it as best as we could. Second, we would then need to discuss the changes in treatment.

When we met next, I told her what I had learned. Initially, she was frightened and upset. Then, to her credit, after some discussion, she settled down and we talked about the possible changes in treatment. First, we reduced the frequency and type of therapy. I suggested that we meet only once a week and focus on those issues that currently were most relevant in her life now, with less emphasis on her past. I explained that I would ask more questions and make more comments during the session, and that we would focus on problem-solving strategies. Second, I raised the possibility of using a little medicine if it seemed right at some time in the future. Mrs. Davis agreed to the change in therapy, but was concerned about medication. I told her we would not rush into the use of a medication, but wait until we had more information. That was fine with her.

As therapy progressed, I slowly gained a clearer picture of the complexity of Mrs. Davis's problems. A pattern gradually emerged from the ways that she dealt with her daily life, her relationship with her husband, challenges at work, and her "homesickness." For example, she was often very angry with her husband for not devoting more time to her in the evening and on weekends, rather than studying the law. This was one source of many arguments with him. In part, she understood that he needed to study to do well in school. However, she was rarely able to overcome the empty feeling that this caused and the fear that he didn't care about her. These feelings would grow stronger and stronger, until she reached the point where she was extremely angry and desperate for attention. Occasionally at these times she would go to the airport, fly back home, and have a two- or three-day affair with an old boyfriend from college. She told me after one of these impulsive trips that this young man was very kind to her, appreciated her, and spent quite a bit of time with her. Then we would discuss the consequences of this trip on her relationship with her husband—and on her job, if she left during the workweek. We also discussed what alternatives were available to her to deal with her anger and sense of desperation in ways that were not harmful.

It took many months of work in therapy for us to recognize when she was at greatest risk for making these trips. We struggled to help her find better ways to deal with her feelings of rejection by her husband, the sense of abandonment, desperation, and other feelings that put her at risk. Also, we agreed that she would call me at any time of the day or night *before* she left. But nothing seemed to help.

Another recurring problem was her relationship with her section head at work. As she described her, she seemed to be a well-intentioned, highly motivated woman who ran a pretty tight ship. Through Mrs. Davis's eyes, she did not seem at all warm and supportive, but often overly critical. Mrs. Davis's responses to any real or perceived criticisms from her were either sullen withdrawal or temper outbursts. She told me that during one such incident, in a fit of rage, she went to the hospital parking lot to look for this person's car so that she could put a few dents in it. Fortunately, she could not find it. As usual, we discussed the incidents leading up to the outbursts of anger, how much she needed the job, and alternative ways of dealing with these situations. Again, none of this seemed to have any clear effect on how she felt or how she behaved. By now, I was getting a little desperate myself, because her behaviors were understandably placing both her marriage and her job in great jeopardy.

My supervisor was supportive, but he could not offer me any treatment alternatives. He did encourage me to not become discouraged, and to press on in therapy with Mrs. Davis.

At this point, I recalled a patient I had treated the previous year on the inpatient service. This man, a dentist, suffered from recurring anxiety attacks that were so severe that he was left unable to work, or even to care for himself. Psychotherapy did not reduce these episodes, nor did the usual antianxiety agents or antidepressants available at the time. Therefore, he required frequent short-term hospitalization until he was functional again. Because he had never been tried on a major tranquilizer (we now call them **antipsychotic agents**), I proposed to my faculty supervisor that we do so, but at very low doses. The treatment worked very well, reducing his symptoms, the number of hospitalizations, and improving his work performance. I describe this patient in more detail at the end of Chapter 9.

Based on that experience, I thought that this class of medications, in very low doses, might help Mrs. Davis bring her behavior under better control, although this result had not been reported in the scientific literature. I raised the issue with Mrs. Davis and told her that I had reviewed the scientific journals thoroughly, searching for some help for her. Most studies on the use of medications in borderline disorder reported negative results and were very pessimistic. Medications just did not seem to help people with this disorder. If anything, many people with borderline disorder abused the antianxiety agents (then called minor tranquilizers) such as Valium, Librium, and meprobomate. The standard doses of antidepressants and antipsychotic agents typically produced only intolerable side-effects.

However, because of my experience the year before, I told Mrs. Davis that I thought it was worth trying a very low dose of a major tranquilizer, especially because she had experienced at least that one break with reality early in treatment. She asked more about the medicine and then said "absolutely no" when I told her that the class of medicine I was recommending was usually used for people who suffered from schizophrenia or severe manic-depressive (bipolar) disorder, although at much higher doses.

Therapy continued for several more months with little improvement.

Then, for reasons that are still unclear to me, Mrs. Davis agreed to try the medicine. After carefully describing the potential side-effects of the medication, I started her on a very low dose of a medicine called Stelazine (trifluoperazine), 1 mg each morning. The usual dose of this medicine is 20 to 40 mg a day. After one week, she reported she felt a little less anxious and angry. We waited another week. There was no further improvement, so we increased the dose to 2 mg a day. She then reported a noticeable decrease in her emotional reactions, angry outbursts, and impulsive behaviors, and some improvement in her ability to have fairly calm and reasonable discussions with her husband about their problems.

Our first breakthrough in psychotherapy occurred not too long after that. She called me late one night from the airport just before boarding the plane for one of her trips. She had never done that before. We talked for some time about the events that had occurred over the previous few days, the consequences of her leaving, the need for an emergency therapy session the next day, and anything else I could think of to keep her off that plane. Finally, she agreed to return home and to see me the next day. She made very few unscheduled flights after that.

Progress in other areas also occurred. There were fewer flare-ups at work, and she missed fewer days due to severe headaches and other physical symptoms resulting from stress. Her impulsive buying sprees, another source of difficulty at home, decreased in frequency and degree. She seemed better able to remember and apply the work we did in therapy.

For example, I was stopped in the hospital one day by a young lady who introduced herself as a friend and neighbor of Mrs. Davis. She said that she understood I could not say anything about Mrs. Davis, but she simply wanted me to know that she was doing much better. I said it was very kind of her to tell me this. I mentioned I would need to tell Mrs. Davis she had done so, and she said that was fine. She went on to say that when she had first met Mrs. Davis, she would come to her home, tell her of her emotional troubles, her impulsive actions, and the resulting problems. She said she had been very worried about Mrs. Davis and felt helpless as she tried to help her. (I understood that feeling very well.) She went on to say that now when Mrs. Davis comes to visit, she tells her of the impulsive things she has thought of doing, but has not yet done. "Before I do it, I can hear Dr. Friedel say 'Well, what is going on in your life, what are your alternatives, and what are the consequences?' Then he'll ask 'So, what is the best choice?' So now I try to figure that all out before I see him, and try to do it."

After another year in therapy, Mrs. Davis reached the point where her emotions had stabilized quite well, and most of her decisions were appropriate. She and her husband had worked out a mutually satisfactory relationship; she was doing well at work, and she no longer felt desperate living so far from her parents. She had made a number of nice friends.

I suggested that we gradually reduce the frequency of therapy sessions, but was careful to let her know that we could always increase them again if needed. In another year she was seeing me only for medication checks, when she had a problem that needed my help, or just to touch base with me to assure herself that I was available if necessary. By then, I had completed my training and was a member of the faculty at Duke. This pattern of treatment continued for several more years. I then accepted a faculty position at the University of Washington in Seattle. I was fully aware by now of the extraordinary sensitivity that Mrs. Davis, and other people with borderline disorder, have to separations. Therefore, months before I was scheduled to leave, I asked her to come in to see me, to discuss my leaving. We spent the next few months working through her feelings and concerns about my departure. I recommended a few of my colleagues to her so that she could continue her medicine and get other help when needed. Fortunately, she seemed to feel comfortable with one of these psychiatrists and permitted me to brief him on our work together.

About two years after I left Duke, Mrs. Davis called me in Seattle. She said she was doing well and liked her new doctor. However, she had a big decision to make and wanted my help as well. Her doctor had said this was fine with him. She then went on to tell me that she and her husband were considering moving to another city, and possibly starting a family, but they had a number of concerns about doing so. We set up several phone therapy sessions, and she filled me in on the details. She, her husband, and her therapist had worked through the issues very well, so I had little to add. Finally, it dawned on me that her main reasons for calling me were to support their decisions, and to be reassured that I would be available if she needed my help.

Over the next ten years or so, Mrs. Davis called me every few years, usually whenever she and her husband were about to make a significant change in their lives. (I've had a number of patients with borderline disorder do this, and I believe that it's very supportive and doesn't harm them or their relationship with their current physician or therapist.) She remained on her medicine and continued to do well.

I now have not heard from Mrs. Davis in over fifteen years. It has been my hope that this means she is still doing well. I think of her from time to time, and am grateful for all that we learned together about borderline disorder.

I think you may now understand why these two stories are very personal to me. Although there are similarities in these stories, the outcomes are very different. Denise's illness ultimately resulted in her early death, but it didn't have to be that way. I wonder what course Denise's life would have taken if she had received the medications and therapy now available for people with borderline disorder. Most were not available at that time to the average patient with the disorder. Denise also eventually turned to alcohol in an attempt to reduce her suffering. Mrs. Davis did not reach this level of desperation, to the best of my knowledge. This was a critical difference, as we will discuss further.

If you receive proper help, you will not reach this level of desperation either. You have a much better opportunity to receive effective treatment for your disorder than has ever been available before. Chapters 8 to 10 discuss how you can make this happen. However, in order to make full use of the information on treatment, it's helpful to learn more about the history, nature, and causes of borderline disorder.

THREE

The History of Borderline Personality Disorder

■ FTEN, WHEN MY patients and I arrive at the diagnosis of borderline disorder, they become quite concerned about the meaning of the term *borderline*. It's not uncommon for them to have researched the topic on the Internet and come across terms like **borderline psychotic**, **borderline schizophrenia**, and **pre-schizophrenia**. Understandably, these terms can be frightening and require an explanation.

The meanings of the term *borderline* and the diagnostic criteria of borderline disorder have changed considerably over the past sixty-five years. Borderline psychotic, borderline schizophrenia, pre-schizophrenia, as well as other terms and different definitions of *borderline*, have been used at some point during this evolution. In this chapter, I trace the development of the main concepts about the diagnostic characteristics of borderline disorder, in order to distinguish those ideas that have stood the test of time from those that have been discarded as the result of further experience and research. I also contrast the concepts of the major diagnostic issues involving borderline disorder with those that are currently under review by experts in the area.

I realize that some of the material in this chapter may seem a bit abstract and not particularly relevant to dealing with the problems that borderline disorder causes in your life. Trust me here for a while, as I will continue to use and build on this information in many of the chapters that follow. I deeply believe that the effort you devote to learning as much as you can about borderline disorder ultimately will be well rewarded by your gaining a great deal more control over your life than you have experienced in the past. Knowledge is the edge that gives you an advantage in life.

The Evolution of Borderline Disorder

The term *borderline personality disorder* came into official use in 1980 with its inclusion in the third edition of the *Diagnostic and Statistical Manual* of the American Psychiatric Association (DSM-III). However, the disorder has been recognized for almost three thousand years.

Theodore Millon, a psychologist at the University of Miami and Harvard, and an expert in the evaluation of personality and personality disorders, has uncovered a number of early historical literary and medical references that describe individuals with symptoms that we would now consider to be consistent with borderline disorder. Some of these descriptions appear in the writings of Homer, Hippocrates, and Aretaeus. More recently, Bonet in 1684, Schacht and Herschel in the eighteenth century, and Baillarger, the Fabrets, and Kahlbaum in the nineteenth century, described medical conditions that closely resemble borderline disorder. However, during this period, there was no consistent behavioral descriptive or diagnostic term for those patients.

The early decades of the twentieth century were marked by a modest increase in attention by the medical community to the people for whom we now use the diagnosis of borderline disorder. In 1921, the German psychiatrist Emil Kraepelin, noted for his brilliant work on describing and classifying mental disorders, defined a group of patients who demonstrated the core symptoms of borderline disorder. Two years later, the European psychiatrist Schneider provided another description of patients who now would probably be diagnosed with borderline disorder.

The Psychoanalytic Origins of Borderline Disorder

In the early part of the twentieth century, the psychoanalytic concepts of the neurologist and psychiatrist Sigmund Freud, the founder of psychoanalysis, were dominant in American psychiatry. So it makes sense that it was psychoanalysts who made the next significant contributions to our understanding of borderline disorder.

During the early part of the last century, psychoanalysts recognized a population of patients that did not fit into any existing diagnostic category. During the course of their clinical practices, they treated patients in psychoanalysis who initially appeared to suffer from anxiety, depression, and other symptoms that were thought to be **neurotic** in origin. At that time, all mental disorders that did not have psychotic symptoms fell into the category of neuroses. Although these patients at first appeared the same as other neurotic patients, their therapists noticed several important differences as treatment progressed. For example, some of these patients developed psychotic features for brief periods during the treatment session. In addition, they did not seem to improve from psychoanalysis. Although they appeared to understand the meanings of the information and the general concepts that arose in treatment, and even seemed to improve at times, the improvement was temporary. If progress did occur, relapses were commonplace and usually complete.

Based on these experiences, some psychoanalysts began to report their observations in the medical literature. In doing so, they speculated on the diagnostic category, nature, and causes of the disorder that affected these patients. It was during this period that terms like *borderline psychosis*, *pre-schizophrenia*, **pseudoneurotic schizophrenia,** and **latent schizophrenia** emerged in attempts to accurately classify this group of patients. These disorders made up the early borders between core borderline disorder and other disorders (see Figure 3.1 on next page). However, no clear consensus developed in the field regarding the proper diagnostic name and criteria, the causes, or the most effective treatments of borderline disorder. Some psychoanalysts at the time even suggested that the borderline diagnosis lacked validity and integrity. They called it a "wastebasket diagnosis" and suggested it was only used because people with these symptoms did not fit neatly into any existing diagnostic classification. Unfortunately, there are still some mental health professionals who don't believe that borderline disorder exists.

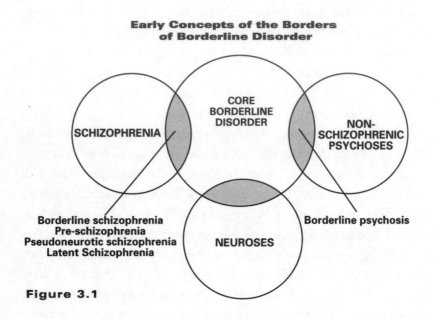

Early Concepts of the Borders of Borderline Disorder

Figure 3.1

Adolph Stern and the Border Line Group

In 1938, in the midst of this confusion, the American psychoanalyst Adolph Stern published a landmark article. In it, he defined what he believed were the main characteristics of borderline disorder, described why he thought these people reacted the way they did, both in and out of therapy, and provided guidelines for treatment that he found were more effective than traditional psychoanalysis. Stern referred to these patients as the "border line group." Because of his clear and comprehensive description of these patients, Stern is credited by many as the person most responsible for the popularization and continued use of "border line," now *borderline*, as a diagnostic term.

In this article, Stern listed ten characteristics of his border line group:

1. narcissism;
2. psychic bleeding;
3. inordinate hypersensitivity;
4. psychic and body rigidity—"the rigid personality";
5. negative therapeutic reactions;
6. what looks like constitutionally rooted feelings of inferiority, deeply embedded in the personality of the patients;
7. masochism;
8. what can be described as a state of deep organic insecurity or anxiety;
9. the use of projection mechanisms; and
10. difficulties in reality thinking, particularly in personal relationships.

Since this article was written primarily for other psychoanalysts, the meanings of some of these terms are probably not clear to you, but I think it would be helpful for you to understand them as Stern meant them, for several reasons.

First, you'll see a considerable number of similarities between these characteristics and the current diagnostic criteria and characteristics of borderline disorder that I described in Chapter 1. The consistency of the symptoms of borderline disorder over a sixty-five-year period of careful observation and research is a major indication that this diagnosis has validity and integrity.

Second, Stern's article was the first of very few articles that significantly influenced and stimulated later thinking and research on borderline disorder. This is what's referred to in research literature as a **seminal article**. For example, when discussing the possible causes of borderline disorder, Stern writes "this group never develops a sense of security acquired by being loved, which is the birthright of every child. These patients suffer from affective (narcissistic) malnutrition." The word **narcissism** refers to one's capacity to value or "love" oneself. Those who regard themselves too highly are above the normal range of self-value, and we refer to them as narcissistic. People plagued with chronic self-doubt and poor self-esteem are generally below the normal range of narcissism. The concepts of early maternal deprivation and other early traumas were noted by Stern as risk factors for developing borderline disorder. Since then, these concepts have been supported by a number of research studies.

Third, Stern indicated that he believed that one of the underlying causes of the disorder was an inherent or inborn tendency for an individual to develop it. In doing so, he correctly anticipated by fifty years the identification of genetic and other biological risk factors for borderline disorder.

Fourth, Stern believed that identifying the border line group of patients was essential if psychotherapy was to be successful. Although he maintained that psychoanalysis was still possible, he believed several modifications in therapy were required. He believed it was important that the therapist be very supportive of the patient and be very careful not to appear critical. He stressed that attention should be focused on the relationship issues between the patient and therapist, not on historical issues or interpretations of feelings or actions. This meant the issues of excessive dependency, clinging behaviors, unrealistic expectations, and overly negative reactions had to be dealt with consistently and in a nonjudgmental manner. Many of these principles still apply in the treatment of patients with borderline disorder.

So without further ado, here is a breakdown of the characteristics of borderline disorder as defined by Stern.

1. **Narcissism.** Stern reported that at least 75 percent of his patients in the border line group did not receive wholesome and spontaneous affection from their mothers in the early years of their life. He believed that this, either alone or with other early deprivations, resulted in a fundamental deficit in the self-assurance and self-worth of these patients that made them much more prone to high levels of anxiety in response to stress. Stern considered the anxiety resulting from this fundamental deficit in self-assurance to be "the motor" that produced the other symptoms of patients in the border line group.

2. **Psychic bleeding.** Stern coined this term to describe patients in the border line group who were not resilient to painful and traumatic experiences, who collapsed under pressure.

3. **Inordinate hypersensitivity.** Patients in Stern's border line group were "consistently insulted and injured by trifling remarks . . . and occasionally develop mildly paranoid ideas." He considered the hypersensitivity to be the result of the deeply rooted insecurity in character noted above, which "necessitated undue caution and awareness to danger." This characteristic clearly resembles the symptoms of emotional instability and stress-related paranoid ideation included in the current diagnostic criteria of borderline disorder (Table 1.2 on page 19).

4. **Psychic rigidity or "the rigid personality."** People in Stern's border line group reacted to external and internal anxiety-producing stress with both physical and psychological rigidity. He emphasized their lack of tolerance to change and inflexible responses to stress, conditions present from childhood.

5. **Negative therapeutic reactions.** Stern observed that his patients in the border line group operated within a very narrow margin of security. This caused patients to respond with anxiety, anger, discouragement, and depression to any comments by the therapist that they perceived as harmful to their self-esteem. Patients more often reacted negatively (as though they'd been rejected), rather than favorably, to potentially helpful discoveries and comments made by the therapist in therapy. Many therapists are still reluctant to treat patients with borderline disorder because of this common response in therapy. This characteristic is similar to the symptoms of inappropriate anger and affective instability that are current criteria of borderline disorder (Table 1.2 on page 19).

6. **Feelings of inferiority.** According to Stern, patients in the border line group had persistent feelings of inferiority that affected almost the entire personality. These feelings of inferiority were not influenced by any accomplishments, no matter how significant, and created a wide gap between the normal

expectations of mature performance and their own perceived abilities. This gap resulted in severe anxiety, protests of inability to perform, and then collapses into inaction.

7. **Masochism.** Stern noticed that self-inflicted harm of all types was prevalent in the personal, professional, and social lives of this group of patients. Self-destructive behaviors and self-injurious or parasuicidal acts now constitute diagnostic criteria of borderline disorder (Table 1.2 on page 19).

8. **"Somatic" insecurity or anxiety.** This refers to a lack of self-assurance or self-confidence that appears to have always existed in this group of patients. Stern implies that it appears to be of "somatic"—that is, of biological—origin. This inherent deficit would explain the difficulties that patients with borderline disorder have in developing self-assurance through experience, improved performance, and personal growth. This characteristic has some similarities to the criterion on identity disturbance in the current diagnostic criteria for borderline disorder (Table 1.2 on page 19).

9. **The use of projection mechanisms.** In Stern's view, this was the link between people in the border line group with those patients who suffer from psychotic disorders (Figure 3.1). **Projection** is the unconscious psychological attempt to deal with anxiety by attributing one's own unacceptable attributes to the outside world. In people in the border line group, this could result in an expectation of malevolence in others, and, when under severe stress, in paranoid thinking. This characteristic is related to the paranoid ideation listed in current diagnostic criteria of borderline disorder (Table 1.2 on page 19).

10. **Difficulties in reality thinking.** Stern suggested that the border line group had considerable difficulty in perceiving their environment accurately and thinking realistically. The chief examples he used to illustrate this difficulty were the distorted attitudes and behaviors of his patients toward the therapist. He found that on the one hand, the border line group viewed the therapist as an omnipotent, all-knowing, and extremely powerful figure who made them feel happy and secure, and to whom they would cling with desperate dependency; on the other hand, they responded

very negatively to any clarifying or instructive comments by the therapist, which they usually perceived as an attack on their fragile self-esteem. Under these circumstances, the patients often responded with anxiety, anger, discouragement, and emotional withdrawal from the therapist. You probably recognize these responses as being similar to the pattern of unstable and intense interpersonal relationships that is a current criterion of borderline disorder (Table 1.2 on page 19).

Seven of the nine criteria we now use to diagnose borderline disorder are included in these ten characteristics described by Stern in 1938. I think it's remarkable that he did so based mainly on the sparse medical literature existing then and on his personal clinical observations.

In the decades following Stern's article, a small but growing number of other articles and book chapters about borderline disorder appeared and made significant contributions to the medical literature. I think you'll find that the evolution of thinking about borderline disorder is an informative and interesting story. At the very least, it will dispel a number of myths about the disorder, especially the myth that there is no validity to a borderline disorder diagnosis.

Robert Knight and Borderline States

The next major contribution to our recognition and understanding of borderline disorder was made by the psychoanalyst Robert Knight in the 1940s. Knight introduced concepts from the field of **ego psychology** into Stern's psychoanalytic conceptual framework of borderline disorder. Ego psychology deals with those mental processes that enable us to deal effectively with our thoughts, feelings, and responses to life around us. These are called **ego functions**.

Knight believed that the ego functions impaired in borderline disorder include emotional regulation; rational thinking; integration of feelings, impulses, and thoughts; realistic planning; successful adaptation to the world around us; involvement in mature relationships; and effectively subduing and re-channeling the energy from primitive and basic impulses. He also believed that other ego functions were spared in borderline disorder, including memory, calculations, and certain habitual performances. We now know that these latter functions are also subtly impaired in borderline disorder. Knight referred to the symptoms of these patients and the ego dysfunctions he described as *borderline states*.

Otto Kernberg and Borderline Personality Organization

Two decades later, the American psychoanalyst Otto Kernberg made the next important advances in the area. Kernberg proposed that people with borderline disorder represented a distinct population of individuals who could be defined by the characteristic organization of their personalities. He suggested using a model of mental illness, which was determined by three distinct personality types: *psychotic personality organization,* consisting of individuals predisposed to psychotic disorders such as schizophrenia; *neurotic personality organization,* those individuals predisposed to less-severe mental illnesses such as anxiety and depressive neuroses; and *borderline personality organization,* represented by people who fell between the first two types and show the symptoms that we now refer to as borderline disorder. His work further elaborated on Knight's conclusions that borderline personality organization represented fundamental and persistent impairments of ego functions.

In addition, Kernberg, who is still professionally active, remains more optimistic about the effectiveness of psychoanalytic psychotherapy for patients with borderline personality organization than many of his colleagues. He believes that if treated properly in psychoanalysis, positive and lasting changes can be made in the fundamental organization of the personalities of people with the disorder. The combination of Kernberg's model, his optimism about treatment, and his lucid contributions to the medical literature sparked a badly needed increase in interest in borderline disorder among psychiatrists.

How Borderline Disorder Became
a Valid Diagnosis

Roy Grinker and the Borderline Syndrome

The next seminal contribution to our understanding of borderline disorder was made by Roy Grinker and his colleagues in 1968. In that year, they published the results of the first **empirical research** involving people with borderline disorder. Rather than base their research on psychoanalytic concepts and strategies, Grinker and his research team decided that verbal and nonverbal behavior are the basic data of scientific psychiatry. So they attempted to describe, classify, and quantify the ego functions that are disturbed in borderline disorder in behavioral terms.

From their data, Grinker and his colleagues concluded that specific impairments of ego function differentiate the *borderline syndrome,* as they named it, from other mental disturbances. These ego dysfunctions were manifested in four behavioral characteristics that best identify patients with the disorder. They are: (1) a predominant emotional state of *expressed anger;* (2) a defect in *emotional relationships;* (3) impairments in *self-identity;* and (4) *depressive loneliness.*

The four behavioral characteristics of Grinker's borderline syndrome remain valid criteria of borderline disorder, as you can see from Table 1.2 on page 19 in Chapter 1. The empirical research of Grinker and his colleagues was critical because it provided an empirical approach to the identification of characteristics of borderline disorder, and it spurred on further research in an effort to clarify and validate the main diagnostic features of the disorder.

John Gunderson and Borderline Patients / Borderline Personality Disorder

John Gunderson is a psychiatrist at Harvard's McLean Hospital. His first major contribution to the field of borderline disorder was in 1975 when he published, with Margaret Singer, an important article called "Defining Borderline Patients: An Overview." This widely acclaimed article reviewed and synthesized all of the relevant literature that existed on borderline disorder and redefined the main characteristics of the disorder. The enthusiastic response to the article prompted Gunderson to develop a structured research instrument, the Diagnostic Interview for Borderline Patients (DIB). This instrument enabled researchers around the world to conduct studies with a reasonably homogeneous population of borderline patients, and validly compare results from these studies. This was a major research breakthrough, and it stimulated a significant amount of research of all types on borderline disorder.

Much of the initial research conducted by Gunderson and his colleagues focused on defining a set of diagnostic criteria of borderline disorder that clearly distinguished it from other mental disorders. This work was followed up by a large empirical research study led by Robert Spitzer, a psychiatrist from Columbia University. Together, these studies provided the initial scientific rationale for confirming the existence of borderline disorder and its inclusion in the third edition of the *Diagnostic and Statistical Manual* of the American Psychiatric Association (DSM-III), published in 1980. This listing of borderline personality disorder (its official name) in DSM-III was the culmination of the efforts of the psychiatrists I mentioned, and of others, to define and authenticate the existence of a mental illness that caused much suffering but had not yet received adequate attention by the medical community. An indication of the recognition of borderline disorder as a valid clinical entity is the increasing number of research articles about the disorder in the medical literature. In the mid-1970s, about a hundred articles had been published on borderline disorder. By the mid-1980s, the number had jumped to approximately a thousand, and now the total number is almost three thousand.

So, you now can see that the term *borderline personality disorder* evolved first from Stern's term *border line group*, then Knight's *borderline states*, Kernberg's *borderline personality organization*, and then Grinker's *borderline syndrome*. In addition, the legitimacy of the current criteria for borderline disorder, and of the disorder itself, are supported by a number of well-conducted empirical research studies.

Recent Changes in the Borders of Borderline Disorder

A major result of the research inspired by Gunderson's diagnostic rating instrument for borderline disorder has been the changes in the borders—the overlap of symptoms—of borderline disorder with other mental disorders. Initially, the borders with schizophrenia and non-schizophrenic psychotic disorders were considered most important (Figure 3.1). This remained the predominant concept until the late 1970s.

Data resulting from a number of different research strategies, including genetic, epidemiological, and descriptive studies, have dramatically altered our thinking in this area. First, it now seems clear that borderline disorder is not related to schizophrenic disorders. Second, there appears to be some fundamental, but as yet unknown, connection of borderline disorder to other mental disorders such as affective disorders (major depressive disorder and **bipolar II disorder**); alcoholism and other substance-abuse disorders; **posttraumatic stress disorder; attention deficit hyperactivity disorder;** and other personality disorders, especially **antisocial, schizotypal, histrionic,** and **narcissistic personality disorders** (see Figure 3.2 for more information). I discuss many of these mental disorders in detail in Chapter 7.

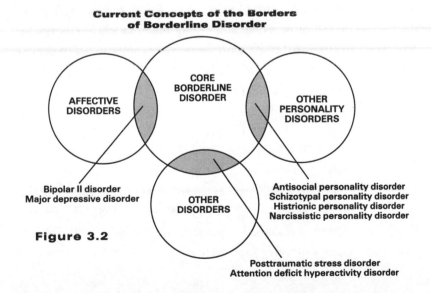

Current Concepts of the Borders of Borderline Disorder

AFFECTIVE DISORDERS

CORE BORDERLINE DISORDER

OTHER PERSONALITY DISORDERS

OTHER DISORDERS

Bipolar II disorder
Major depressive disorder

Antisocial personality disorder
Schizotypal personality disorder
Histrionic personality disorder
Narcissistic personality disorder

Posttraumatic stress disorder
Attention deficit hyperactivity disorder

Figure 3.2

The Future Classification of Borderline Disorder

The problem with the current system of classification of personality disorders is that it uses a *categorical* approach. What this means is that either you meet the criteria for borderline disorder as described in Table 1.2 on page 19, or you don't. If you demonstrate five or more of the nine criteria, you are diagnosed with borderline disorder; if you have four or less, you are not. If you meet one to four criteria, you are considered to have borderline "traits," but not the disorder. But if these traits are moderate to severe in intensity, and cause you serious problems, what should be the appropriate diagnosis and treatment?

Another problem that results from the categorical approach is that a significant number of patients will meet current diagnostic criteria for two or more personality disorders. How do we make sense of this? These and other problems with the current diagnostic approach do not mean that borderline disorder is not a valid clinical disorder, but rather that we may well need another approach to conceptualizing and applying the most discriminating diagnostic criteria.

Over the past decade, a number of experts in the field have questioned the usefulness of the current categorical approach used in the Diagnostic and Statistical Manual of Mental Disorders (DSM-IV) to classify personality disorders. They have suggested an alternative approach that evaluates a number of distinct behavioral *dimensions* of personality that extend across the spectrum of both normal and disordered behavioral patterns. For example, emotional stability and impulse control are two personality dimensions that are components of everyone's personalities. It's the *degree* to which one exhibits these and other personality dimensions that determines normal or disordered behavior. Several models using this approach have emerged from extensive research investigations, but no final consensus has yet developed.

In an effort to deal with the lack of a clear consensus on this issue, the American Psychiatric Association has decided to assemble a panel of experts. Their task will be to determine if the next edition of the *Diagnostic and Statistical Manual of Mental Disorders* (DSM-V) should change the current categorical approach to the diagnosis of personality disorders to a dimensional approach. If that occurs, there's no need for you to be confused by the new system of classification—just look at Table 1.1 on page 2. I've already placed the DSM-IV criteria and other characteristics of borderline disorder in four groups, or dimensions: poorly regulated emotions, impulsivity, cognitive perceptual impairment, and impaired relationships. Some of these dimensions of borderline disorder will most likely be used in the new system of classification, if it is adopted. The characteristics of borderline disorder have been observed for almost three thousand years, across many nationalities and cultures, and there is strong evidence of an inherent biological basis to borderline disorder. Changes in our diagnostic approaches will not change the fundamental nature of the disorder.

It's the opinion of many experts in the field, an opinion that I share, that a scientifically based, rational diagnostic description of personality disorders is more likely to result from a dimensional than from a categorical diagnostic approach. The dimensional approach will be advantageous for a number of reasons. For example, it will provide a clearer description of the overall pattern of each person's specific personality. In doing so, it will define those personality behavioral dimensions that fall within the normal range, and distinguish them from those that fall outside of this range. For example, the degrees of impairment of emotional regulation, impulse control, and perceptual-cognitive function need to be more precisely determined. This is important because people with borderline disorder demonstrate different combinations of symptoms of the disorder and levels of severity of each symptom.

A more precise description of the degree of impairment in the behavioral dimensions of borderline disorder for each patient will enable clinicians to better focus treatment efforts. In addition, experimental efforts to study the behavioral dimensions of borderline disorder from a number of perspectives should prove more effective and revealing than attempts to study a complex diagnostic category.

For example, in order to better understand the **etiology** (the causes or origins) of borderline disorder, we need to analyze the behavioral dimensions of the disorder at the levels at which those dimensions are represented in the brain. Although I believe a dimensional approach to the diagnosis of personality disorders seems reasonable, the models proposed so far have not been tightly bound to our current knowledge about the neural systems of the brain that mediate the psychological and behavioral dimensions of personality. Nonetheless, I think it's a good idea to change the current categorical system of diagnosis to a dimensional system, as this would be more likely to place borderline disorder on a firmer foundation in modern neural science than does the current categorical system.

This historical review of the origins of borderline disorder reveals an extraordinary evolution, over the past century, of the diagnostic criteria of the disorder. Our concepts about the borders of the disorder have changed significantly. Many early proposals considered the disorder to border on schizophrenia. A substantial amount of research has essentially eliminated that possibility. Current concepts emphasize the connections of borderline disorder with other disorders such as alcoholism, posttraumatic stress disorder, and affective disorders, or emphasize the overlap of the behavioral dimensions of the disorder with other personality disorders.

Currently, experts in the field are working to develop more effective diagnostic tools for borderline disorder. As this work progresses, so will our understanding about the causes, the course, and the development of more effective treatments of the disorder.

In a Nutshell

Here's what you should take away from this chapter:

- The symptoms of borderline disorder have been recognized since the time of Hippocrates.
- Since the term *borderline* came into popular use in 1938, borderline disorder has been referred to as the *border line group, borderline states, borderline personality organization, borderline syndrome*, and now *borderline personality disorder*.
- The early descriptions of borderline disorder proposed that the fundamental symptoms of the disorder bordered on a number of different classes of mental disorders, including

schizophrenia, affective disorders, psychotic states in general, and other personality disorders.

- Since then, research has demonstrated no significant relationship between borderline disorder and schizophrenia. However, there is some evidence that borderline disorder may be related to affective disorders such as bipolar disorder, to other disorders such as posttraumatic stress disorder and alcoholism, and to other personality disorders.

- Research on the characteristics of people with borderline disorder has resulted in a set of diagnostic criteria of borderline disorder that appear to distinguish it from other disorders (see Table 1.2 on page 19).

- This and other research strongly suggests that the diagnosis of borderline disorder has reasonable validity and integrity as a mental illness.

- Finally, experts in the field of personality and personality disorders have proposed a substantial departure from our current *categorical* diagnostic approach. They suggest that personality is best described by a limited number of behavioral *dimensions,* such as emotional stability and impulse control, and that the degree of departure of one's behaviors from the normal range in each of these dimensions best characterizes personality disorders.

FOUR

What Are
the Causes?

ONCE MY PATIENTS are reassured that they're not suffering from a disorder that will result in their developing schizophrenia or other severe psychotic conditions, many of them and their families naturally want to know what causes borderline disorder. You may have read or heard that borderline disorder is caused by the way you were raised, that you didn't receive enough love and affection from your mother, or that your father was too cold, critical, and distant. You may have also learned that the parents of people with borderline disorder don't provide a consistent, supportive, non-chaotic home life for their children, and that there are frequent arguing, anger, and temper outbursts in the family, much of it directed at the child with borderline disorder. In addition, it's often said that emotional, physical, and sexual abuses in childhood are common experiences of people with borderline disorder. Unfortunately, you may have even suffered from one or more of these traumas as a child and have concluded, quite reasonably, that your early experiences are the causes of your current difficulties.

These early concepts of the causes of borderline disorder were dominant for many decades, in spite of the fact that they were based mainly on the reports of patients to their therapists, and that there was little empirical research to support these beliefs. Then, when research studies in this area were conducted, the results partially validated the original observations. But it is not that simple. A number of people with borderline disorder have experienced these early traumas. Others with borderline disorder did not have these childhood experiences, and yet developed the disorder. In addition, many children have experienced these traumas, but have not developed borderline disorder. What are we to make of these findings?

Does Borderline Disorder have Environmental or Biological Causes?

Research efforts over the past two decades have uncovered biological alterations in specific neural pathways of people with borderline disorder, compared with people without the disorder. These pathways are known to control the core behaviors that are impaired in people with borderline disorder, such as emotional regulation, impulse control, perception, and thinking. This work has revealed consistent and specific structural and functional changes in these critical pathways in those with borderline disorder. There is evidence that genetic factors also play a significant role in the development of the disorder.

Does this mean that borderline disorder has biological, rather than environmental, causes? The problem with this question is that it suggests a split between the *mind* and the *brain*. There is no such split. All psychological functions of the mind depend totally on the activity of specific neural pathways in the brain. I will explore in detail the relationships between the psychological functions that are disturbed in borderline disorder, and the specific neural pathways controlling these functions, in Chapter 6. For now, I think it's useful to explore what we know about the biological and environmental predispositions to borderline disorder, and to what extent they interact and contribute to the development of the disorder.

Risk Factors versus Causes

Based on the research, it's reasonable to conclude that borderline disorder is the result of the interaction of biological *and* environmental risk factors. Risk factors are not exactly the same as causes. When situation A is said to *cause* situation B, a direct, one-to-one relationship is implied. Each time situation A occurs, it will result in situation B. For instance, if someone inherits the gene for Huntington's disease, a fatal, degenerative disease of the brain, to the best of our current knowledge, they will inevitably develop the disorder. In this case, one defective gene causes the disorder.

But that's not true for most medical disorders. For example, in the case of diabetes, we know of approximately twenty genes that, if abnormal, place a person *at risk* for developing the disorder. It appears that the combination of at least four or five of these abnormal genes is required to put the individual at serious risk for developing diabetes. In addition, it is possible that some people with genetic risk factors will develop diabetes, and others with a similar genetic makeup will not. In part, developing diabetes also depends on the *behavior* of these individuals. Those individuals with additional environmental risk factors for diabetes, such as a poor diet, excessive weight, and little exercise, will have an added risk of developing diabetes. These environmental factors may make the difference between developing and not developing diabetes.

In other words, there is an interaction between the *degree* of genetic and environmental risk factors. The more severe the genetic risk, the less environmental risk is required. The less severe the genetic risk, the more severe the environmental risk is required to develop the disorder. Nonetheless, mutations in a number of genes appear to be necessary in order to develop many medical disorders, including borderline disorder. These are referred to as **multigenic disorders**, that is, disorders that require a number of genetic mutations before the disorder manifests itself.

It now appears likely that genetic, other biological, and environmental disturbances all serve as risk factors for borderline disorder.

Biological Risk Factors

When I was about twenty years old, I remember asking my maternal grandmother what she thought about the significant differences in the personalities of all of the members of our family—my brothers, sisters, cousins, other members of the extended family, and me. She said "Robert, I have seen about one hundred babies born into the entire family over my lifetime. [She came from a large French-Canadian Roman Catholic family.] With very few exceptions, the way you were as babies is the same as you were as children, then adolescents, then adults. I have not seen any of you change very much throughout your lives. I believe to a large extent, we are born the way we are."

My grandmother was forced to leave school at the age of twelve to cook, clean, and care for her father and six older brothers after her mother left them. What she lacked in formal education, she made up for with remarkably keen observations and astute insights. We now know that at least 50 percent of the characteristics of our personality can be attributed to genetic factors.

There are two types of biological risk factors that contribute to the development and course of any medical illness. They are inherited (genetic) factors, and developmental factors resulting in the abnormal development of one or more body organs. Either of these biological factors could place a person at risk for developing borderline disorder.

Genetic Risk Factors

A recently published study provides evidence that there is a significant genetic predisposition to borderline disorder. Experts in the field now believe that what is inherited are genetic mutations that impair the normal functions of those neural systems that control the core behavioral dimensions of borderline disorder: regulation of emotion; impulse control; and perception and reasoning. These genetic alterations are believed to place individuals at risk for developing the disorder.

Borderline disorder does appear to be more common in families in which other family members have borderline disorder and/or other disorders that share some of the traits of borderline disorder, such as affective disorders, posttraumatic stress disorder, alcoholism and other substance-related disorders, and several other personality disorders. This is not surprising, because these disorders also appear to be genetically transmitted and have been associated with abnormalities that occur in some of the same neural pathways as those affected in borderline disorder. (See Chapter 6 for more information on the neural pathways that appear to regulate the behavioral dimensions affected in borderline disorder.)

Developmental Risk Factors

In addition to genetic risk factors, it's also possible that the neural systems associated with the major symptoms of borderline disorder develop abnormally in some people with the disorder, either before or shortly after birth. These developmental abnormalities may then increase the risk for developing borderline disorder if they affect the neural systems that control emotional regulation, impulse control, and perception, memory, thinking, and reasoning. But what could cause such early alterations of intrauterine and infant development? There are at least two possibilities. First, it's estimated that the brain contains approximately 10^{11}, or one hundred billion, neurons (nerve cells). In order for the brain to carry out all of its functions properly, these nerve cells must be arranged in a very specific way. They must be lined up correctly in each of the many pathways and circuits that control all of the functions of the brain, such as vision, hearing, motor activities, emotion, motivation, and thinking. Developmental disorders (for example, some forms of mental retardation and learning disabilities) occur when certain neural pathways are not aligned correctly and do not function properly. Considering the enormous number of neural pathways and connections in the brain, it is not surprising that some of these pathways and connections do not always develop correctly. The greater the number of incorrect neural connections in the brain, the greater is the likelihood that a developmental disorder will occur.

Second, such developmental abnormalities may be caused by external physical factors that impair normal brain development during pregnancy or at the time of delivery. These factors may include nutritional deficiencies; congenital infections; the use of substances by the mother that are toxic to the fetus, such as alcohol, nicotine, and certain medicines; and decreased blood flow to the baby at birth. My mother may well have been correct in her belief that the use of an anesthetic during the delivery of my sister Denise contributed to her developing borderline disorder.

If genetic or developmental disturbances affect the neural systems that control the behavioral dimensions of borderline disorder, a person may have one or more inborn risk factors for the disorder. Genetic and early developmental disturbances could account for the reports of some parents of people with borderline disorder that these children were "different" since birth or early childhood.

Environmental Risk Factors

It's clear that biological risk factors are not the only factors that predispose people to borderline disorder. Research studies have shown repeatedly that environmental risk factors also increase the risk of individuals to the disorder. The environmental risk factors most frequently observed among people with borderline disorder are early separations or loss, trauma, ineffective parenting, and possibly adverse social customs.

EARLY SEPARATIONS OR LOSS

About 50 percent of people with borderline disorder have a history of early childhood separation from one or both of their parents. In these families, parents separate, divorce, or one parent deserts early in the child's life. Some parents of borderline patients have mental disorders themselves, including bipolar disorder, severe depression, alcoholism, and antisocial behaviors including criminality. These disorders clearly affect the capacity of these parents to provide good parental care, and can separate them physically and/or functionally from the child.

TRAUMA

Emotional, physical, and sexual abuses are the most commonly occurring traumas in people with borderline disorder. Repeated sexual abuse is more common in the histories of women with borderline disorder, while long-term physical abuse is more common in men with the disorder. Sexual and physical abuse can occur by a member of the family, or by a person outside the family. Sustained sexual abuse, especially incest, is associated with a high incidence of self-injurious behavior and suicide in people with borderline disorder.

INEFFECTIVE PARENTING

There is considerable evidence in the research literature that many people with borderline disorder have suffered from poor parenting. In these cases, there is a broad spectrum of parental failures. They include unresponsive, unloving, inconsistent, and unsupportive care from one or both parents. Poor parenting also includes providing poor role models for children. Frequent arguments, fights, and separations fail to provide children with a safe harbor at home. They also fail to equip children with examples of how to deal effectively with life's problems, and with strategies and skills to deal with their own internal emotional tensions and conflicts. Finally, poor parenting can involve the failure to protect the child from repeated abuse by the other parent, another member of the family, or an outsider.

It is important to understand that these identical environmental risk factors might result in different mental and physical disorders, based on the person's unique set of biological risk factors. Also, in the absence of significant biological risk factors for mental disorders, remarkably, some children can tolerate even severe environmental stress without apparent serious long-term psychological consequences.

ADVERSE SOCIAL CUSTOMS

Theodore Millon has recently proposed that two social and cultural trends in Western culture place people at additional risk for borderline disorder. These are: (1) social customs that worsen rather than remedy damaged parent-child relationships; and (2) a decrease in the capacity of institutions to compensate for the harm done by these impaired relationships.

Children with inherent difficulties integrating information and feelings, and with poor parenting, may be subjected to constantly shifting cultural styles and values that add to their lack of a coherent and stable view of themselves and their lives. Their relationships are also less stable than in former generations. They have little understanding of the value of their father's work, and the work of others, which is typically more abstract than in previous generations. Their mothers are often working and not able to help encourage appropriate behavior and support a stable environment for them. Society rarely provides children at risk for borderline disorder with values that they can emulate and that would help stabilize their precarious view of life. In such an unstable environment, they are unable to feel secure about their fate and what the future holds for them. The brief and often disruptive images on television are probably, on balance, more harmful than helpful in establishing clear and consistent boundaries of behavior for children who desperately need such boundaries. It is estimated that the typical eighteen-year-old American teenager has spent more time watching television than relating with his or her parents or attending school. Finally, the availability of drugs and the lax attitude about them by their peers further decrease the capacity of these children and teenagers to properly modulate their emotions and impulsive behaviors, to think clearly, and to develop increasingly mature and sound relationships.

Traditional customs of society that are meant to back up those of home and peer groups no longer do so with consistency. For example, the structure and support of the extended family members, who are now often dispersed across the country, neighbors, and schools, churches, and other community organizations do not play the pivotal roles in helping mold the value systems of children that they did in prior generations. In modern American society, they do not provide the same safety net for children at risk as they did in the past.

As is the case for all environmental risk factors, no one is suggesting that social-cultural risk factors cause borderline disorder. However, it's possible that they add to the total environmental burden of risk of children and adolescents already at high risk for the disorder.

How Environmental Risk Factors
Affect the Brain

Are there permanent consequences on brain development for children who are exposed to long-term harmful experiences early in life? More specifically, does the occurrence very early in life of continuous environmental stress permanently alter the critical neural systems involved in borderline disorder? Answering these questions requires some knowledge of how the brain develops and is affected by experience.

The human brain continues to develop well into the first decade of life. It is now known that the brain has many more neurons during childhood than even a few years later. This early "surplus" of neurons appears to provide exceptional adaptability and survival value to humans. We use, and thereby highly develop, certain neural pathways critical to survival in our peculiar environments. Under certain circumstances, these pathways may be the ones that control physical abilities that enable us to hunt, fight, plant, or build. In an environment requiring such skills, the neural pathways mediating these functions will develop more than ones that are used less. Also, people with superior inherent talents in these areas will have a better chance at survival and procreation than individuals less naturally gifted in this way. In other societies, intellectual abilities are more in demand than are physical talents. As a result of environmental need and emphasis, the neural pathways that control intellectual processes will develop preferentially, and those individuals most talented in these skills will be best rewarded.

Regardless of the degree of inherent talents, the brain responds to the demands of the environment by diverting nourishment from underused neural pathways to those more heavily in use. This process "prunes" the less frequently used neural pathways in the brain, thus assuring optimal learning and performance in the needed areas. The development of essential abilities and the pruning of less essential abilities enable the brain to function most efficiently and effectively.

Now, let's return to the issue raised above. What effects do environmental risk factors have on brain function in children? The answers to this question are just coming to light. For example, recent research has demonstrated abnormal brain function in certain regions of the brain of women with borderline disorder who have been sexually abused as children, that is not present in women who do not have the disorder. Although there are different interpretations of these findings, they raise the possibility that long-term changes in critical neural pathways may be the result, in part, of early traumatic experiences. These and similar changes in brain function resulting from other harmful environmental experiences could serve as one mechanism by which environmental risk factors interact with the biological risk factors noted earlier. This would increase the probability that individuals who have been exposed to these harmful environmental experiences will develop borderline disorder.

For example, from a biological perspective, unsupportive behavior by the parent of a frequently abused and frightened child may cause the fear system of the child to become permanently hypersensitive and over-reactive. In addition, long-term abuse may damage the function of certain memory pathways and thus protect the child from the emotional pain of thinking about these assaults. However, later in life, suppressing unpleasant events from memory may be maladaptive, and even result in dissociative episodes during which critical experiences are not remembered.

Early separation from, or impaired parenting by, one's mother or father may result in a lifelong dread of separations, or a poor sense of personal worth. Although changes in the brain caused by repeated fearful experiences appear to be very difficult to reverse totally, they can be modified considerably. There are a number of ways to produce these modifications in people with borderline disorder, and I discuss them at greater length in Chapters 9 and 10.

How Do Biological and Environmental Risk Factors Interact?

For the most part, environmental stresses such as those described above are harmful to children, including those who are born without any genetic or developmental impairments. However, when added to biological risk factors for borderline disorder, environmental risk factors appear to significantly increase the risk of these children developing the disorder. This is referred to as a **stress–diathesis model**.

One question raised by the stress-diathesis model is: "Which life experiences most increase the risk of developing borderline disorder?" As I mentioned before, any long-term psychological consequences of harmful experiences of people with borderline disorder are controlled by changes in the neural pathways that are involved in the symptoms of the disorder. However, it is not known to what extent each of the environmental risk factors for borderline disorder causes long-lasting psychological and biological changes. Experts in the field disagree about which specific biological and environmental risk factors are most critical. For example, Marsha Linehan, a psychologist at the University of Washington who has developed a specific form of therapy for borderline disorder, believes that people with the disorder have a biological predisposition for poorly regulated emotions. She contends that this inherent biological deficit is aggravated by parents who punish or demean these children, rather than attempt to understand them and help them deal with their poor emotional control (validate them). Mary Zanarini, a prominent researcher from Harvard University, suggests that inherently inadequate and poorly learned impulse control is the main feature of the disorder. Patricia Judd and Thomas McGlashan from Yale University assert that the central mechanism for the development of borderline disorder is faulty bonding to the parents, bonding that fails to maintain the infant's safety and survival through caring and nurturing parental protection.

It's very important for those with borderline disorder, as well as their parents, siblings, and marital families, to understand that none of the environmental risk factors I've discussed has been shown to *cause* borderline disorder. Many people who are exposed to the same abuse, separations, and bad parenting do not develop borderline disorder, and some borderline patients have not experienced any of these environmental risk factors. It's most likely that some critical combination of biological and environmental risk factors is necessary in order for a person to develop borderline disorder. Much more research is needed to determine the precise interactions and influences of these risk factors on the development of this disorder.

The Main Implications

There's a growing body of research evidence indicating that both biological and environmental factors increase the risk of developing borderline disorder. One of the important conclusions that we can draw from these findings is that they provide a scientific basis for the use of both medications *and* psychotherapy in the treatment of patients with borderline disorder.

It's important that you fully recognize the implications of this. I treat some patients with borderline disorder who are initially very opposed to the use of appropriate medications. As I described in Chapter 2, Mrs. Davis significantly reduced the rate of her recovery by resisting medication during the early phase of her treatment. She was not able to benefit adequately from the issues worked on in psychotherapy until she began her medication. I also see patients with borderline disorder who are quite willing to take medication, hoping for a magical cure of their difficulties. However, they are resistant to engaging in psychotherapy and the difficult work and changes that therapy involves. So they don't benefit from this type of treatment, and they fail to learn the skills they should have learned at an earlier age but didn't. In my experience, many patients become less resistant to either form of treatment when they come to understand the importance of both the biological and the psychological factors associated with borderline disorder that we have discussed in this chapter.

FIVE

Tracing the Course of the Disorder

☐ NE OF THE fundamental features of any medical illness is the natural course it will take. The course of a disorder is defined by several characteristics: the etiology; the typical age of onset, or of maximum vulnerability; the nature, severity, and progression of symptoms; the acute, chronic, or episodic occurrence of the symptoms; the responses of the symptoms to treatment; and the prognosis or likely outcome of the disorder.

Borderline Disorder in Adolescents

If behavioral symptoms resembling borderline disorder develop in children, they will often continue to evolve as these young people enter pre-adolescence and adolescence, but not always into borderline disorder. For in-depth information on borderline disorder and children, see Chapter 11. However, the full spectrum of symptoms of borderline disorder appears most commonly during the teenage years and young adulthood. This period of life is the time of maximal vulnerability for those people who are at high risk for developing borderline disorder. The symptoms that mark the onset of borderline disorder in teenagers closely resemble those seen in adults (Chapter 1). Therefore, the correct diagnosis of borderline disorder is more likely to occur during this period of life than during childhood.

Although adolescents with borderline disorder typically have symptoms that are similar to adults, they are modified in age-specific ways. In a recent study of hospitalized adolescents with borderline disorder, two thirds of them demonstrated symptoms of emotional instability, uncontrolled anger, feelings of emptiness or boredom, impulsiveness, and suicidal threats or gestures. Surprisingly, only one third had unstable relationships, and even fewer had identity disturbances. Overall, in this study, the rate of occurrence of borderline disorder among all admissions, and the symptom profiles of individuals with the disorder, were similar in adolescents and adults.

Follow-up studies suggest that less than half of adolescents with borderline disorder when first seen, still meet criteria for the disorder several years later. This does not mean that those who no longer meet criteria are without symptoms; they just do not have enough symptoms to meet categorical criteria. They may have four of the nine criteria in Table 1.2 on page 19, and they still may have significant difficulties. For example, in one study, three symptoms of borderline disorder were found to be more persistent and stable over time than other symptoms. They are emptiness or boredom; inappropriate, intense anger; and emotional instability. These symptoms can be quite disabling.

Poor Emotional Control

In adolescents with borderline disorder, arguments with parents and siblings may occur more frequently than they did in childhood and become very heated, far out of proportion to the source of the disagreement. In addition to severe outbursts of anger, other symptoms of poor emotional control may appear, such as significant episodes of moodiness, sadness, or anxiety. Some adolescents may show a tendency toward rapid boredom with activities after great, initial enthusiasm. Their interests will shift rapidly from one area to another. They often have difficulty in completing projects that require persistence.

Impulsivity

Serious and generally rebellious misbehaviors may first appear in adolescence. These may include failure to do homework, driving the family car before obtaining a license, drinking and taking drugs, staying out past curfew, dressing and appearing in hair styles and other bodily adornments that are at the fringe of family standards and social norms and acceptability, sexual misconduct, truancy from school, stealing, and developing friendships with other teenagers who engage in similar behaviors. Some teenagers with borderline disorder may perform destructive acts such as breaking furniture or other people's possessions, or even physically attacking their parents or siblings.

Adolescents with borderline disorder may also demonstrate self-injurious behavior for the first time. These behaviors are usually scratching or cutting their wrists or arms with sharp instruments, physically hurting themselves in other ways, or taking overdoses of aspirin or other medications that are available around the house. These self-injurious acts are often in response to arguments with their parents or boyfriend or girlfriend; actual or threatened separation from these and other people important to them; or being caught at, and held accountable, for serious misbehaviors.

Perception and Reasoning

There are very few studies that examine this group of symptoms in adolescents. These and anecdotal reports suggest that identity disturbance, suspiciousness, and paranoid thinking may occur in adolescents with borderline disorder, though they may not be as apparent as in adults. Clinical experience suggests that adolescents with borderline disorder also have difficulty with their ability to reason as well as their peers, especially while under emotional stress.

Relationships

Adolescents as a group are caught in a major dilemma of normal development. On the one hand, they continue to be largely dependent on their parents and others for many of their daily essentials. On the other hand, they strive for increasing independence, often beyond their capacity to use this independence wisely.

Gradually achieving independence and mature relationships is a difficult task for adolescents, even if they don't have borderline disorder. Because major characteristics of the disorder are severe conflicts over dependency and a significant impairment of forming sound and balanced relationships with anyone, it should not be surprising that adolescents with borderline disorder have even more difficulty with these normal processes of maturation than do those without the disorder.

Therefore, relationships with parents, other family members, friends, and boyfriends or girlfriends may become increasingly tumultuous. Parents often become "the enemy," seemingly overnight, as adolescents with borderline disorder shift their dependent, clinging, and ambivalent relationships from parents to their peers. They may first develop one or two very close friendships with other teenagers of the same sex. However, it is usually not too long before the relationships shift to boyfriends or girlfriends. These relationships are often intense and brief, may involve premature sexual activity, and, when over, for whatever reason, often result in dramatic functional collapses. For example, the adolescent may not be able to attend school or do his/her homework, may withdraw from interacting with family and friends, and may develop physical symptoms such as headaches and abdominal pain.

Borderline Disorder in Early Adulthood

For some people, the symptoms of borderline disorder don't significantly disrupt their lives until the late teenage years or the early twenties. Life for everyone during this period becomes more complex and challenging. The stresses of leaving home, and the demands of higher education, work, marriage, and child-rearing require increasing self-reliance, self-discipline, and independence. People with borderline disorder typically have great difficulty developing these adaptive skills during this critical period in their lives. This inability to deal effectively and consistently with the normal stresses of maturity is the result of the emotional, impulsive, cognitive, and physical symptoms of the disorder, which may occur for the first time, or increase to a higher level of severity and frequency if already present. The severity of these symptoms of borderline disorder can vary considerably among young people with the disorder, and, therefore, will cause varying degrees of disturbance to their lives.

The Episodic Nature of Symptoms

Regardless of when symptoms of borderline disorder first appear, they often appear episodically on a background of otherwise fairly normal behavior. These episodes are usually precipitated by stressful experiences involving significant personal losses or disagreements, or in response to severe consequences of destructive behaviors such as failure at school or work, stealing, reckless driving or driving while intoxicated, and alcohol and drug abuse. Family gatherings at holidays or other occasions may also result in a flare-up of symptoms.

Families of people with borderline disorder gradually learn under what circumstances symptomatic episodes are most likely to occur, and begin to dread these occasions. It becomes increasingly frustrating and discouraging for people with borderline disorder and their families to repeatedly go through these episodes, which usually worsen and occur more frequently over time. It's especially bewildering because between episodes, people with borderline disorder may be relatively free of symptoms and appear to be doing very well. These periods of symptom-free behavior make it more difficult to endure the next relapse, because it appears that the relapses are deliberate and intentionally provocative.

The Misdiagnosis of Borderline Disorder

It's during this period of their lives that many people with borderline disorder first seek—or are brought by parents or spouses for—medical help. Some consult psychiatrists or other mental health professionals about emotional and behavioral symptoms, while others go to their primary care physicians with complaints about physical symptoms. Unfortunately, the core problem of borderline disorder is often initially unrecognized. If this is the case, the person with borderline disorder then begins a frustrating and unsuccessful series of psychiatric evaluations and medical tests. These often result in incorrect diagnoses and ineffective treatments that bring, at best, only partial and temporary relief.

At this point, people with borderline disorder are at a critical juncture in their lives. If the correct diagnosis is made, and if skilled clinicians provide effective treatment, the prognosis can be quite good. The symptoms of the disorder may be brought under control and the lives of patients with borderline disorder can be stabilized to a considerable extent. However, in the absence of the correct diagnosis and effective care, the outcome is generally much less favorable.

The Prognosis

Until recently, many psychiatrists and other mental health clinicians thought that the prognosis for patients with borderline disorder was very poor. This pessimism was based, in part, on the chronic, episodic, and recurring nature of the symptoms of the disorder. Also, pessimism was supported by the apparent failure of many patients to respond well to the standard uses of psychotherapy and medications that had proven helpful to patients with other mental disorders, such as depression and anxiety. Finally, the widely held perception of poor outcome of borderline disorder may have been due to a variety of flaws in the design of early research studies evaluating the outcome of borderline disorder. These studies typically involved relatively few patients with severe borderline disorder who were in treatment, and the studies did not include a comparison group. In general, the findings from these early studies were that many borderline patients did poorly in the short term, but better over the long term.

However, more recent studies suggest that such pessimism is not warranted. These studies show that many people with borderline disorder respond well to specific medication regimens and to special forms of psychotherapy designed specifically for the treatment of the disorder. Recent research suggests that 60 to 75 percent of people with borderline disorder improve significantly over time as the effects of treatment are realized. This doesn't mean that they no longer have any symptoms, but that the symptoms are significantly reduced in severity, and that they cause less disruption in the patients' lives and their family's lives.

The Effects of Treatment on Outcome

I've stressed that if you or a family member has borderline disorder, you should be hopeful, but I know that that's easier said than done. What you want is proof, some solid reason to be hopeful. In the medical community, the best tangible reason to believe anything is because the results of well-conducted research support the belief. Here are three important studies of people with borderline disorder who were followed over many years, each of which will give you reason to be hopeful.

THE McLEAN STUDY

MARY ZANARINI and her colleagues at Harvard's McLean Hospital in Boston have very recently reported the results of a six-year prospective follow-up study of 290 patients with borderline disorder and 72 patients with other personality disorders. A prospective study is one designed to gather the intended information prior to the study, rather than after the patients have been treated. Such studies increase the accuracy and validity of the results. All patients were carefully diagnosed with appropriate rating instruments and met DSM-III (the previous edition of the *Diagnostic and Statistical Manual of Mental Disorders*) diagnostic criteria. Patients were studied at two, four, and six years after their initial hospitalization and entrance into the study, and remained in treatment during the course of the study. At the times of follow-up, they received extensive evaluations of symptoms and treatment history.

The authors report three major findings:

1. Remission, which means an individual no longer meets DSM-III criteria for borderline disorder, was common. The remission rates of borderline patients were about 35 percent at the two-year mark,

50 percent at the four-year mark, and 75 percent at six years. These results are very consistent with those found at similar times in earlier, smaller studies.

2. Recurrences of borderline disorder in patients who had achieved remission were rare. This suggests that in this intensively treated group of borderline patients, once they felt understood and learned how to control and adapt more effectively to their symptoms, their progress was not easily lost.

3. Borderline patients experienced significant reductions in symptoms of each of the four dimensions of borderline disorder. However, different symptoms demonstrated different patterns of improvement over time. For example, emotional disturbances were more persistent and were still present in 60 to 80 percent of patients in six years.

Some impulsive behaviors, especially self-mutilation, suicidal efforts, substance abuse, and sexual promiscuity, declined dramatically, often to one third of their initial rate of occurrence. Other impulsive behaviors, such as binge eating, verbal outbursts, and spending sprees, declined only about 30 percent at the six-year follow-up.

Over time, cognitive and interpersonal symptoms of borderline disorder declined more than emotional symptoms, but less than impulsive symptoms. While psychotic-like thoughts dropped from about 50 percent to 20 percent of the patients at six years, odd thinking declined from 85 percent to 50 percent.

Some areas of interpersonal relationships also improved more than others. Over six years, difficulties with therapists declined from 50 percent to 10 percent of patients. Stormy relationships/manipulation/sadism, and demandingness/entitlement declined from 60–80 percent to 25–50 percent, and reported intolerance of aloneness, abandonment, or dependency concerns decreased from 90 percent of borderline patients to 60 percent.

The authors conclude that the results of this study suggest that borderline disorder is characterized by two distinct types of symptoms. One type of symptom represents the more temperamental or enduring aspects of borderline disorder. These symptoms, such as chronic feelings of anger or emptiness, suspicion, difficulty tolerating aloneness, and abandonment concerns, seem to resolve more slowly and were still reported by a majority of borderline patients six years after their initial admission. The other type, including self-mutilation, suicide efforts, quasi-psychotic thought, treatment regressions, and problems in relationships with the therapist, is a manifestation of acute illness. These seem to disappear relatively quickly over time.

THE COLLABORATIVE LONGITUDINAL PERSONALITY DISORDER STUDY

THE COLLABORATIVE Longitudinal Personality Disorder Study (CLPDS) is funded by the National Institute of Mental Health (NIMH) and involves the collaboration of research sites in the departments of psychiatry at Brown, Columbia, Harvard, Texas A&M, Vanderbilt, and Yale Universities. It is designed to study prospectively the outcomes of four personality disorders, including borderline disorder.

This group recently reported on the possible reasons for sudden "remissions" in the 160 borderline patients enrolled in the study. Eighteen patients who initially met five or more diagnostic criteria fell to two or fewer criteria during the first six months of the study. Of these 18 patients, only one had suffered a relapse at a two-year follow-up evaluation.

Rapid improvement in ten of the patients was judged to be due to situational changes resulting in relief from extremely stressful situations. Such relief typically involved either establishing relationships with new partners, or leaving very stressful relationships.

In five other patients, rapid remission from borderline disorder was associated with successful treatment of acute mental disorders that occurred with borderline disorder. These included **panic disorder**, substance abuse, major depressive disorder, and bipolar disorder (see Chapter 7 for more information on these disorders).

The important findings from this study are that about 10 percent of a large sample of borderline patients experienced a significant remission in six months, and all but one remained in remission for two years. The authors note that these very positive findings contrast favorably against the estimated suicide rate of about 10 percent of patients with borderline disorder.

THE LINKS AND HESLEGRAVE STUDY

PAUL LINKS and Ronald Heslegrave of Toronto, Canada, have published a series of reports of prospective studies of the outcomes of 88 patients with borderline disorder. In these studies, patients with borderline disorder were evaluated at two and seven years after the initial assessment.

A major finding of this study was that 47 percent of the patients were described as having persistent or stable borderline disorder at the seven-year follow-up. This finding is very consistent with those of other researchers who estimate the long-term stability of borderline disorder between 51 percent and 57 percent.

Links and Heslegrave were also able to identify factors that were highly predictive of long-term outcome of borderline disorder. The initial level of impulsivity accounted for 25 percent of the variations in outcome at the seven-year follow-up; in other words, a high initial level of impulsivity predicted a greater likelihood of persistent borderline disorder than a low initial level. Patients initially diagnosed with borderline disorder who also were diagnosed with substance abuse were twice as likely to have borderline disorder at follow-up than were those patients without substance abuse. There were two other significant predictors of the course and outcome of borderline disorder found in this study. A severe level of symptoms of borderline disorder and a history of childhood sexual abuse predicted poorer outcome than less severe symptoms and no childhood sexual abuse.

The authors conclude from their findings that people with persistent borderline disorder typically demonstrate high levels of impulsivity, and that impulsivity is the engine that appears to perpetuate the disorder over the course of their life. They go on to suggest that modification of impulsive behavior with medications, for example, may enable patients with borderline disorder to develop stable and meaningful relationships.

Taken as a whole, these studies are very encouraging about the prognosis of borderline disorder and help dispel the myth that the dis-order is typically chronic and poorly responsive to treatment. They strongly suggest that with good treatment and with better control over impulsive behavior, you will experience a significant improvement in many of your symptoms. All symptoms do not improve to the same degree, but they all do improve. One of the main factors that deter-mines the rate and degree of your improvement is your remaining in treatment as long as is necessary.

What Happens If You Drop Out of Treatment?

Unfortunately, for one reason or another, many people with bor-derline disorder leave treatment prematurely. It may be that their treatment program is not working as well as they would like. Others may no longer be able to afford the proper care, or don't receive badly needed support from their family or spouse. For some, it's that they're unwilling or unable to give up the alcohol, drugs, or other activities and behaviors that prevent them from benefiting from treat-ment. Regrettably, for others, they are unable to find a psychiatrist in their community who is skilled in the diagnosis and treatment of borderline disorder, and dedicated to working with patients with the disorder. Not surprisingly, the prognosis is not nearly as good for these people as it is for those who have been stabilized on a success-ful medication regimen and who remain in treatment until they have learned to consistently manage their lives more skillfully and effec-tively. My main purpose in reviewing the studies of the course of borderline disorder is to provide you with sound reasons for enter-ing and remaining in therapy. These studies show that proper treat-ment is your best hope of gaining control over your life.

There Are Different Levels of Severity

It's important to understand that the severity of borderline disorder is not the same for everyone who has it. Some people have very mild forms of the disorder and respond extremely well to treatment. Oth-ers have more severe forms of the disorder. For them, the treatment plan may be more complex and treatment may take longer. This difference in severity is a common characteristic of many medical illnesses. For example, some people with mild forms of diabetes may respond well to changes in diet, or require only oral medications, and suffer very few consequences of their illness. Other diabetic patients require severe dietary restrictions and multiple daily injections of insulin, and may still remain in poor control and develop serious secondary medical problems. As Links and Heslegrave discovered in their study, severity is an important indicator of the long-term outcome of borderline disorder. However, if you or a loved one suffers from severe borderline disorder, the situation is not hopeless. It does mean that you'll have to expend more effort and patience to get better.

Regardless of the severity of borderline disorder, psychiatrists and other physicians and mental health professionals who specialize in the treatment of people with this illness are now much more optimistic about successful outcomes than they were even a decade ago. This optimism is based, in part, on the research findings I discussed in this chapter. In addition, our understanding of the fundamental nature of borderline disorder is increasing more rapidly now than at any time in the past. Advances continue to be made in treatments specifically designed for people with borderline disorder, and we now see that significant improvements can result from the combined efforts of the person with borderline disorder and his or her spouse and family.

SIX

Borderline Personality Disorder and the Brain

I 'VE FOUND THAT it helps people with borderline disorder and their families if they understand the relationship between their symptoms and behaviors and the systems of the brain that are involved in the disorder. It's important to find out as much as possible about the fundamental nature of your symptoms. That way, you can understand in plain language *why* you feel and behave as you do. Learning about the biological basis of borderline disorder can help make it seem less mysterious and a little more acceptable.

We now know enough about the functions of the brain to begin to understand what is occurring in the central nervous system of people with borderline disorder that produces your symptoms. Even though we can't define exactly the differences in brain function that distinguish you from people without the disorder, we are able to describe some of the main features of the problem. Research over the past two decades has used advances in modern medical technology to begin to uncover the neural basis of borderline disorder. What we've found is that the symptoms of borderline disorder appear to be the result of biochemical and physiological abnormalities in the neural systems that regulate emotional activity, impulse control, and thinking.

Core Behavioral Dimensions of Borderline Disorder

In one of his excellent books on understanding the relationships between behavior and brain function, Joseph LeDoux, a prominent neuroscientist at Cornell University, states "...the proper level of analysis of a psychological function is the level at which that function is represented in the brain." In order to understand the brain structures and functions that are believed to be involved in borderline disorder, we should review briefly the major groups or dimensions of behavior that are affected by the disorder.

Poorly Regulated Emotions

You may have observed that your emotions are affected in three ways: the degree of your emotional response; the rate of change in your emotions; and the rate of return to normal levels.

DISPROPORTIONAL EMOTIONAL RESPONSES

In the average person, emotional responses are proportional to the events that cause them. For example, a small negative incident will usually produce a comparably small negative response, whether it is anger, sadness, or anxiety. Likewise, a stronger stimulus will cause a proportionally stronger response. The emotional response is reasonably equivalent to the event that caused it.

When you have borderline disorder, you often don't have proportional responses to situations. You may overreact emotionally to many life events. For example, a minor constructive criticism by a husband or boyfriend may evoke a violently angry response from you, which leads to a major argument. A brief separation from someone important to you may produce an excessive amount of anxiety, sadness, or anger. More serious events, such as the breakup of a close relationship, could cause severe emotional reactions and behavioral consequences, including a variety of damaging and self-injurious actions. Less often, you may underreact emotionally to a disturbing situation, then later feel badly and not know why.

EMOTIONAL LABILITY

In addition to difficulty in controlling the degree of your emotional responses, you may experience rapid changes in your emotions: for example, you may swing from feeling anxious to feeling depressed or angry. As you may recall from Chapter 1, these rapid swings in mood could have caused you to be inaccurately diagnosed with bipolar disorder.

DELAYED RETURN OF EMOTIONS TO THEIR NORMAL LEVEL

Once in a hyperemotional state, you may have found that it takes your emotions longer to return to their usual level than it does other people. This is another characteristic of emotional dysregulation experienced by people with borderline disorder.

Therefore, it appears that in people with borderline disorder, the mechanisms in the brain that control these three characteristics of emotional response do not function properly. This results in emotional responses that are at times so severe and prolonged that they have been referred to as "emotional storms."

Impulsivity

Many people with borderline disorder have difficulty effectively controlling their impulses and behaving in a reasonable and rational manner, especially when they are in a highly emotional state. At such times, you may find it extremely difficult, if not impossible, to calm yourself down, and to reassure yourself. Because of this, you don't have time to think through the situation you're in carefully in order to make a well-balanced decision on how to handle it.

Most people can recall experiences when emotions briefly overcome their reason and self-control, and they say or do things impulsively that they later regret. Nonetheless, most of the time, even under stress, they are able to keep their emotions and impulses in check and to behave appropriately. In people with borderline disorder, however, the brain mechanisms that are responsible for regulating impulsive behavior are impaired, making it difficult to develop and to carry out well-reasoned and appropriate responses.

Impaired Perception and Reasoning

A number of problems with perception and reasoning occur in people with borderline disorder. These problems are especially evident when you are under stress and your emotions are running high. However, many of them may be present to a less noticeable degree most of the time.

The major symptoms in this dimension of borderline disorder are temporary, stress-related paranoid thinking and dissociative episodes. You may also generally expect others to behave badly toward you, and be uncertain about your core values and beliefs. You may not have a well-thought-out and reasonable plan for your future. You may have difficulty in seeing, balancing, and resolving the complex problems of everyday life, but rather perceive and react as if people and situations are either black or white, all good or all bad. Finally, you may have difficulty in reasoning through complex problems, in identifying your alternatives, the advantages and disadvantages of these alternatives, and then choosing the most appropriate response, rather than the action that you "want" to take.

Again, there is evidence that the brain systems that control these cognitive activities do not function properly in people with borderline disorder.

The Study of Behavior at the Brain Level

Why do people with borderline disorder have more difficulty controlling their emotions and impulses, and thinking and reasoning, than people without the disorder? To understand the answer to this question, you need a basic understanding of how the brain functions. Again, bear with me here for a while. I believe you may find this a little easier and more interesting than you think.

It's estimated that the brain contains approximately 100 billion neurons. Neurons, or nerve cells, have one primary function: to discharge impulses to other neurons by chemical messengers (to "fire") when they are stimulated to a certain critical level themselves by other neurons. This fact immediately raises a question. If the brain is made up of cells that function simply by firing or not firing, how are the different actions or functions of the brain produced? In other words, how can the firing of these nerve cells produce different sensations such as vision, smell, and touch, as well as physical movements, emotions, motivations, and thoughts? Are the neurons that produce these actions inherently different, or do they use different chemical messengers, called **neurotransmitters**? To some degree, different types of neurons do have different functions in each neural pathway, but these neurons typically exist in all pathways and use essentially the same neurotransmitters. Therefore, differences in cell type and in chemical messenger are not the primary reasons for the different functions of the brain.

The Relationship Between Neural Pathways and Behavior

It's not fully understood how the activity of neurons in the brain produces different functions, but it appears that they do so primarily because of their location in the brain and their connections to other neurons and body organs. For example, the stimulation of neurons that connect the retina of the eye with the part of the cortex of the brain devoted to processing visual information (the visual cortex) results in visual images. If this pathway is impaired at any point along its course, we will not see well, or at all. Similarly, activity in neurons that connect the cortex of the brain with muscles produces contraction of the muscles, and therefore movement.

These examples are fairly straightforward, but they don't answer the more difficult question of how the activity in neurons in the brain produces emotions, memories, thinking, and impulse control. The answer to this is only partially known. To a significant degree, it seems that activity in very specific neural pathways and circuits controls these and other functions. That is, just as occurs in vision and movement, brain activity in certain other pathways results in specific emotions, while activity in yet other pathways results in impulse control, memories, and thoughts. Therefore, the importance of the *location* in the brain of neural pathways is critical in determining the functions of these pathways.

Interactions Between Brain Pathways

A second principle of brain function is also important to understand at this point. Although specific brain functions are determined by the activity of neurons in specific pathways, these pathways do not operate in isolation from one another, but interact at specific locations in the brain. This enables information in one pathway to be integrated with, and to influence the activity of, other pathways.

For example, activity in specific memory pathways produces specific memories. But it may also have effects on the activity of pathways that produce emotions. Therefore, the memory of a pleasant event may also produce a pleasant feeling. The memory of another event may cause a very unpleasant feeling. The converse is also true. An emotional state may produce memories that are consistent with that emotion. When we are happy, we tend to have pleasant, happy memories. When we are sad, we are likely to recall sad and unhappy events in our life.

Finally, emotions appear to alter our ability to remember certain events. Those events that are associated with strong emotions are often remembered more vividly and for a longer time than events with little emotional significance. We also know that if an event produces very strong and disturbing emotions, accurate memory of that event may be impaired, and it may be forgotten or "repressed."

Neurotransmitters and Brain Function

You need to know one more important fact about brain function to understand what is currently known about the biological basis of borderline disorder. Neurons cause one another to fire or not fire by releasing neurotransmitters, which interact with specific receptors for these chemicals on the next neuron. The interaction of these chemical messengers with their receptors on another neuron has one of two effects. It either increases or decreases the likelihood that the next neuron receiving the neurotransmitter will fire. That is, the effect is either stimulatory or inhibitory. The two most abundant neurotransmitters produced in the brain are **glutamate**, a stimulatory neurotransmitter, and **gamma aminobutyric acid (GABA)**, an inhibitory neurotransmitter. These two chemical messengers are used by all brain pathways and circuits.

In addition, activity in brain pathways is stimulated or inhibited by other neurotransmitters that are called **neuromodulators**, such as **dopamine**, serotonin, **acetylcholine**, and norepinephrine. In contrast to the hundreds of millions of neurons in the brain that utilize the neurotransmitters glutamate and GABA, relatively few neurons utilize the neuromodulators. It's estimated that the brain contains about 100,000 dopamine-producing neurons. Nonetheless, dopamine and other neuromodulators exert a strong influence on brain activity and function. The loss of dopamine neurons in only one of its pathways results in Parkinson's disease, and Alzheimer's disease is associated with the loss of neurons that secrete acetylcholine.

The Neural Systems Involved in Borderline Disorder

Now that you have a basic understanding of the relationship between the neural pathways of the brain and behavior, you are prepared to consider the specific neural systems and neurotransmitter disturbances that are associated with the symptoms and behaviors of borderline disorder. Data from a number of different research studies support three conclusions. First, the pathways in the brain that process emotional responses do not appear to function correctly. Second, the pathways in the brain that process impulse control appear to be underactive. Third, there is evidence that a critical area of the brain responsible for rational thought and reasoning is impaired in borderline disorder. The abnormal function in these three important and distinct neural systems could account for the core behavioral dimensions of borderline disorder. To break it down even further, here's a list of the neural circuits that appear to be disturbed in borderline disorder:

- Emotional dysregulation: *amygdala* system
- Impulsivity: *anterior cingulate* and *orbitomedial prefrontal* systems
- Cognitive–perceptual impairment: *dorsolateral prefrontal* system

The Neural Systems of Emotion

Researchers have consistently reported abnormal emotional responses in people with borderline disorder. For example, people with borderline disorder typically demonstrate a greater reaction to pictures of faces that have fearful and angry expressions compared to pictures of faces that have emotionally neutral expressions. This "fear response" is controlled by a structure in the medial (middle) region of the anterior temporal lobe of the brain called the **amygdala** (Figure 6.1). The amygdala is the central structure in a neural system that processes emotions, and its main functions are to:

- *Determine the emotional significance* of new information in light of past experience and provide this information to other neural circuits for further interpretation and appropriate action.
- Rapidly organize and initiate *subconsciously* both inborn and acquired responses to stimuli.
- Provide the essential first step in developing conditioned emotional responses.

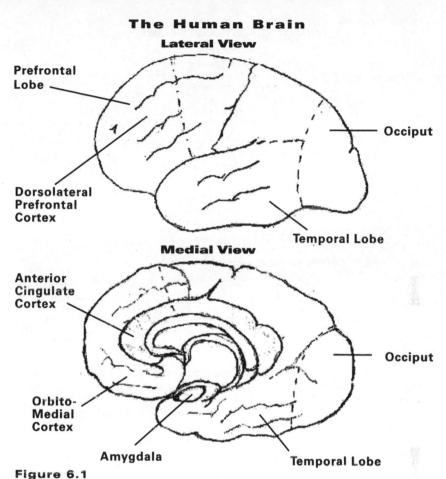

The Human Brain

Lateral View

Prefrontal Lobe

Dorsolateral Prefrontal Cortex

Occiput

Temporal Lobe

Medial View

Anterior Cingulate Cortex

Orbito-Medial Cortex

Amygdala

Occiput

Temporal Lobe

Figure 6.1

Lateral and medial (middle) views of the brain demonstrate regions that are important in the neural systems and pathways that control emotion (amygdala and orbital prefrontal cortex), impulse control (anterior cingulate and orbitomedial prefrontal cortex), and perception-reasoning (dorsolateral prefrontal cortex).

Information travels through and is processed by the main pathways and structures of the amygdala system as shown in Figure 6.2. Incoming sensory information is split at one of the relay and processing structures in the brain called the **thalamus**. Part of the signal is sent to the amygdala and processed rapidly to determine its emotional significance as a result of past experiences. The amygdala then initiates the appropriate automatic emotional responses. These include programmed physical, physiological, and hormonal responses that are most adaptive to the situation.

Neural Circuits of Emotion

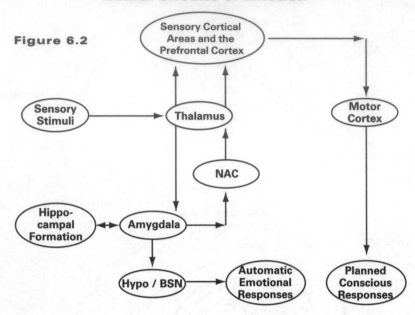

Figure 6.2

Information from sensory stimuli are processed and split at a deep brain structure, the thalamus. Part of the signal is transmitted to the amygdala, where its emotional significance is determined and appropriate automatic responses are initiated. Some of this information from the amygdala is transmitted to the nucleus accumbens (NAC) where it is processed further for the assignment of the appropriate levels of motivation and reward, both positive and negative. Pathways from all of the deep brain structures transmit information to the orbital prefrontal cortex for conscious perceptions of emotional responses that we refer to as feelings.

Finally, part of the original sensory information that was split at the thalamus is transmitted to sensory cortical areas for more precise, conscious evaluation than occurred at the faster, though less precise, subconscious subcortical levels.

(NAC: nucleus accumbens; Hypo: hypothalamus; BSN: brain stem nuclei.)

The cerebral cortex also receives part of the sensory information from the thalamus for processing at a conscious level in the sensory cortical areas. The conscious perception of emotions appears to take place in the orbital prefrontal cortex (Figure 6.1). The recognition and processing of emotion at the cortical level provides for some degree of conscious control over emotional responses. The structures and pathways involved in this control are related to impulsivity.

CONDITIONED FEAR RESPONSES

One of the best-studied emotional responses controlled by the amygdala system are conditioned fear responses. These are the automatic and rapid responses we develop when we are exposed to harmful situations. For example, a young girl who is being repeatedly sexually abused may develop a conditioned fear response to footsteps coming down the hall to her bedroom at night. Her conditioned fear response could be an inability to move, increased blood pressure and heart rate, an endocrine response such as increased cortisol and norepinephrine levels, or all of them. Endocrines are hormones that are secreted into the bloodstream and produce widespread effects throughout the body.

It's important to understand that these emotional responses are automatic and not under conscious control. In addition, once a conditioned fear response occurs, it appears to be permanently embedded in the brain. It may lessen substantially over time, but it remains in place and may be reactivated by a variety of circumstances and situations. It is not surprising, then, that recent research has shown that the amygdala is more reactive in response to stressful stimuli in people with borderline disorder than it is in people who do not have the disorder.

This hyperreactivity of the amygdala is not specific to individuals with borderline disorder. For examples, veterans with **posttraumatic stress disorder** (PTSD) have very vivid emotional memories of and "relive" past traumatic combat experiences. Their brain scans demonstrate greater activity of the amygdala when they are exposed to combat pictures than occurs in veterans who have had similar combat experience, but who do not have PTSD. It appears that people with borderline disorder and the veterans with PTSD in the study are either born with a fear system that is hyperreactive, or it became hyperreactive in response to early fear-provoking trauma, or both.

People with borderline disorder are more likely to develop PTSD, panic disorder, and chronic anxiety than the general population.

MOTIVATION/REWARD PATHWAYS

Research has shown that the amygdala neural system is critical in the generation of other emotions as well as fear. For example, the experiences of motivation and reward are tightly linked in the brain to emotion. We are motivated to perform those acts that result in positive rewards and feelings. We avoid those that produce negative responses and unpleasant feelings. The brain pathway that controls motivation and reward runs through a structure deep in the brain called the **nucleus accumbens**, which is closely associated with the amygdala.

As you can see in Figure 6.2, a major pathway from the amygdala, where the emotional significance of an experience is determined, connects directly to the nucleus accumbens. It's possible that the motivation/reward component of the amygdala system does not perform normally in people with borderline disorder. The decreased sense of self-assurance and self-worth that are characteristic of borderline disorder appear to be related to not feeling a sense of reward from accomplishments. This blunted response to positive rewards may be due to impaired function in the nucleus accumbens motivation/reward component of the amygdala system.

Normal dopamine activity in the nucleus acumens is essential for the motivation/reward system to function properly (Figure 6.5). There is evidence that the activity of this neuromodulator is disturbed in people with borderline disorder. Abnormal dopamine activity in the nucleus accumbens may also account for the high rates of depression and substance abuse associated with borderline disorder. Alcohol and many addictive drugs have been shown to stimulate dopamine activity in this area of the brain.

EMOTION AND MEMORY

As noted above, memory and emotions are very closely related. A very important structure in the brain related to memory is the **hippocampal formation**. This is located anatomically adjacent to the amygdala and connected to it structurally and functionally by strong neural pathways (Figures 6.1 and 6.2). Low to moderate levels of stress and emotional response appear to increase memory, while high levels interfere with memory formation and recall. This close relationship may explain why some people with borderline disorder have episodes of long lapses of memory when under high stress.

All of this is to say that the emotional symptoms of borderline disorder, and other disorders that co-occur with borderline disorder, may be related in part to dysfunctions in the amygdala system.

The Neural Systems of Impulse Control

Research studies have shown that people with borderline disorder have a clear decrease in function in the prefrontal lobes of the brain (Figure 6.1). Nerve pathways and circuits in the prefrontal lobes are responsible for thinking, planning, reasoning, and evaluating what to do, and then for acting accordingly. Control over impulses appears to be associated especially with activity in the middle portions of the prefrontal lobes, especially those pathways arising from the **anterior cingulate cortex** and the **orbitomedial cortex** (Figure 6.1). These circuits perform several functions, including:

- *Consciously* evaluating the significance of emotionally charged information relayed directly from sensory systems, and indirectly from the amygdala system
- Assessing the potential consequences of behavioral responses to these stimuli
- Integrating and modulating these responses prior to and during action
- Storing this information for future use

These functions of the **orbitomedial** and anterior cingulate prefrontal *circuits* are clearly very important in the control of impulsive behavior (Figure 6.3). These circuits exert a "top-down" modulation of the activity of structures situated deep in the brain. Depending on conclusions and decisions made at the higher cortical level, the lower-level systems, such as the amygdala system, can be either stimulated or inhibited. However, this top-down control is not complete. Attempts to make ourselves relax when highly anxious rarely work, unless we have received specialized treatment such as biofeedback training. Therefore, impairment of these circuits could result in diminished impulse control. But is there any evidence of abnormal activity in this area of the brain in people with borderline disorder?

Neural Circuits of Impulse Control

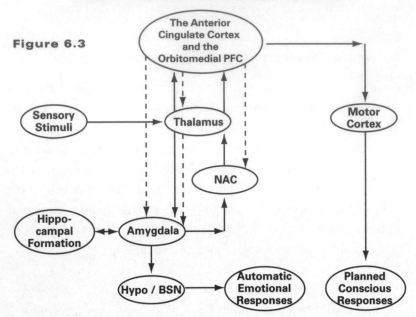

Figure 6.3

Once information is processed at the cortical level for factual and emotional content (see Figure 6.2), prefrontal cortical areas, especially the anterior cingulate and orbitomedial prefrontal cortex, exert "top-down" control through pathways that connect with, and stimulate or inhibit, the subcortical systems (described in Figure 6.2). These pathways are represented by the dashed lines (- - - - - -) on the diagram.

Positron emission tomography (PET) scans (three-dimensional pictures of the brain that can demonstrate regional levels of activity or function in a living person) of the brains of people with borderline disorder show a decrease in activity in the medial aspects of the prefrontal lobes, especially the anterior cingulate cortex (Figure 6.1), compared to people without the disorder. The degree of impairment in activity in this area of the brain in people with borderline disorder is associated with the degree of impulsivity that they demonstrate.

The level of impulsivity in people with borderline disorder is also related to a decrease in activity of the neuromodulator serotonin in the pathways that control impulsive behavior. This may be why medications that increase serotonin activity in the brain often help people with borderline disorder gain better control over impulsive behavior.

The Neural Systems of Perception and Reasoning

We know that parts of the lateral (right and left side) areas of the pre-frontal lobes of the brain are associated with thinking, planning, and reasoning, also referred to as cognitive behaviors. The **dorsolateral prefrontal cortex and circuits** are especially important in controlling cognition (Figures 6.1 and 6.4). The dorsolateral prefrontal circuits enable us to:

- Reason
- Develop strategies for solving complex problems
- Think abstractly
- Facilitate working memory and learning

The dorsolateral prefrontal cortex interacts closely with the medial and orbital prefrontal cortices to enable the full expression of working memory, thinking, and reasoning (Figure 6.4). This strongly suggests the possibility that some of the symptoms and behaviors of borderline disorder are due to disturbances in pathways that connect these and other structures in the brain that are described above.

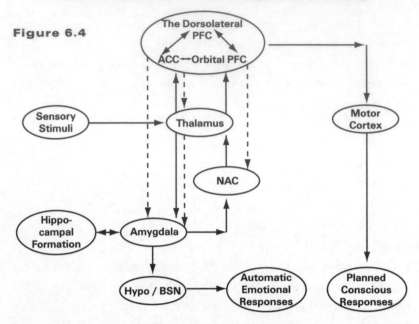

Figure 6.4

Accurate and clear thinking and consciously processing information depend on activity in the dorsolateral prefrontal cortex. This information is integrated with, and processed further by, the anterior cingulate cortex and orbital prefrontal cortex. Pathways from these latter brain regions exert "top-down" control on behaviors generated by the deeper brain structures shown in figures 6.2 and 6.3.

(PFC: prefrontal cortex; ACC: anterior cingulate cortex; NAC: nucleus accumbens; Hypo: hypothalamus; BSN: brain stem nuclei.)

There are neuropsychological tests that are specifically designed to evaluate cognitive brain functions. These tests consistently show that many people with borderline disorder have impairment of these functions, compared to individuals who do not have the disorder. In addition, a recent brain imaging study of people with borderline disorder has demonstrated a significant decrease in neuronal activity in the dorsolateral prefrontal region of the brain.

Neuromodulator Dysfunction

Other research findings give us clues about the specific chemical disturbances in the brains of people with borderline disorder, disturbances that may account for impaired emotional and impulse control and disturbed thinking and reasoning. There's evidence of abnormal **serotonergic** and **dopaminergic activity** in certain pathways in the brains of patients with borderline disorder. The serotonergic and dopaminergic pathways originate in the brain stem and are distributed widely to many cortical and subcortical structures of the brain. These include the three neural systems involved in borderline disorder (Figure 6.5).

Dopamine & Serotonin Modulatory Pathways

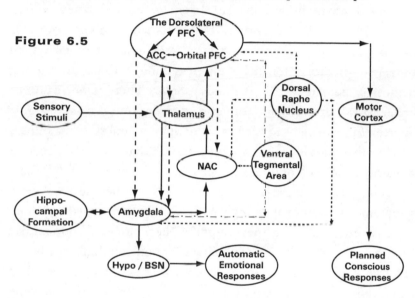

The pathways diagrammed in Figures 6.2–6.4 utilize the stimulatory and inhibitory neurotransmitters glutamate and GABA, respectively. Activity in these pathways is modulated (stimulated or inhibited) by a number of other neurotransmitters, also referred to as neuromodulators. The neurons of two of these neuromodulators have their origins in the ventral tegmental area (dopamine) and the dorsal raphe nucleus (serotonin), both located in the brain stem. There is evidence that both of these neuromodulator systems do not function properly in borderline disorder.

⋯⋯ represent serotonin pathways; — • — represent dopamine pathways; - - - - - represent "top-down" control pathways.

(PFC: prefrontal cortex; ACC: anterior cingulate cortex; NAC: nucleus accumbens; Hypo: hypothalamus; BSN: brain stem nuclei.)

Neuromodulators selectively increase or decrease the level of activity in neural circuits in order to enhance appropriate responses of all types. Abnormal activity of serotonergic and dopaminergic activity may seriously affect the neural pathways controlling the behavioral functions that are impaired in people with borderline disorder. The evidence that these chemical abnormalities exist in people with borderline disorder provides physicians with the opportunity to develop and use new and more effective pharmacological treatment approaches (see Chapter 9).

In Simple Terms

Abnormal activity in the amygdala system (emotional dysregulation), along with decreased activity in the orbitomedial and anterior cingulate systems (impulsivity) and the dorsolateral prefrontal system (impaired memory, learning, and reasoning), occurs in varying degrees in people with borderline disorder. There is no reason to believe that everyone with borderline disorder suffers from the same degree of impairment in each of these three neural systems. In fact, it's clear that people with borderline disorder have different levels of impairment in each of the three behavioral dimensions of the disorder controlled by these neural pathways. Some people have more symptoms of emotional dysregulation, while others may have more difficulty in controlling their impulsive behavior. Still others may have the most difficulty in their ability to reason and think clearly and rationally, especially under stress. Indeed, at times of severe stress, they may briefly lose contact with reality to the point where they become very suspicious of people, or feel as if they are having "out-of-body" experiences or other unusual thoughts and sensations.

Here are the two most important facts to take away from this chapter:

1. Borderline disorder is the result of disturbances in specific neural pathways in the brain, and is not the result of intentional or willful behavior.
2. Research continues to give us a better understanding of these disturbances, which will result in new and more effective treatments of borderline disorder.

SEVEN

Common Co-occurring Disorders

I F YOU HAVE borderline disorder, you suffer from many distressing symptoms and behavioral problems. For reasons not well understood, you are also more prone to develop other mental disorders than people without borderline disorder. These disorders include.

- Mood disorders, particularly major depressive disorder, dysthymia, and bipolar disorder
- Substance use disorders
- Anxiety/panic disorders
- Posttraumatic stress disorder
- Eating disorders, particularly bulimia and anorexia nervosa
- Attention deficit hyperactivity disorder
- Other personality disorders

These disorders are often correctly diagnosed in people with borderline disorder, but the diagnosis of co-existing borderline disorder is missed. When this occurs, treatment for the other condition is typically less successful than it might otherwise be, mainly because the appropriate treatments for borderline disorder are not implemented.

On the other hand, in order to effectively treat borderline disorder, your doctor needs to recognize other disorders if they are also present, and prescribe the appropriate additional treatment. As I mentioned in Chapter 5, the early detection and effective treatment of a mental disorder co-occurring with borderline disorder often results in a rapid remission of the symptoms of borderline disorder itself. So it's extremely important that you and your psychiatrist try to determine the presence of these co-occurring conditions and promptly begin the appropriate additional treatments if indicated.

In order to provide you with the most accurate definitions of the disorders that commonly co-occur with borderline disorder, throughout this chapter I have used and adapted the diagnostic criteria for these disorders from the *Diagnostic and Statistical Manual of Mental Disorders*, Fourth Edition (DSM-IV), published by the American Psychiatric Association, with their permission. This manual is used across most of the world and is considered the "gold standard" in defining mental disorders.

Mood Disorders

Research has shown that the prevalence of major depressive disorder, dysthymia, and bipolar disorder are all increased in people with borderline disorder. **Major depressive disorder** occurs at some time in more than 80 percent of people with borderline disorder, whereas it occurs in 5 to 12 percent of men and 10 to 25 percent of women in the general population. Almost 40 percent of people with borderline disorder will develop dysthymia.

Major Depressive Disorder

Because major depressive episodes and dysthymia occur so commonly with borderline disorder, it's essential that you know and recognize their symptoms and immediately alert your physician if they occur.

If you have major depressive disorder, you will have experienced five or more of the following symptoms for at least two weeks:

- You are depressed most of the day, nearly every day. You feel sad or empty, or break out into tears for no apparent reason. In children and adolescents, a depressed mood can come across as an irritable mood.
- You've lost interest, or no longer find pleasure, in many or all of the activities that usually bring you enjoyment.
- You've lost a significant amount of weight, but you're not dieting. Or conversely, you've gained a lot of weight, typically more than 5 percent of your body weight, in a month. You've also seen a decrease or increase in your appetite nearly every day.
- Your sleep pattern is disturbed by insomnia or excessive sleep. When you do sleep, it's not restful and you have disturbing dreams or even nightmares.
- You notice physical and mental agitation or retardation most of the time that may be observable to others as well.
- You feel fatigued or have low energy levels nearly every day. This may have resulted in a significant decrease in your usual activities.
- You have feelings of worthlessness, or excessive or inappropriate guilt. These feelings are not merely self-reproach or guilt about being sick.
- You have significant difficulty in thinking or concentrating, or you're indecisive, to the point that it interferes with your ability to function normally each day.
- You have recurrent thoughts of death and of dying, recurrent thoughts about suicide, a specific plan for committing suicide, or have attempted suicide.

The symptoms of major depressive disorder will most likely cause you significant distress and/or hinder your ability to function socially, at work, or in other important ways. Before you jump to any conclusions, you should be clear that the symptoms you're experiencing are not due to the effects of a substance, for example, a drug of abuse or a medication, a general medical condition, or bereavement you feel for the loss of a loved one.

Dysthymic Disorder

The symptoms of dysthymic disorder are similar to major depressive disorder, but there are fewer of them, they are less severe, and you must experience them for a longer period of time to be diagnosed.

If you suffer from dysthymic disorder, you will have been depressed for at least the last two years. Your depression lasts for most of the day, and for more days than you feel normal.

While depressed, you will have experienced two or more of the following symptoms:

- Poor appetite or overeating
- Insomnia or excessive sleeping
- Low energy or fatigue
- Low self-esteem
- Poor concentration or difficulty making decisions
- Feelings of hopelessness

During this two-year period, you have never been without the above symptoms for more than two months at a time, and the symptoms have caused you significant distress or have interfered with your performance socially, at work, or in other important areas of your life.

In order to be diagnosed, you can't have suffered from a major depressive episode (see above) during the first two years of this disturbance or had a manic episode, a mixed episode, a hypomanic episode, or cyclothymic disorder (see below).

It must be clear that your symptoms are not due to the effects of a substance, for example, a drug of abuse or a medication, or a general medical condition.

Differences Between Borderline Disorder, Major Depressive Disorder, and Dysthymia

There's a considerable overlap of symptoms between borderline disorder, major depression, and dysthymia. So at times, it may be difficult to determine if you have developed an episode of major depressive disorder or dysthymia, or you're simply experiencing an increase in your symptoms of borderline disorder. But there are some differences between the symptoms of these mood disorders and of borderline disorder that help distinguish one from the other.

The sad, depressed, and lonely feelings associated with borderline disorder are frequently triggered by some life event and occur soon afterward. There is also a difference in the *quality* of the depressed mood. When due to borderline disorder, the depressed mood is often associated with strong feelings of emptiness, loneliness, and fears of abandonment. The episodes of depressed mood in borderline disorder typically do not last for two weeks (like major depressive disorder) or two years (like dysthymia), and they can be easily reversed if the situation causing them improves.

People with borderline disorder may have difficulty falling asleep, or they may sleep excessively. However, these episodes of sleep disturbance are usually related to an identifiable life stress and stop when the stress is managed successfully.

Also, severe suicidal thoughts and self-injurious behavior that are the direct result of a personal problem (for example, an argument with a parent, boyfriend, spouse, or boss) are usually symptomatic of borderline disorder rather than of mood disorders.

When you have borderline disorder, you may experience many of the symptoms of major depressive disorder and dysthymia, especially when you are in a highly emotional state and under severe stress. But your symptoms could be the result of poor emotional control, a core feature of borderline disorder, and not an indication of a mood disorder.

However, if you think you have the symptoms of either of these disorders, it's best that you immediately alert your psychiatrist so you can figure out what's going on and if additional treatment is appropriate.

This treatment frequently involves the addition of an antidepressant, or an increase in dosage if one is already being used. Cognitive Behavioral Therapy (see Chapter 10) focusing on depression may also prove useful to help identify thought patterns and behaviors that operate as risk factors for mood disorders, and to encourage new, more successful behaviors.

Bipolar Disorder

Bipolar disorder occurs in about 10 percent of those with borderline disorder, whereas it occurs in about 1 percent of the general population. Bipolar disorder is essentially major depressive disorder accompanied by manic and hypomanic episodes. Manic episodes are periods of distinctly elevated, expansive, or irritable moods that last at least one week. Hypomanic episodes consist of four days of mild to moderate elevation of mood, improved and positive thinking, and increased energy levels. There are also periods during which symptoms of mania or hypomania occur with symptoms of depression, which are called mixed episodes. If an individual meets the criteria for both a major depressive and a manic episode, they are considered to have bipolar I disorder. If the criteria for both a major depressive episode and a hypomanic episode are met, they are diagnosed with **bipolar II disorder.**

Major Bipolar Symptoms

MANIC EPISODES

Having a manic episode means you experience a distinct, abnormal, and persistent period of elevated, expansive, or irritable mood that lasts at least one week.

In order to be diagnosed as having a manic episode, you must have had three or more of the following symptoms during your period of mood disturbance. They must have been present to a significant degree and have persisted for the entire time.

- An inflated self-esteem or grandiosity
- A decreased need for sleep

- Increased talking or a pressure to keep talking
- A crowding of ideas or the impression that your thoughts are racing
- Excessive distractibility
- An increase in purposeful activity, socially or sexually, or at work or school
- An excessive pursuit of pleasurable activities that often results in harmful consequences such as buying sprees, sexual indiscretions, or ill-advised business investments.

These episodes can be quite severe, and usually cause obvious problems in your performance at work and in relationships with others. Sometimes manic episodes require hospitalization to prevent harm to you or others, or if you experience psychotic symptoms.

As with the other mood disorders I described above, you need to be clear that your symptoms are not due to the effects of a substance (a drug of abuse or a medication) or a general medical condition. The symptoms must also be differentiated from those of a mixed episode (see page 112).

HYPOMANIC EPISODE

Having a hypomanic episode means you experience a distinct, sustained period of elevated, expansive, or irritable mood that lasts at least four days, and is clearly different from your normal, everyday mood.

The symptoms are exactly the same as for a manic episode, and you will need to have experienced three or more of them in order to be diagnosed. The symptoms must have been persistent and present to a significant degree for the whole time.

If you have a hypomanic episode, there will be a clear change in your functioning that is not characteristic of you, and the changes are observable by others.

Unlike a manic episode, a hypomanic episode will not hinder your performance at work, socially, or in relationships with others, or require hospitalization to prevent harm to you or others. You will also not experience psychotic symptoms.

Again, you must be clear that your symptoms are not due to the effects of a substance (a drug of abuse or a medication) or a general medical condition.

MIXED EPISODE

A mixed episode or mixed state means that you experience the symptoms and meet the criteria for a manic episode and for a major depressive episode (aside from duration) *at the same time.* Your symptoms must be present almost every day for at least one week.

This type of mood disturbance will hinder your performance at work, socially, and in relationships with others. A mixed episode may also require hospitalization to prevent harm to you or others, or if you experience psychotic symptoms.

As always, you must be clear that your symptoms are not due to the effects of a substance (a drug of abuse or a medication) or a general medical condition.

Mixed episodes may be caused by antidepressant treatment, such as medication, electroconvulsive therapy, and light therapy. When that's the case, the episodes should not be considered part of bipolar I disorder.

Because of the significant changes in mood experienced by people with bipolar disorder, this diagnosis is often inappropriately made for people with borderline disorder, which means they receive incorrect and ineffective treatment. However, you and your physician should be on the alert for the development of an episode of true bipolar disorder, especially bipolar II disorder, because the hypomanic symptoms can be subtle and easily missed. If bipolar disorder is detected, additional treatment is then needed. Such treatment usually involves the addition of a mood stabilizer such as lithium, divalproex, or lamotrigine, and an antidepressant when one is needed.

Substance-Related Disorders

The careful evaluation of a large group of people with borderline disorder found that two thirds of them seriously abused alcohol, street drugs, and/or prescribed drugs. There appear to be a variety of reasons for this. Many people with borderline disorder say that such behaviors temporarily relieve the severe emotional pain that they experience when under stress. Predictably, this relief is short-lived. Even worse, the use of these substances often drastically decreases their already impaired reasoning ability and increases their emotional hyper-reactivity and impulsive behavior. The use of alcohol and street drugs leads to a dramatic worsening of the symptoms of borderline disorder, and also decreases the effectiveness of medications and psychotherapy. In addition, the repeated use of alcohol and drugs by those with borderline disorder frequently leads to addiction and sustained craving for these substances. A number of people in the medical community believe it's possible that some of the genetic alterations that predispose people to borderline disorder may also be among the group of genes that are risk factors for alcoholism and drug abuse.

For all of these reasons, I strongly advise my patients not to use alcohol or take any street drugs, and to take prescribed medications only as ordered by their physicians. I encourage those patients who have a substance-use disorder to enroll in an alcohol or drug treatment program. I also suggest to some of them that they may benefit from a trial on the mood-stabilizer topiramate because of its potential to reduce alcohol and drug craving in addicted patients. You should keep in mind that the use of topiramate for the treatment of alcoholism is an off-label use of the drug (meaning it hasn't been approved by the Food and Drug Administration [FDA] for this type of use), and the potential side-effects, such as decreased memory and a lowering of blood bicarbonate levels, should be carefully considered by you and your physician.

The bottom line is that there is little or no hope of gaining control over the symptoms of borderline disorder while alcohol and other drugs are being used. Substance dependence and substance abuse are among the strongest predictors of poor short- and long-term outcome of borderline disorder. To better acquaint you with the symptoms, here are the official definitions of these disorders.

Substance Dependence

Substance dependence is defined as a harmful pattern of substance use that leads to significant impairment or distress. If you have substance dependence, you will experience three or more of the following symptoms during any time in the same twelve-month period:

- You develop a tolerance to the substance. This means you either need to significantly increase the amounts of the substance to achieve the desired effect, or you experience a significantly diminished effect with the use of the same amount of the substance.
- You experience withdrawal symptoms that are characteristic of the substance, or you need to take the substance, or a closely related substance to relieve or avoid withdrawal symptoms.
- You take the substance in larger amounts or over a longer period than was intended.
- You have a persistent desire, or are unsuccessful in your efforts, to cut down or control your use of the substance.
- You spend a great deal of time in activities that involve obtaining or using the substance, or recovering from its effects.
- You reduce or give up important social, work, or recreational activities because of your substance use.
- You continue to use the substance despite the fact that you experience persistent or recurrent psychological or physical problems that are caused or made worse by the substance. For example, you continue to use cocaine although you know that it causes you to become depressed, or you continue to drink even though you know it will make your ulcer worse.

Substance Abuse

Substance abuse is also defined as a harmful pattern of substance use that leads to significant impairment or distress, but it has a less immediately devastating effect on your life. If you have substance abuse, you will experience one or more of the following symptoms within a twelve-month period. In addition, your symptoms should never have met the criteria for substance dependence for this class of substance noted above.

- Recurrent substance use results in your failure to fulfill your obligations at work, school, or home. For example, due to substance use you have repeated absences from work, or poor work, absences, suspensions, or expulsions from school, or you neglect your children or household duties.
- You continue to use the substance in situations in which it may cause you physical harm. For example, you drive an automobile or operate a machine when impaired by the substance.
- Substance use results in legal problems, such as arrests for driving under the influence or for disorderly conduct.
- You continue to use the substance even though it causes repeated social or interpersonal problems, such as arguments with your spouse about the consequences of intoxication, or physical fights.

Anxiety and Panic Disorders

Anxiety is a common symptom of borderline disorder. You may experience it especially during times of stress—for example, when you have felt personally criticized and rejected—or during periods of separation from people who are very important to you. Moderate to severe anxiety can also lead to other symptoms, like physical pain, headaches, abdominal pain, and irritable bowel syndrome.

You should be aware of the fact that anxiety disorders occur in about 90 percent of people with borderline disorder. A very severe form of anxiety, called panic disorder, occurs in about 50 percent of people with borderline disorder. Panic disorder is when you have recurrent, unexpected panic attacks that are followed by at least one month of persistent concern about having another attack and the possible consequences of the attacks, or you have a significant change in behavior that's related to the attacks.

Symptoms can appear unexpectedly and suddenly, for no apparent reason, and disappear either rapidly or slowly. People who suffer from panic attacks may also be fearful of finding themselves in circumstances from which escape may be difficult or embarrassing, such as elevators, shopping malls, and movie theaters. This is referred to as claustrophobia.

Panic Attacks

Panic attacks are when you experience periods of intense fear during which four or more of the following symptoms develop suddenly and reach a peak within ten minutes:

- Palpitations
- A pounding heart, or an accelerated heart rate
- Sweating; trembling or shaking
- Shortness of breath or a sense of smothering
- The feeling that you are choking
- Chest pain or discomfort
- Nausea or abdominal discomfort
- Feeling dizzy, unsteady, lightheaded, or faint
- A feeling of unreality or of being detached from yourself
- The fear of losing control or going crazy
- The fear of dying; numbness or tingling sensations
- Chills or hot flushes

If you're experiencing disabling anxiety disorders and panic attacks, you should seek treatment immediately. Treatment must proceed with care, however, because these disorders are commonly treated with certain medications, such as benzodiazepines (like Xanax, Klonopin, or Valium), that have been found to be harmful in most people with borderline disorder because of their addictive potential. Therefore, other approaches are often required, such as a temporary increase in the neuroleptic, atypical antipsychotic, or antidepressant medication if it's already being used. Initiating the use of an antipsychotic agent or an antidepressant may prove effective for moderate to severe anxiety or panic attacks if one is not already prescribed. In addition, a course of Cognitive Behavioral Therapy specifically tailored to target the symptoms of anxiety and panic attacks should be considered as part of the long-term treatment of these problems.

Posttraumatic Stress Disorder

The occurrence of **posttraumatic stress disorder** (PTSD) in people with borderline disorder ranges from 26 percent in a mixed population of inpatients and outpatients to 57 percent in a totally inpatient population. PTSD significantly complicates the diagnosis and treatment of borderline disorder because of the overlap of some of the symptoms of these disorders. The fact that a history of trauma is present in everyone with PTSD and about 50 percent of those with borderline disorder also complicates the diagnosis both of these disorders.

The high rate of PTSD in people with borderline disorder is not surprising, considering the exposure of many people with the disorder to early and repeated traumas. Although some medical professionals have speculated that borderline disorder is a variation of PTSD, recent research suggests that they are separate disorders.

The term PTSD has gained considerable popularity recently and, unfortunately, it's frequently misused. The following definition of PTSD will help you determine whether you suffer from the disorder.

If you have PTSD, you must have been exposed to a traumatic event in which both of the following occurred:

- You experienced or witnessed an event that involved actual or threatened death or serious injury to yourself or others
- Your response involved intense fear, a sense of helplessness, or horror

In addition, you frequently re-experience the traumatic event in one or more of the following ways:

- You have recurrent distressing recollections of the event, including images or thoughts
- You have distressing dreams, the contents of which are unrecognizable
- You act or feel as if you are reliving the traumatic event or having flashback episodes
- You have intense psychological or physical distress when exposed to situations that remind you of the traumatic event

Also, you avoid situations associated with the trauma, and attempt to numb your general level of responsiveness in three or more of the following ways:

- You avoid thoughts, feelings, or conversations about the trauma
- You make efforts to avoid activities, places, or people that cause you to recall the trauma
- You are unable to recall an important part of the trauma
- You have a noticeable decrease in interest, or participation, in important activities
- You feel detached from other people
- Your feelings are restricted; for example, you are unable to have loving feelings
- Your sense of your future has become limited; for example, you do not expect to have a career, marriage, children, or a normal life span

You have an increased level of arousal, which is indicated by two or more of the following:

- You have difficulty falling or staying asleep
- You are irritable or have outbursts of anger
- You have difficulty concentrating or you are hypervigilant
- You have an increased startle response

Finally, the disorder causes you significant distress or interferes with your life socially, at work, or in other important ways, and has been present for more than one month.

It's important to determine if you have both borderline disorder and PTSD. If you do have both, your treatment plan should be re-evaluated by your psychiatrist or primary care clinician (see Chapter 8).

Eating Disorders

A recent large study of people with borderline disorder who required hospitalization determined that the rate of eating disorders of all types is over 50 percent among these patients. The rate of the two most common eating disorders, bulimia nervosa and anorexia nervosa, was found to be 26 percent and 21 percent, respectively.

Bulimia Nervosa

Bulimia is characterized by episodes of significant overeating (also known as binging) and purging (self-induced vomiting and excessive use of laxatives), over-concern about body weight and dieting, and dissatisfaction with body size and shape. Bulimia is commonly and effectively treated with antidepressants (especially the selective serotonin reuptake inhibitors [SSRIs]), Cognitive Behavioral Therapy, and other therapies. A trial on topiramate could also be considered because of its effect on appetite stabilization, but keep in mind the cautions I list on page 113.

When you have bulimia nervosa, you have repeated episodes of binge eating that involve:

- Eating, in a specific period of time (for example, within two hours), an amount of food that is much larger than most people would eat during this period of time
- Lack of control over eating during the episode

After the binges, in order to prevent weight gain, you attempt to compensate by inducing vomiting; misusing laxatives, diuretics, enemas, or other medications; or resorting to excessive fasting or exercise.

In order to be diagnosed with bulimia, you must have episodes of binge eating and compensatory behaviors, on average, at least twice a week for three months.

Another key factor is that your self-esteem is inappropriately influenced by your body shape and weight, and that the disturbance does not occur only during episodes of anorexia nervosa (see below).

Anorexia Nervosa

Anorexia nervosa is a very severe, sometimes fatal, eating disorder that predominantly affects women. People who suffer from anorexia nervosa have an extreme concern about body weight and a preoccupation with food and calories. They believe they are overweight even when actually underweight, have a tendency to over-exercise, and stop menstruating. Antidepressants (SSRIs), Cognitive Behavioral Therapy, and other therapies are commonly used to treat this disorder.

When you have anorexia nervosa, you refuse to maintain your body weight at or above a minimally normal weight for your age. For example, you have weight loss that results in a body weight less than 85 percent of that expected for your age and height; or you fail to gain weight during a period of growth, also leading to a body weight less than 85 percent of normal.

You have a real fear of gaining weight or becoming fat, even though you are seriously underweight. You view your body weight or shape incorrectly, and your self-esteem is unduly influenced by your body weight or shape. If you are a woman, you have missed at least three consecutive menstrual cycles. You also strongly deny the seriousness of your precariously low body weight.

Attention Deficit Hyperactivity Disorder

There is some evidence that **attention deficit hyperactivity disorder** (ADHD) is more common in people with borderline disorder than it is in the general population.

ADHD is characterized by poor control of attention, easy distractibility, and poor school, work, and social performance. There are three subtypes of ADHD: one is associated with inattention and hyperactivity plus impulsivity: the second predominantly with inattention; and the third predominantly with hyperactivity and impulsivity. ADHD is estimated to occur in about 5 percent of school-age children. It's more common in boys than in girls. The hyperactive subtype is much more common in boys, while the inattentive subtype (the subtype with normal activity levels) is somewhat more evenly distributed among boys and girls. The disorder is now known to persist into adulthood in many people and to require continued treatment. There is often a strong family history of ADHD.

It's not uncommon for children with borderline disorder to be misdiagnosed with ADHD and treated with stimulants such as **methylphenidate** (Ritalin) or an amphetamine derivative, such as Adderall. Children and adults with borderline disorder treated with these medications typically do not respond well, and may even do worse than without these medications. However, if borderline disorder and ADHD co-occur, there are some anecdotal reports that the combination of a low dose of a **neuroleptic** or antipsychotic **agent** for the symptoms of borderline disorder enables a stimulant to produce a beneficial effect on the symptoms of ADHD. In some instances, behavioral treatments alone are effective in ADHD.

Inattention

In order to meet the ADHD criteria for inattention, you must have had six or more of the following symptoms of inattention that have persisted for at least six months:

- You frequently fail to give careful attention to details, or you make careless mistakes in schoolwork, work, or other activities
- You have difficulty maintaining your attention in tasks or recreational activities
- You consistently fail to follow through on instructions and to finish schoolwork, chores, or tasks at work

- You have difficulty organizing tasks and activities
- You frequently avoid tasks that require sustained mental effort
- You often lose items necessary for tasks or activities, for example, school and work assignments, pencils, books, or tools
- You are easily distracted by unimportant thoughts or events
- You are often forgetful during daily activities

Hyperactivity

In order to meet the ADHD criteria for hyperactivity, you must have had six or more of the following nine symptoms of hyperactivity and impulsivity that have persisted for at least six months:

HYPERACTIVITY
- You frequently fidget with your hands or feet, or squirm in your seat
- You have difficulty remaining seated in a classroom, at work, or in other situations where doing so is expected
- Your activity level is excessive in situations in which it is inappropriate, or you often feel restless
- You have difficulty quietly engaging in leisure activities
- You often feel driven or compelled to do something
- You frequently talk excessively

IMPULSIVITY
- You frequently blurt out answers before others have a chance to complete their questions
- You have difficulty waiting for your turn
- You often interrupt or intrude on others, for example, by barging into conversations or other activities

Whichever symptoms you suffer from, they must have resulted in maladaptive behavior that is inconsistent with your stage of development in order to qualify for an ADHD diagnosis. In addition, some of these hyperactive–impulsive or inattentive symptoms need to have been present before age seven; there must be impairment in social, academic, or occupational performance; and current impairment from the above symptoms occurs in two or more settings, for example, at school, work, or at home.

Other Personality Disorders

Clinicians have observed for many decades that people with border-line disorder also have symptoms of other personality disorders. At times, the number of these symptoms reached the point where a diagnosis could be made for a second and even a third personality disorder. At other times, the number of symptoms of other personality disorders doesn't meet the diagnostic requirements, and the person is said to have "traits" of these disorders.

There are ten personality disorders listed in DSM-IV-TR. They are grouped into three clusters based on their most prominent characteristics. The following is a summary of the main features of each of these disorders adapted from DSM-IV-TR.

Cluster A (odd—eccentric)

PARANOID

Paranoid personality disorder is characterized by a persistent pattern of severe mistrust and suspiciousness of others, associated with an unjustified expectation of malevolent behavior that began by early adulthood. This mistrust is accompanied by a reluctance to confide in others, a strong tendency to bear grudges and counterattack angrily at the slightest perceived provocation, and unjustified suspicions of the fidelity of spouse or sexual partner.

SCHIZOID

Schizoid personality disorder involves a pattern of detached social relationships associated with a decreased range of expressed feelings toward others beginning in early adulthood. The individual with schizoid personality disorder typically:

- Does not seek or enjoy close relationships, even with family
- Chooses solitary activities
- Has little desire for sexual relationships
- Derives little pleasure from any activity
- Lacks close friends
- Seems indifferent to praise or criticism
- Is emotionally cold and detached

SCHIZOTYPAL

An individual with **schizotypal personality disorder** has difficulty developing close relationships due to odd perceptions, distortions, and eccentric behavior that began in early adulthood. This person has odd beliefs or magical thinking, odd thinking and speech, is suspicious or paranoid, has a decreased range of and inappropriate emotions, exhibits eccentric or peculiar behavior, lacks close friends, and has excessive social anxiety associated with paranoid fears.

Cluster B (dramatic—emotional)

ANTISOCIAL

People with **antisocial personality disorder** have a pervasive pattern of disregarding and violating the rights of others. This pattern usually has been present since the age of fifteen, and the diagnosed individual is usually at least eighteen years old. Common behaviors are:

- Repeated illegal acts that are grounds for arrest
- Repeated lies
- Using aliases and "conning" others for personal gain
- Impulsive acts and not planning ahead
- Reckless disregard for personal safety or that of others
- Repeated irresponsibility regarding work, behavior, or financial obligations
- A lack of remorse

HISTRIONIC

Histrionic personality disorder is marked by a pattern of emotional and attention-seeking behavior that begins in early adulthood. This person is uncomfortable unless he or she is the center of attention and draws attention by using physical appearance. He or she has a vague style of speech and his or her behaviors are dramatic and can be theatrical with an exaggerated expression of emotion. This individual is often inappropriately sexually seductive or provocative, has a shallow expression of emotions that shift rapidly, is suggestible, and overestimates the intimacy of relationships.

NARCISSISTIC

A person suffering from **narcissistic personality disorder** has a pervasive pattern of grandiosity, the need for admiration, and a lack of empathy that began by early adulthood. Typical behaviors and attitudes include:

- An exaggerated sense of importance
- A preoccupation with fantasies of great success, wealth, power, beauty, and perfect love
- A strong sense of being unique and capable of being understood by, or should relate only to, people of high status
- A sense of entitlement
- Exploitation of others
- An unwillingness or inability to identify or understand the needs and feelings of others
- Envious behavior
- Arrogance

Borderline disorder is also included in Cluster B.

Cluster C (anxious—fearful)

AVOIDANT

Avoidant personality disorder involves a pattern of feeling inadequate and being socially inhibited and hypersensitive to criticism that begins by early adulthood. This person avoids work situations that require social contact because of fear of disapproval or rejection, is reluctant to engage with others unless certain of being liked, is restrained in intimate relationships for fear of ridicule, feels inadequate and inferior and is inhibited in new situations because of these feelings, and rarely takes risks or engages in new activities for fear of embarrassment.

DEPENDENT

Dependent personality disorder is characterized by strong feelings of the need for care, resulting in a pervasive pattern of submissive and clinging behaviors and separation fears that begin by early adulthood. This person typically:

- Requires excessive reassurance in making everyday decisions
- Wants others to assume responsibility for most major life situations
- Is fearful of disagreeing because of fear of lack of support
- Fears starting projects because of lack of confidence
- Goes to extremes to gain nurturance and support
- Is uncomfortable when alone because of unrealistic fears of inadequacy
- Urgently seeks another close relationship when one ends
- Is overly preoccupied by the fear of being left to care for herself or himself

OBSESSIVE-COMPULSIVE

Obsessive-compulsive personality disorder is characterized by a preoccupation with orderliness, perfection, and internal and interpersonal control at the cost of being flexible, open, and efficient, beginning by early adulthood. This person is so preoccupied with organization that the main point of the activity is lost. He or she is perfectionistic to a degree that interferes with completion of the task, devotes excessive time to work at the expense of leisure activities and friendships, is overly conscientious and inflexible about morality, ethics, or values, hoards worthless items of no sentimental value, is reluctant to assign tasks or work to others unless they will perform them exactly his or her way, spends money reluctantly, and is rigid and stubborn.

In a recent study, adolescents with borderline disorder displayed a broader array of symptoms of other personality disorders than did adults, especially schizotypal and passive–aggressive (no longer listed as a personality disorder). In a different study of adults with borderline disorder, antisocial personality disorder co-occurred more commonly than other personality disorders. In a large study of adults, men and women with borderline disorder demonstrated different patterns of co-occurrence. Men were more likely than women to meet criteria for paranoid, passive–aggressive, narcissistic, and antisocial personality disorder.

The high rate of co-occurrence of borderline disorder and other personality disorders can be a major complication in its diagnosis and treatment. As I mentioned in Chapter 4, the significant overlap of symptoms between personality disorders is a major reason why a diagnostic approach to personality disorders based on symptom *dimensions,* such as emotional dysregulation and impulsivity, is thought to be more accurate and useful than the current approach of defining distinct *categories* of personality disorders.

Why is the Issue of Co-occurrence Important?

There's one major point that I want you to take away from this chapter: It's a very real possibility that some of your symptoms are caused by one or more of the disorders I've described above, especially if the symptoms don't match up with the typical borderline disorder symptoms. It's essential to keep this in the back of your mind, because it may well save you a lot of trouble. Many people simply assume that these symptoms come from their borderline disorder and then think that their treatment plan is failing. This in turn causes many people to drop out of treatment, which is the worst choice you can make.

These co-occurring disorders *can* be treated, and there's evidence that their successful treatment may also significantly reduce the severity of the symptoms of your borderline disorder, which of course would be a great relief.

EIGHT

The Key Elements of Treatment

PROPER TREATMENT OF borderline disorder involves the following components: locating a **primary clinician**, determining the most appropriate level of care for you, evaluating your need for medication, and selecting the type of psychotherapy that will be most effective for you. This chapter will give you an overview of these components of treatment, so you can make more informed decisions about your care. I will also describe in detail the role your primary clinician plays in the treatment, and the process you both go through to determine your proper level of care at any time. The following two chapters will cover the topics of medication and psychotherapy.

Borderline Disorder Treatment Components

The most important step in getting proper treatment for borderline disorder is selecting a psychiatrist or other mental health professional skilled in the diagnosis and treatment of the disorder. This person will serve as your primary clinician. Together, you will determine the level of care that is the least restrictive and provides optimal safety and support at any given time during treatment. Once you figure this out, you may need to try a number of medications before you find the one medication or the combination of medications that yields the best results with the fewest side-effects. Although there is no "magic medical bullet" for borderline disorder, medications can help lessen the severity of the symptoms, and can also set the stage for the best possible results from the work of psychotherapy.

Abstaining from alcohol and street drugs is essential if you want to make any progress in your treatment. It's also essential that psychotherapy be part of your total treatment plan. Therefore, the most appropriate psychotherapeutic approaches for you need to be determined. Individual psychotherapy still provides the basic long-term therapeutic experience for patients with borderline disorder.

In addition, working in group therapy and participating in support groups with other people with borderline disorder can be very helpful. Realizing that others also suffer from this disorder and learning ways to deal with emotional crises and to better control impulsive behaviors can be very beneficial to you. Group therapy may facilitate the work you accomplish in individual psychotherapy and shorten the process. It's also very helpful to work with parents, spouses, and other family members to build and strengthen these critical relationships. But this work can't occur without your strong commitment and effort, and those of involved family members.

In order to be effective, all forms of psychotherapy require changes in old behavioral habits that do not work well. Habits are difficult to break, especially when they need to be replaced by new behaviors that are at first a little strange and frightening.

I realize that many of my patients initially find the process of getting started in treatment a bit overwhelming, but I try to reassure them that they are not alone in their struggle to gain control over their lives. In addition to my help, the team of skilled professionals and the strategies that can be assembled to help them are very extensive, and these approaches have been proven over time to be extremely helpful. Gradually increasing the number and intensity of treatment approaches is an effective way to help you gain a better understanding of your illness and control over it, and to learn new skills at a reasonable and tolerable pace.

Taking Responsibility

The successful journey to a more stable, happy, productive, and satisfying life for people suffering from borderline disorder depends on a number of factors, but it's essential that you understand clearly and believe deeply that you, more than anyone or anything else, have the ability and responsibility for gaining control over your own life.

You need to seek out the best clinicians to help you understand more about the characteristics and nature of your disorder, the specific ways it affects your life, and what you can do to minimize its effects. You must learn to exert the self-discipline required to do what needs to be done. It is important that you encourage and allow your family to learn how to best help you. In other words, you have to take responsibility for building the foundation for your own recovery. Patience and persistence are crucial to your success, and these behaviors are usually not strong points in people with borderline disorder. However, they *can* be developed, especially with the proper help, and as you achieve small and large successes, failures become less common.

Finding a Primary Clinician

Finding the right clinician to help you is critical. Given the number and complexity of issues, mental health providers, and decisions involved in the proper treatment of a person with borderline disorder, you need a single clinician to assume a central role in helping you. This person is referred to as your primary clinician. In his most recent book on borderline disorder, John Gunderson has described well the responsibilities of the primary clinician. They are:

- To educate the patient about the nature and causes of borderline disorder
- To ensure that all appropriate evaluations are performed in order to determine the patient's specific needs

- To develop with the patient a comprehensive treatment plan that best meets these needs
- To ensure that the plan is implemented
- To routinely determine the patient's safety and progress in treatment
- To implement changes in the treatment plan when indicated
- To ensure communication among other therapists, if any, who are involved in the patient's treatment.

There is some controversy, even among experts, as to the qualifications and skills required to serve most effectively as the primary clinician for people with borderline disorder. My experience has led me to side with those who believe that the optimal choice for the role is a psychiatrist well trained and experienced in this area. Because of our training in the discipline of medicine, psychiatrists are best able to understand and explain to patients with borderline disorder the biological, as well as the environmental, bases of the disorder. As physicians, psychiatrists are accustomed to making judgments about the safety of patients and taking prompt action when indicated. Also, psychiatrists are trained in most aspects of treatment, have unique knowledge about the appropriate use of medications, and are experienced in most of the psychotherapies effective in treating borderline disorder. Finally, as is the case for all physicians, psychiatrists are traditionally trained and generally expected to serve as the leader of multidisciplinary treatment teams and to make the final clinical decisions.

Having said this, I know that in many communities there are no psychiatrists who have sufficient training and experience with borderline disorder to fill the role of primary clinician. Under these circumstances, you should go with the clinician who is best trained and most experienced in borderline disorder. He or she is preferable to a clinician of lesser training and experience, and may serve well as your primary clinician.

Once you locate and team up with a primary clinician, a treatment plan should be developed. There are several components of a successful treatment plan for borderline disorder that need to be considered. These include the determination of the proper level of care (e.g., hospital, residential, or outpatient), and the selection of the appropriate combination of medications, psychotherapy, group therapy, and participation in support groups.

Levels of Care

A careful evaluation by a psychiatrist or other skilled physician will lead to the determination of the level of care that is most appropriate for you. If the risk is high for self-harm or harm to others, you may require hospitalization and close supervision. If this is not the case, but your symptoms are severe and can't be managed effectively on an outpatient basis, you may require a partial hospitalization program or residential care. But most often, outpatient care will be the most appropriate setting for your treatment. At times, making the best decision on the appropriate level of care can be difficult for you, your physician, and your family, especially early in the treatment process when your knowledge of one another is limited.

Changing your level of care may be necessary at any time during the treatment process. After you have been in treatment for a while, the decision to change the level of care is a little easier than early in treatment, because of the degree of knowledge and trust that has been built among you, your physician, and your family. Under most circumstances, whenever a change in level of care is considered, everyone should engage in a thorough discussion of the alternatives and the relative benefits and risks in order to make the best decision.

Once you and your primary clinician have determined the level of care that is most appropriate for you, it's time to make important decisions about medications and psychotherapy. The following two chapters will provide you with information about these two important areas of your treatment.

NINE

Medications

THERE ARE TWO reasons why medications are used in the treatment of borderline disorder. First, they've proven to be very helpful in stabilizing the emotional reactions, reducing impulsivity, and enhancing thinking and reasoning abilities in people with the disorder. Second, medications are also effective in treating the other emotional disorders that are frequently associated with borderline disorder, like depression, panic attacks, and physical disorders such as migraine headaches.

It's very difficult for people with borderline disorder to learn about themselves and their disorder, to deal effectively with their problems, and to make real progress in psychotherapy when they can't adequately control their emotional reactions and impulsivity, when they can't think rationally and clearly. Many people with borderline disorder feel as if they are fighting a losing battle because they know they shouldn't allow their emotions and behavior to get out of control, but they can't seem to stop it. You may know very well how it feels to be continually frustrated because you're unable to exert adequate control over your feelings and impulses, unable to reason well under stress.

For example, it's important that you remain connected to your feelings and internal conflicts, and not attempt to escape from them when dealing with a particularly difficult issue, such as separation, and the grief and other painful feelings that accompany the loss. These are the times when you're most likely to break off the therapeutic process and act in self-destructive ways, such as excessive drinking or drug use, or such as injuring yourself. The situation is additionally frustrating because other people do not understand why you lose control from time to time. They consider such behavior to be entirely willful.

You and your family may be pleasantly surprised and considerably relieved to learn that medications can help reduce some of the most troublesome symptoms of the disorder to a more tolerable level. Then you will be better able to remain engaged in difficult situations, and to learn to handle conflicts and other problems more effectively than you have in the past. Remember that Mrs. Davis, the first patient with borderline disorder who I treated with psychotherapy, did not benefit very much from therapy until she agreed to take a small dose of medication.

The Classes of Medications Used to Treat Borderline Disorder

Neuroleptics and Atypical Antipsychotic Agents

The group of medications that have been studied most for the treatment of borderline disorder are neuroleptics and atypical antipsychotic agents (Table 9.1). The neuroleptics were the first generation of medications used to treat psychotic disorders. They included chlorpromazine (Thorazine), trifluoperazine (Stelazine), haloperidol (Haldol), thiothixene (Navane), and a few others. The atypical antipsychotics are the second generation of medications developed to treat psychotic disorders. They include the first drug discovered in this group, clozapine (Clozaril), and olanzapine (Zyprexa), risperidone (Risperdal), quetiapine (Seroquel), ziprasidone (Geodon), and aripiprazole (Abilify).

TABLE 9.1

Medications Studied and Used in the Treatment of Borderline Disorder

Drug Class	Medications	Symptoms Improved by One or More Medications in the Class
Antipsychotics		
Neuroleptics	thiothixene (Navane)* haloperidol (Haldol)* trifluoperazine (Stelazine)* flupenthixol*	anxiety, obsessive-compulsivity, depression, suicide attempts, hostility, self-injury/assaultiveness, illusions, paranoid thinking, psychoticism, poor general functioning
Atypical	olanzapine (Zyprexa)* risperidone (Risperdal)° clozapine (Clozaril)*	anxiety, anger/hostility, paranoid thinking, self-injury, impulsive aggression, interpersonal sensitivity
Antidepressants		
SSRIs (selective serotonin reuptake inhibitors) and related antidepressants	fluoxetine (Prozac)* fluvoxamine (Luvox)* sertraline (Zoloft)° venlafaxine (Effexor)°	anxiety, depression, mood swings, impulsivity, anger/hostility, self-injury, impulsive aggression, poor general functioning
MAOIs (monoamine oxidase inhibitors)	phenelzine (Nardil)*	depression, anger/hostility, mood swings, rejection sensitivity, impulsivity
Other antidepressants	bupropion (Wellbutrin)	
Mood Stabilizers		
	divalproex (Depakote)* lamotrigine (Lamictal)° carbamazepine (Tegretol)° lithium°	unstable mood, anxiety, depression, anger, irritability, impulsivity, aggression, suicidality, poor general functioning
Nutriceutical Agents		
	Omega 3 fatty acids	agression, depression

* placebo-controlled studies; ° open label studies

At their usual doses, these medications are very effective in improving the disordered thinking, emotional responses, and behavior of people with other mental disorders, such as bipolar disorder and schizophrenia. However, at smaller doses they are helpful in decreasing the overreactive emotional responses and impulsivity, and in improving the abilities to think and reason of people with borderline disorder. Low doses of these medications often reduce depressed moods, anger, and anxiety, and decrease the severity and frequency of impulsive actions. In addition, patients with borderline disorder report a considerable improvement in their ability to think rationally. There's also a reduction in, or elimination of, paranoid thinking, if this is a problem.

There are now seven published placebo-controlled clinical research studies of neuroleptics and atypical antipsychotic agents in people with borderline disorder. Six of these studies have shown positive results. The American Psychiatric Association has recently published a supplement to their journal, *The American Journal of Psychiatry*, entitled "Practice Guideline for the Treatment of Patients with Borderline Personality Disorder." In this guideline, neuroleptics and antipsychotic agents are recommended for people with borderline disorder who have symptoms of disturbed thinking, such as paranoia, depressed mood, anxiety, impulsivity, and self-destructive behavior.

The use of neuroleptics and atypical antipsychotics for treating borderline disorder is also supported by research findings that suggest these medications may exert their therapeutic effects by actions on specific dopamine, or dopamine and serotonin, receptors. Abnormal activities of these two neurotransmitters have been implicated as risk factors for borderline disorder. Based on all this, a therapeutic trial on one of these medications is an important treatment option to consider for many people with borderline disorder.

For example, one of my patients with borderline disorder, a lady in her mid-twenties, initially came to see me because of increasing bouts of depression and the rapid deterioration of her marriage. After two years of marriage, her husband was ready to leave her because of her extreme jealousy, her continual demands for attention and reassurance, their frequent arguments, and her severe outbursts of temper. He said that because of her jealousy and continual need of reassurance, she called him at work several times a day. He often found it impossible to discuss problems with her in a thoughtful way, because at these times her reasoning just did not make sense. Prior attempts to treat her depression with antidepressants were only mildly and briefly effective.

Once the diagnosis of borderline disorder was made, and after a thorough discussion of the problem, a treatment plan was developed. In addition to the antidepressant she had been taking for some time, she was started on a low dose of a neuroleptic every night. Two weeks later, both she and her husband reported a significant improvement in her temper, jealousy, and oversensitivity to criticism. She was sleeping more restfully, and her nightmares had stopped. Also, there was a noticeable improvement in their ability to discuss and work out their problems. Finally, she was able to sustain this level of improvement over time and to engage in meaningful psychotherapy.

Some people who are started on a low dose of a neuroleptic are concerned about taking a medication that is typically used for people with more severe mental disorders. In the practice of medicine, physicians often use medications for problems other than the usual indications, mainly because there is evidence that they also work well for these other problems. Despite the research that demonstrates the usefulness of this class of medications for people with borderline disorder, some physicians are reluctant to prescribe and some people are reluctant to take a neuroleptic for the disorder because of a specific side-effect that neuroleptics may produce called **tardive dyskinesia**. This is an abnormal, involuntary movement disorder that typically occurs in those receiving average to large doses of neuroleptics.

To the best of my knowledge, there is no scientific evidence that indicates that low doses of neuroleptics cause tardive dyskinesia in people with borderline disorder. Nonetheless, although the risk appears to be small, it is still a concern. The atypical antipsychotic agents appear to carry a lower risk of causing tardive dyskinesia than traditional neuroleptics, when prescribed at the usual doses for those with more severe mental illnesses. These medications are now probably more commonly prescribed for people with borderline disorder than are the neuroleptics.

There are two recent studies of low doses of one of these newer medicines, olanzapine, compared to a placebo, in people with borderline disorder. Collectively, the results of these studies suggest that this atypical antipsychotic agent is effective in reducing anxiety, suspicious thinking, and impulsivity, and in improving relationships in people with borderline disorder. There is preliminary evidence from **open label trials** (research studies in which the medicine used is known to the patient and to the research team) that other atypical antipsychotic agents such as risperidone and clozapine are also effective in the treatment of borderline disorder (Table 9.1, page 137).

In spite of the fact that atypical antipsychotics may be less likely to cause side-effects than traditional neuroleptics, both have the ability to produce such effects. These include weight gain, drowsiness, insomnia, breast engorgement and discomfort, lactation, and restlessness. Some of these side-effects are temporary and others are persistent. Before you start on a traditional neuroleptic or atypical antipsychotic, you should review its side-effect profile with your psychiatrist.

Antidepressants

Depression and other symptoms of poor emotional control are common in borderline disorder. And as you may remember from Chapter 7, episodes of severe mood disorders are much more common in people with borderline disorder than in the average person. In addition, certain antidepressants may be helpful in alleviating several of the other major symptoms of borderline disorder, especially impulsive behavior. So it's not surprising that antidepressants are often prescribed for patients with borderline disorder.

SELECTIVE SEROTONIN REUPTAKE INHIBITORS (SSRIs)

In the *American Psychiatric Association Practice Guideline for the Treatment of Borderline Personality Disorder*, a class of antidepressants called selective serotonin reuptake inhibitors (SSRIs), and related medications such as venlafaxine (Effexor), are recommended as the initial pharmacological treatment for people with borderline disorder who are suffering from emotional symptoms and impulsivity. A number of research studies have demonstrated disturbances in serotonin function in patients with borderline disorder, which provides a good rationale for the use of SSRIs in the treatment of this disorder, as the SSRIs increase serotonin activity in the brain (Table 9.1).

A recent placebo-controlled trial of the SSRI fluvoxamine (Luvox) in women with borderline disorder demonstrated that the medication improved rapid mood shifts, but not impulsivity and aggression. Other SSRIs and related antidepressants have been found to be useful in open label trials in people with borderline disorder. These medications include sertraline (Zoloft) and venlafaxine (Effexor).

The main side-effects you may encounter when taking an SSRI are decreases in **libido**, that is, your interest in sexual activity, and in your capacity to perform and respond sexually. Not everyone taking SSRIs experience these side-effects, and many who do experience them consider them a tolerable tradeoff to the reduction of their symptoms.

The Monoamine Oxidase Inhibitors (MAOIs)

Another class of antidepressants, the monoamine oxidase inhibitors (MAOIs), can also be useful in treating borderline disorder. In one placebo-controlled clinical study, the MAOI phenelzine (Nardil) was shown to be effective. However, MAOIs have the potential to produce very serious, even life-threatening, side-effects if used improperly. Most physicians use an MAOI for people with borderline disorder only after other medications have been tried, and the physician feels confident that the patient will follow the necessary rules that have been clearly outlined to him or her.

Bupropion

Bupropion (Wellbutrin) works differently than the other classes of antidepressants I've mentioned. It's an **activating antidepressant** that appears to work through its action on dopamine and norepinephrine neurotransmitter pathways. Evidence has recently been reported that dopamine dysfunction may be a risk factor for borderline disorder.

Although there are no studies of the effectiveness of bupropion in borderline disorder, in my experience it's often useful for those who suffer from recurrent depressions characterized by an increased need for sleep; increased appetite, often with carbohydrate craving; a decrease in energy; and decreased memory and ability to think clearly. This is also the typical symptom profile of people who suffer from recurrent depressions due to bipolar disorder. If the SSRIs are not effective in relieving these episodes of depression, I believe a trial on bupropion is worth serious consideration, even before a trial on an MAOI. An added benefit to the use of bupropion is that it rarely produces the decrease in sexual interest and function often associated with SSRIs. Bupropion stimulates brain activity, so it must be used cautiously with people who have a personal or family history of seizures, or who have suffered brain trauma.

THE TRICYCLIC ANTIDEPRESSANTS

You should also be aware that not all antidepressants are useful in treating borderline disorder. One study has shown that the tricyclic antidepressants amitriptyline (Elavil, Amitriptyline, Endep) and nortriptyline (Pamelor, Aventyl) may actually worsen your condition. Other tricyclic antidepressants should also be used with caution in people with borderline disorder.

Mood-Stabilizing Agents

Not everyone with borderline disorder responds adequately to neuroleptics, atypical antipsychotic agents, or antidepressants. Under these circumstances, other medications can be useful, either taken alone or in conjunction with one or more of the other medications I've described. In preliminary clinical trials, a group of medications referred to as mood-stabilizing agents has been shown to help reduce symptoms in some people with borderline disorder.

THE ANTIEPILEPTICS

This class of mood stabilizer includes divalproex (Depakote), carbamazepine (Tegretol), lamotrigine (Lamictal), and topiramate (Topamax). These medications are commonly used for people suffering from partial complex seizure disorder, and they are referred to as antiepileptic drugs. Partial complex seizure disorder originates in the temporal lobes of the brain. As you know, this brain region is closely tied to borderline disorder because it contains the amygdala, a brain structure important in the generation of emotions.

Divalproex and lamotrigine have been designated by the Food and Drug Administration (FDA) as effective and safe in people with bipolar disorder. They are used as alternatives to lithium, another mood stabilizer I describe later in this chapter. One of the primary symptoms of bipolar disorder is extreme fluctuation of emotions, usually from euphoria to utter depression. Other abnormalities of emotional control are also present in people with bipolar disorder, including irritability and anger outbursts. It seems reasonable that if these medications can calm down seizure activity in a region of the brain involved in producing emotions, and if they are useful in the treatment of bipolar disorder, they may also be able to reduce the emotional turmoil and related behaviors in people with borderline disorder. Although research trials with divalproex, carbamazepine, and lamotrigine in relation to borderline disorder are limited in number, these medications appear to be quite helpful for some people with the disorder (Table 9.1).

Although this class of mood stabilizers is the least studied of the medications commonly used in the treatment of borderline disorder, it is interesting for two reasons. First, antiepileptic drugs appear to exert their therapeutic effects by altering different neurotransmitter pathways than neuroleptics, atypical antipsychotic agents, and antidepressants do. These latter medications primarily affect the activity of dopamine and serotonin in the brain. The antiepileptic drugs appear to work by affecting the activity of GABA and glutamate pathways in the central nervous system.

Glutamate is the major excitatory neurotransmitter in the brain, and GABA is the major inhibitory neurotransmitter. There is no direct evidence of abnormal activity of either of these two neurotransmitters in people with borderline disorder, but the normal activity of the brain is so dependent on the proper function of glutamate and GABA that it seems quite possible that abnormalities in the activity of either or both of these neurotransmitters may be risk factors for borderline disorder. Therefore, the use of these medications provides physicians with a class of medications that operate through brain mechanisms that are complementary to other medications more commonly used for borderline disorder, thus increasing the chance of additional therapeutic benefit.

The second reason that antiepileptic drugs are important in the treatment of borderline disorder is that they appear to have secondary therapeutic effects and side-effects that differ significantly within the group. For example, lamotrigine has antidepressant effects that are superior to those of divalproex and carbamazepine. Therefore, lamotrigine may be more useful for those who have frequent depressive episodes that are not well controlled by other medications. Another antiepileptic drug, topiramate, seems very effective in reducing food, alcohol, and drug craving for those who have difficulties in these areas.

Many people with borderline disorder are dependent on alcohol and street drugs and have eating disorders. I've found that topiramate significantly reduces food, alcohol, and drug craving and eating disturbances in some people with borderline disorder that have these difficulties. Finally, while divalproex and carbamazepine may cause significant weight gain, lamotrigine appears to be weight-neutral, and topiramate often reduces weight. These medications are not approved by the FDA for the treatment of borderline disorder, so this is an off-label use of these drugs. Therefore, you should review their benefits and risks carefully with your psychiatrist before using any of them. Of course, that's true for any medication that is prescribed for you.

LITHIUM

Lithium is another mood-stabilizing medication that can be helpful in treating borderline disorder. This medication is most commonly used to treat people with bipolar disorder. There are similarities in many of the symptoms of depression and other mood disturbances in bipolar disorder and borderline disorder, and these similarities suggest that lithium could be useful for people with borderline disorder. In open label clinical research trials, lithium does appear to be effective in some patients with borderline disorder (Table 9.1). It's less commonly used in treating borderline disorder than the other mood stabilizers I've already mentioned, because lithium can be toxic at blood levels that are not much higher than those that are therapeutic. This requires close monitoring of lithium blood levels when treatment is initiated, and at least once or twice a year when levels are stabilized. Even so, if other mood stabilizers fail to help, and a medication in this group appears to be indicated by the symptoms of a patient with borderline disorder, a trial on lithium is a reasonable alternative.

Antianxiety Agents and Sedatives

Anxiety and poor sleep are common symptoms of borderline disorder. The class of medications most frequently used for these symptoms is benzodiazepines, such as diazepam (Valium), alprazolam (Xanax), temazepam (Restoril), flurazepam (Dalmane), and triazolam (Halcion). Research studies and clinical experience indicate that these medications should be used very rarely and with great caution in people with borderline disorder, because of their high addictive potential and a reported capacity to increase impulsive behavior.

Some people also experience adverse responses to the non-benzodiazepine sedative zolpidem (Ambien), such as aggressiveness, extroversion, agitation, hallucinations, and depersonalization. So if this medication is prescribed for you, be aware of this possible problem.

Nutriceutical Agents

Mary Zanarini and Frances Frankenburg at Harvard's McLean Hospital have recently reported the results of a creative therapeutic approach to the treatment of women with borderline disorder. Cross-national studies had shown that higher rates of seafood consumption were associated with lower rates of bipolar disorder and depression. Also, in placebo-controlled trials, people with depression and bipolar disorder had benefited from mixtures of certain fatty acids found in fish oil. Building on these discoveries, Zanarini and Frankenburg conducted a placebo-controlled study of the effects of omega-3 fatty acid on women with borderline disorder. Their results showed a significant reduction in aggression and depression in women treated with the fatty acid compared to the control group. If these results are replicated in a larger trial, this is a promising finding because the treated women did not report significant side effects. Also, the mechanism of action, though unknown, is probably new, and may lead to other innovative treatment approaches in borderline disorder.

How Medications Are Selected for Treating You

After looking at Table 9.1 (page 137), you can see that the three main classes of medications used for people with borderline disorder appear to produce similar overall results in improving the symptoms of the disorder. This raises two questions:

Why are different classes of medications effective for similar symptoms of borderline disorder?

How does your doctor decide which medications or combination of medications are right for you?

The Scientific Rationale

You'll remember from Chapter 6 that the neural systems in the brain that regulate emotional control, impulsivity, and cognitive functions (memory, reasoning, and planning) appear to be impaired in people with borderline disorder. To function properly, each of these neural systems uses the stimulatory neurotransmitter glutamate and the inhibitory neurotransmitter GABA. The actions of these two neurotransmitters are modified by other neurotransmitters, such as serotonin and dopamine, also called neuromodulators. The different classes of medicines described in Table 9.1 each have different sites of action and different effects on the activity of the neurotransmitters glutamate and GABA, or on the neuromodulators such as dopamine and serotonin. Therefore, the same behaviors can be affected by the activities of different medications at their specific chemical sites of action in each of the specific neural systems controlling these behaviors.

It now seems likely that borderline disorder is the result of the interaction of genetic, developmental, and environmental risk factors. As is true for many medical disorders, including mental disorders, *multiple* genetic mutations are probably necessary for borderline disorder to develop. These genetic abnormalities could impair the three neural systems that are involved in borderline disorder at multiple locations in their neural pathways. In doing so, they could affect the function of several neurotransmitter mechanisms. These multiple points of neurotransmitter dysfunction along critical neural pathways then become the chemical targets of the different classes of medications used in the treatment of borderline disorder. Because there may well be many sites and types of disturbances, often more than one medication may be required to achieve the desired therapeutic effects. In other words, if the neural pathways are "broken" at several different sites, different medications may be necessary to help restore these sites to more normal function.

The Sequential Selection of Medications

The most appropriate selection of medications for you will depend on at least three factors: proven effectiveness, tolerance, and cost. First, the main symptoms that affect you suggest which medication class may be most helpful. For example, if you're mainly experiencing symptoms of anxiety, depression, irritability, and impulsivity, an SSRI might be prescribed initially. However, if you also have paranoid thinking, dissociative episodes, self-destructive behaviors, or difficulty in reasoning, a neuroleptic or atypical antipsychotic agent may be a more appropriate first choice. If a medicine from both groups is tried, and if emotional dysregulation and impulsivity persist, a mood stabilizer could be added. You may require two or three medications, one from each class, in order to adequately control your symptoms because of their severity or resistance to treatment.

The second factor determining the appropriate selection of medications for you is your ability to tolerate a specific medicine or class of medicines. All medicines can cause side-effects, and some people experience more side-effects to a specific medicine or class of medicines than others. The ultimate goal of medication treatment is to achieve the optimal level of therapeutic effect and the smallest number and least severity of side-effects. This often requires some trial and error before the best medications for you are determined.

The final factor in the selection of an appropriate medication is cost. For example, although the atypical antipsychotic agents appear to be effective in treating some symptoms of borderline disorder, and may have a lower risk of tardive dyskinesia than traditional neuroleptics, you may find them too expensive. If so, it's worth discussing with your doctor the relative risks and benefits of using neuroleptics as opposed to atypical antipsychotic agents.

A Personal Note on Antipsychotic Agents

My clinical and research interest in the use of low doses of antipsychotic agents in borderline disorder dates back to my first year of training as a resident in psychiatry at Duke University Medical Center in 1967. This interest was initially sparked by a gentleman who came under my care on the psychiatric inpatient service.

This man was a dentist and a bachelor who was frequently admitted to the hospital with anxiety attacks that were totally disabling. When these attacks occurred, he couldn't work, and he became so paralyzed by fear that he couldn't even care for himself. He would then simply stay in bed for days. He had been treated with the new class of antianxiety agents available at that time, the benzodiazepines diazepam (Valium) and chlordiazepoxide (Librium), but they were of only minimal help. The recently discovered tricyclic antidepressants mainly caused side-effects or made his symptoms worse. He had been in psychotherapy for years. The only treatment that seemed to help temporarily was a week or two on the psychiatric inpatient service. With around-the-clock care and nurturing, his symptoms would gradually decrease to the point that he was able to take care of himself again and return to work. A few months later, he would relapse and be re-admitted to the hospital.

At that time, his diagnosis was severe anxiety neurosis. I knew nothing about borderline disorder as a first-year resident, so I failed to evaluate him for that possibility. He had never demonstrated any symptoms of **psychosis**. However, he was extremely dependent on a few close relatives and on his psychiatrist. When he became symptomatic, he would become so frantic that he would punch himself. He did not have temper outbursts or complain of severe depression, just a deep sense of loneliness. He had never been able to develop a mature relationship of any kind, frequently driving people away with the demands associated with his clinging dependency.

I don't recall the presence or absence of other symptoms of border-line disorder in this man's history. However, I now suspect that he would have met several criteria of the disorder. It was clear that neither the medications that had been used nor the psychotherapy were having any beneficial effect on him. However, I did have one idea. After reading back through his medical records, I realized that he had never been tried on a "major tranquilizer," as we then referred to the new group of medicines that we now refer to as traditional neuroleptics. I suggested to the faculty member supervising me that we try a very low dose of neuroleptic on this patient. At first, he was skeptical, but the dose I proposed was so small, 1 to 2 mg per day as opposed to the usual dose of 10 to 20 mg per day of this medication, that he gave his approval. The patient readily agreed when I discussed it with him.

To our mutual surprise and pleasure, his symptoms rapidly diminished. We finally determined that the optimal therapeutic range of this medication for this patient was 1 to 3 mg per day, depending on his level of stress. I recall vividly that the nursing staff, who had come to know this patient quite well over many hospitalizations, were initially quite skeptical of the plan, and then of the early results. They had become accustomed to using this class of medication at much higher doses.

Although we all thought the observed improvement might be a placebo effect, no other medication tried had caused this improvement. However, the ultimate test was this patient's long-term response. I remained on the inpatient service for another three months and never saw him re-admitted. Later that year, I confirmed with his psychiatrist that he continued to do better than he had in the past. He was able to work regularly and was now rarely re-admitted to the hospital.

The following year, when I was assigned to the outpatient service, I recalled my experience with this patient when my treatment with psychotherapy of a patient with a definite diagnosis of borderline disorder, Mrs. Davis, wasn't working (see chapter 2 for information). Her positive response to a similar medication prompted me to continue to use this approach with other patients with borderline disorder. Many, but certainly not all, improved on low doses of a neuroleptic.

In 1974, I left my faculty position at Duke and accepted an appointment as Director of the Division of Psychopharmacology in the Department of Psychiatry at the University of Washington School of

Medicine in Seattle. While there, two other young faculty psychiatrists and I spent some time discussing our mutual experiences in treating patients with borderline disorder. We quickly discovered that we had observed essentially the same therapeutic results from low-dose neuroleptic treatment of patients with the disorder.

By then, John Gunderson and Margaret Singer had published their seminal article on the diagnosis of borderline disorder. My colleagues, John Brinkley and Bernard Beitman, and I determined that there was no report of this positive therapeutic effect of low-dose neuroleptic therapy for patients with borderline disorder in the medical literature at that time. In fact, the body of literature on the topic generally discouraged the use of any medications for the treatment of borderline disorder. Therefore, we wrote a review of this literature. In order to challenge the prevailing position, we added to this review five cases from our personal clinical experiences of patients with borderline disorder who had responded well to treatment with this medication approach. The article was published in 1979.

The two main reasons we wrote this article were to alert other psychiatrists to the potential benefit of the use of low-dose neuroleptic treatment in patients with borderline disorder, and to suggest that placebo-controlled clinical trials were needed to test our hypothesis. In 1986, my team of researchers at the Medical College of Virginia, and Paul Soloff's team at the University of Pittsburgh, published simultaneously two such studies in the same scientific journal. Together, these studies demonstrated significant improvement in the major behavioral dimensions of borderline disorder in response to low-dose neuroleptic therapy. Since then, five additional controlled studies have been published on this topic. All but one of these studies have demonstrated significant advantages of low-dose antipsychotic treatment compared to placebo in patients with borderline disorder.

It's my expectation and hope that in less than ten years, borderline disorder will be an approved indication by the FDA for one or more of the atypical antipsychotic agents. This will be the final step in the process of firmly establishing the use of this class of medications for people with borderline disorder, a step that I believe will substantially increase their use in, and benefit to, those with the disorder.

TEN

The Psychotherapies

ALTHOUGH BORDERLINE DISORDER is associated with imbalances in brain chemistry and function, some risk factors also appear to be environmental in nature.

Behavioral symptoms are a major part of borderline disorder, and they ultimately cause disruptions in the normal development of effective patterns of behavior and of important relationships. Therefore, it's critical that you have a safe, supportive, and effective relationship with a person who is able to help you learn about your illness, how it affects you, and how to make those changes that will enable you to gain the best possible control over your emotions, impulsive behaviors, thought patterns, and relationships. A good therapist fulfills these needs and other roles too. Based on research and experience, most experts in this field believe that psychotherapy is essential if you are to gain optimal control over your symptoms and your life. I couldn't agree more strongly.

Psychotherapy can be very rewarding, interesting, and even fun at times. Many people initially view psychotherapy as a mysterious and somewhat frightening experience. They think the main discoveries about themselves will be negative. They are pleasantly surprised to discover many positive attributes about themselves. They are also excited and pleased to be able to learn how to use these strengths.

This chapter will provide you with a brief overview of the main types of individual and group psychotherapy that have proven effective in people with borderline disorder. This information is intended to give you a sense of the different types of psychotherapy, and when each seems to be most helpful. You can then discuss these alternatives with prospective therapists in order to determine the most appropriate form of therapy for you.

Psychodynamic Psychotherapy

Psychodynamic psychotherapy involves a close collaboration between you and the therapist to achieve your goals in therapy by exploring your underlying thoughts, feelings, and motivations. In order for psychodynamic psychotherapy to be effective, it is essential that you be able to recognize your problems, be committed to changing these problems, be able to control self-destructive behaviors as the therapy proceeds, and be able to abide by the terms of therapy initially set out with the therapist. Some experts in psychodynamic psychotherapy also believe that in order for such therapy to be effective, therapy sessions must be held two or three times per week for two or more years.

It's clear that this form of therapy is not appropriate for everyone with borderline disorder. Many patients are not able to engage in psychodynamic psychotherapy for a variety of reasons. For example, you may not be able to tolerate the emotions raised in this form of therapy, or be in sufficient control of your impulsive behavior to meet the requirements noted above, or have the time or finances to devote to the process. It's a good idea to find out if your health insurance policy covers this type of treatment. Even if you are well-suited and able to engage in psychodynamic psychotherapy, not all psychotherapists are sufficiently skilled to provide this type of therapy. These issues should be raised with the therapist before such therapy is undertaken.

Individual Supportive Therapy

Individual supportive psychotherapy is probably the most common form of psychotherapy used for people with borderline disorder, either alone or in conjunction with group therapy.

Most forms of supportive psychotherapy focus on a hierarchy of objectives, that is, a list that ranks the most pressing, fundamental objective at the top and the objective with the least immediate importance at the bottom. The first and most critical short-term objectives of supportive therapy are to assure your safety and that of others, and to develop effective techniques that replace those behaviors that place you and others in harm's way. The second objective is to improve your skills in day-to-day, self-sustaining activities such as proper eating, regular sleep habits, routine exercise, self-care, and medication compliance. The third objective is to develop and implement strategies to enhance your self-esteem. Other objectives of supportive psychotherapy are to validate your feelings; to help you to better understand, and deal with, your feelings more effectively; to recognize those situations most likely to result in impulsive behaviors, and to reduce such behaviors; and to identify and modify the recurring thought patterns that cause the worsening of your symptoms. The final, short-term objective of supportive psychotherapy is to help you determine successful ways to enhance your interpersonal skills and to have sound, healthy relationships.

The long-term objective of supportive psychotherapy is for you to acquire and internalize these skills to the point where you're able to use them most of the time in the absence of the therapist. When this goal is met, you will probably require only occasional visits with the therapist in order to deal with particularly difficult situations that may arise.

Individual supportive psychotherapy is often a rather lengthy process, typically involving one session per week for about two years, or even longer. This may seem like a very long time to be in treatment. However, it is important to remember that the symptoms and behaviors of borderline disorder are often severe and have been present for a long time, and that the environmental causes of borderline disorder are complex. So it's reasonable to anticipate that achieving your goals under such conditions will take a considerable amount of time. As therapy progresses, and new understandings and effective skills are developed, the frequency of therapy may decrease to once a month, or only when needed to deal with particularly difficult life stresses.

In the later stages of supportive psychotherapy, some people are able to develop a degree of insight into the origins of their feelings, thoughts, and behaviors. However, the time devoted to enhancing insight in supportive psychotherapy is typically limited. People who have the desire and have developed the capacity to engage in this type of work may then be candidates for psychodynamic psychotherapy.

It's important for you to know that the use of supportive psychotherapy is not well standardized: that is, it doesn't necessarily mean the same thing to, and is not performed in the same way by, every therapist. You should discuss the goals and other conditions of therapy I've described with a potential therapist to determine if there is a good fit between your and the therapist's expectations. It's also important to make sure the therapist you choose is experienced and skilled in treating patients with borderline disorder.

Psychoanalysis

Another form of individual psychotherapy, called psychoanalysis, involves a very intensive and detailed exploration of unconscious memories, thoughts, and feelings that may be causing significant emotional and behavioral symptoms. Psychoanalysis is now rarely used to treat borderline disorder. In fact, except in rare circumstances, research and experience have led to the conclusion that traditional psychoanalysis is not advisable for most people with borderline disorder.

Cognitive Behavioral Therapy

Cognitive behavioral therapy (CBT) was developed on the premise that the abnormal feelings and beliefs, and the maladaptive behaviors, of people with certain mental disorders could be improved by replacing them with more effective thought patterns and behaviors. The CBT therapist and the patient typically construct a list of specific problem areas. They then develop a set of homework tasks or exercises that generate and reinforce new attitudes, behaviors, and interpersonal strategies that will replace the ones that have proven to be ineffective or detrimental. Many of the goals of CBT are the same as those for supportive psychotherapy. However, CBT is a highly structured process, which means issues that are characteristic of borderline disorder, such as resistance to change and strong, conflicting feelings about relationships, including the relationship with the therapist, may not be dealt with and may interfere with progress in CBT.

Dialectical Behavior Therapy

A specific treatment approach that evolved in part from CBT is called Dialectical Behavior Therapy (DBT). Marsha Linehan, a psychologist from the University of Washington in Seattle, developed DBT specifically for people with borderline disorder, especially those who engage in frequent self-destructive and self-injurious behaviors. DBT is based on Linehan's belief that the symptoms of borderline disorder result from biological impairments in the brain mechanisms that regulate emotional responses. The early behavioral effects of this impairment are magnified, as the person with this biological risk factor interacts with people who don't validate their emotional pain and don't help them learn effective coping skills.

DBT has gained considerable favor in the treatment of borderline disorder because of the results it has achieved in several research studies, especially in reducing self-injurious behaviors and the frequency of hospitalization, and in improving social adjustment. It has been shown that DBT can be taught to and be used by many, but not all, mental health therapists. While there are many workshops available for clinicians to learn more about DBT, a fully trained therapist must have attended a ten-day intensive course of training. Each year, more therapists are receiving this "gold standard" of DBT training, but certified DBT therapists are not yet available in many communities. For the time being, this seriously limits the broad use of this effective treatment approach.

The objectives of DBT overlap to some extent with those of individual supportive psychotherapy, but the treatment approach uses a different theoretical concept and therapeutic approach. DBT seeks to validate your feelings and problems, but it balances this acceptance by gently pushing you to make productive changes. DBT therapy also deals with other opposing or "dialectical" tensions or conflicts that arise, such as the patient's perceived need for a high level of dependence on the therapist and others, and the fear and guilt aroused by such "excessive" dependency.

There are other differences that distinguish DBT from other forms of psychotherapy. For example, DBT consists of the combination of once-a-week individual psychotherapy, preferably by a DBT-certified therapist; a two-and-a-half-hour DBT skills training session conducted in a group setting; and weekly team meetings of the therapists involved in the patient's care. Also, in DBT, you are usually discouraged from using the hospital as a means of controlling your emotional tension, since the goal of treatment is to learn to manage the current emotional crisis in more effective ways. Because of the apparent success of DBT for many people with the disorder, some experts in the area of the psychotherapy of borderline disorder believe it should be strongly encouraged for appropriate patients if trained and skilled DBT therapists are available in the community.

Interpersonal Group Therapy

Until fairly recently, some experts in psychotherapy questioned how helpful group therapy was for people with borderline disorder. However, it has now been demonstrated that when a group of people with borderline disorder work together in therapy with one or two skilled therapists, much progress can be achieved. This form of therapy is called interpersonal group therapy (IPG). Even though you know now that borderline disorder is fairly common, it's particularly reassuring to meet other people with the disorder, to listen to their accounts of how the disorder has affected them, to share problems, and to attempt to help one another deal more effectively with these problems by discussing new strategies that have been attempted and their results.

Neither interpersonal group therapy nor DBT skills training groups are intended to replace individual therapy. However, they can serve to complement and to speed up the learning process of individual therapy. IPG is especially suitable for those who don't engage in serious destructive behaviors, who are able to tolerate the emotional content of the sessions, and who have difficulties with interpersonal relationships. When a certified DBT therapist is not available, IPG groups may also be used as an alternative to the skills training component of DBT. IPGs typically meet for one and a half hours a week. Results can be seen in several months, and the total length of IPG typically takes about two years. The cost of IPG is less per session than individual therapy. Because IPG hastens the results of individual therapy, the total cost of therapy may be reduced, and the ultimate benefits achieved by the combination of both individual and group therapy are often greater.

Family Programs

A recent addition to the spectrum of therapeutic opportunities for people with borderline disorder has been the introduction of family programs for patients and their families. This work can be conducted for individual families and for groups of families. These programs use psycho-educational and problem-solving approaches. One program is based on the DBT skills training method where you and your family together learn the new skills.

In another more recent model, experienced family members co-lead a twelve-week series of sessions for other families, offering them information about borderline disorder, teaching coping skills for their own well-being, and providing an opportunity to develop a support network. Preliminary reports from families who have participated in these groups suggest that they are highly valued and have low dropout rates.

The experiences of experts in the field who have developed and use these treatments also suggest that they significantly benefit people and families in developing a greater understanding of the challenges they face, and in finding new and more effective ways of dealing with these challenges.

Support Groups

In some communities, groups of people with borderline disorder meet on a regular basis, without a therapist, to help one another. Such support groups typically do not charge members a fee, and they can provide many of the same benefits as a therapist-assisted group therapy. There are two types of support groups: those for the person with borderline disorder, and those for their family members.

Although it may be helpful, you should approach participation in such groups with caution. Considerable harm can be done if one or more individuals in the group act in an angry, manipulative, malicious, or otherwise inappropriate and destructive way toward another group member or the group as a whole. Without a trained leader or facilitator present to step in to handle the situation promptly and properly, a member of the group, and even the group itself, may be exposed to significant harm.

Prior to joining a support group, you should seek recommendations about local groups from mental health professionals who work with people with borderline disorder. In addition, it may be helpful to request information from members of such groups before joining.

Treatment: The Bottom Line

The major message I have tried to convey to you in these three chapters on treatment is that there are a number of different levels of care, medications, and individual and group therapy approaches that can be used to help you gain more control over your life—*and that they work*. The treatment plan that works best for another person may not be appropriate or work well for you. Therefore, it's very important that you work closely with your psychiatrist and other mental health professionals to formulate that treatment plan that will produce the best results under your specific circumstances.

TABLE 10.1

Psychotherapies Studied and Used in the Treatment of Borderline Disorder

Type of Therapy	Indications	Adjunctive Treatments	Frequency and Duration
Psychoanalysis	Capacity to intensively explore unconscious memories, thoughts, feelings, and motives relevant to symptoms and behaviors. Rarely appropriate.		4 or more sessions per week for 2 or more years.
Psychodynamic Psychotherapy	Desire and ability to recognize and change personal problems. Capacity to control self-destructive behaviors. Ability to abide by the terms of therapy.	Medications, DBT skills training, or IPG therapy.	2 to 3 sessions per week for 2 or more years.
Individual Supportive Psychotherapy	Inconsistent control of behaviors harmful to self and others. Poor self-care skills, self-esteem, and sense of validation. Deficient recognition and regulation of emotions, impulsive behaviors. Disturbed relationships.	Medications, DBT skills training, or IPG therapy.	1 to 2 sessions per week for 1–2 or more years.
Cognitive Behavior Therapy	Capacity to identify specific problems and perform tasks that reinforce new attitudes, behaviors, and interpersonal strategies. Strong commitment to change and to collaborate with therapist.	Medications	Usually 1 session per week plus outside "home-work."
Dialectical Behavior Therapy	Frequent self-destructive and impulsive behaviors. Capacity to engage in a combination of individual therapy and skills training sessions.	Medications. Hospitalization is typically discouraged.	One individual and one 2½ hour group skills training session per week for 1 year.

Type of Therapy	Indications	Adjunctive Treatments	Frequency and Duration
Interpersonal Group Therapy	Poor self-perception and sense of validation. Feelings of isolation. Difficulty recognizing personal difficulties and identifying effective solutions. Impaired interpersonal skills. Ability to control behaviors harmful to self and others and to tolerate the emotional content of sessions with the assistance of the group therapist(s).	Medications. Used in combination with individual psychotherapy.	One session per week of 1½ hours duration for about 2 years.
Family Programs	For individual and groups of families to learn coping skills, work out acute crises and other problems, enhance understanding, and develop a support network. Same abilities as interpersonal group therapy.	Medications. Used in combination with individual psychotherapy.	One to two sessions per week for varying duration.
Support Groups	Same as interpersonal group therapy, plus ability to control behaviors harmful to self and others and to tolerate the emotional content of the sessions without the assistance of a group therapist(s).	Medications. Used in combination with individual and group therapy.	Research data not available.

ELEVEN

Borderline Personality Disorder in Children

BORDERLINE DISORDER IS usually first diag-
nosed in adolescence or early adulthood, but that doesn't mean that
there are no indications of behavioral problems before the full form
of the disorder becomes apparent. Some children do appear to have
symptoms that are very similar to adolescent and adult borderline disorder. In this chapter, I discuss what appear to be the early symptoms
and course of development of borderline disorder in infants and children. I also offer you some suggestions on how to ensure that your
child is properly evaluated for borderline disorder, and effectively
treated if diagnosed.

Does Borderline Disorder Affect Children?

When parents of people with borderline disorder are asked when
they first noticed that something may have been wrong, they give
different answers. Some say that they noticed very little unusual
behavior until their child was an adolescent. However, some report
that they detected problems as early as the first year of life. Mothers

report that they noticed differences in the temperament of the baby compared to their sisters or brothers at the same age. The affected babies seemed more "colicky," cried more, had diminished ability to experience pleasure, slept less restfully, were upset more easily by changes in routine, and were more difficult to soothe when upset.

In early childhood, children who later are diagnosed with borderline disorder are often described as having been more demanding and requiring more attention than their brothers and sisters. Some seem to worry more, have more episodes of sadness, are more sensitive to criticism, more readily upset by changes in routine or plans, and more easily angered. They are more easily frustrated, and when frustrated they may have severe temper tantrums. They may have great difficulty separating from home to attend school, and under stress may demonstrate physical symptoms such as pulling out small strands of their hair, frequent stomach cramps, headaches, problems with eating, and an abnormal sleep pattern.

In spite of these reports from parents, the fact is that we really don't know very much about what people with borderline disorder were like as children. Very few adults with borderline disorder have been seen by psychiatrists as children. Some believe that this is because of the three-to-one female-to-male difference in the prevalence of borderline disorder. Girls are less likely to be seen by psychiatrists and other mental health care workers because they are more likely to keep their problems inside, rather than act them out as often as do boys. Further, if girls were seen as children, they may have received some other diagnosis.

Another reason we're uncertain about the symptoms of children who are later diagnosed with borderline disorder is that recollections of adolescents and adults with borderline disorder, and of their parents, are often distorted due to their difficult interactions over time. Such difficulties cloud peoples' memories and result in information that may not be totally accurate.

It's not surprising, then, that there are very few articles in the medical literature about the characteristics of borderline disorder in children, and there is no clear agreement about whether the disorder is present during childhood and what the diagnostic criteria should be.

In fact, some of the most popular academic books about borderline disorder don't even mention the disorder in children. So if you have a child who's been having significant behavioral problems, I suspect that it has proven difficult to get a clear diagnosis and information about a comprehensive and effective treatment plan. Therefore, before we proceed any further, I believe it will make the information in this chapter most helpful if I list the main points I will cover. They are:

1. The different criteria for borderline disorder in children do not totally agree with one another, and overlap to some extent with other childhood behavioral disorders. I will review the different diagnostic models of borderline disorder in children, and other childhood disorders that resemble borderline disorder. I will also review the course of the illness in children. For example, some, but not all, children who have symptoms of borderline disorder, or another disorder of childhood, appear to continue to suffer from the disorder as adults, especially girls. Therefore, the purpose of this review is to underscore for you the difficulty in making a "correct" diagnosis of severe behavioral disturbances in children, and provide you with information on the most likely diagnostic alternatives in your child. In this section, I will also discuss the importance of making the best possible diagnosis of a significant behavioral disturbance in your child.

2. There are consistent findings of biological impairment in the children diagnosed with borderline disorder in essentially all of the studies that examined this risk factor in these children. I will note these when they occur. Although it is a painful realization, it may help you to understand that your child has a *bona fide* medical problem and is not simply misbehaved and in need of stricter discipline than other children.

3. The environmental risk factors of borderline disorder found in children appear to be similar to those of adults with the disorder. Recognition of these risk factors will help you help your child more effectively.

4. I will provide you with guidelines on when to have your child evaluated professionally, and on how to locate the best help for

your child and for you, so that you can learn new strategies that will make a difference.

5. There is little well-validated information available about the effectiveness of specific pharmacological and psychotherapeutic treatments of children with the disorder. However, there are anecdotal reports in the medical literature that the judicious use of medications in children with severe behavioral disturbances resembling borderline disorder benefits these children, and enhances their therapy and your interventions. This issue will be discussed.

Attempts to Define Borderline Disorder in Children

The early descriptions of borderline disorder in children paralleled the early process in adults described in Chapter 3. For example, there were reports by child psychiatrists, based on their clinical observations, that a group of children had disturbances in the correct perception, and appropriate responses, to many of their daily experiences. These children demonstrated lack of early pleasurable experiences, hypersensitivity, disintegration under stress, low frustration tolerance, aggression toward parents and other family members, and difficulty in reasoning. Many of these symptoms are characteristics and criteria of borderline disorder as described in Chapter 1. A limited number of similar reports subsequently appeared in the medical literature, broadly describing children with these and other characteristics that resemble borderline disorder in adolescents and adults. However, while some of these children later developed borderline disorder, others developed other disorders. This clearly meant that children with these problems did not necessarily have borderline disorder.

Research on the Diagnosis of Borderline Disorder in Children

In an effort to define valid diagnostic criteria for borderline disorder in children, three different sets of criteria based on empirical research were proposed in the 1980s. In 1982, Jules Bemporad and his colleagues at Harvard University systematically reviewed their experiences with twenty-four hospitalized children who had been selected because their symptoms were similar to those described previously in the medical literature as being consistent with borderline disorder. In general, they found that these children had difficulty in functioning in essentially every area, and that no single symptom enabled them to make the diagnosis. The specific symptoms that best described these children were:

- General developmental delay
- Rapid shifts from neurotic to psychotic-like states
- A significant inability to deal effectively with anxiety
- An excessive tendency to move from realistic thinking to fantasy and bizarre thinking
- Significantly disturbed relationships with parents, siblings, other family members, and other children
- Poor self-control marked by difficulty in dealing with frustration and anger, leading to severe temper tantrums and frantic, undirected hyperactivity
- Associated symptoms such as poor social functioning, a noticeable failure to learn from experience, poor self-grooming, difficulty in adapting to change, neurological soft signs (for example, subtle impairments of coordination, perception, and intellectual performance), and significant fluctuations between high and low levels of functioning

The doctors also pointed out that, as disabling as the above symptoms were when they occurred, these children could at other times appear quite normal.

One test of the validity of any set of diagnostic criteria is its ability to define a population of patients who will experience a similar course of illness and outcome. In one of the earliest follow-up studies involving children diagnosed with borderline disorder, Donna Lofgren, Jules Bemporad, and their colleagues followed nineteen children (ages 6–10) who had been hospitalized and who met the Bemporad criteria for the disorder. The major finding in the study was that sixteen of the nineteen children later met diagnostic criteria for a personality disorder, ten to twenty years after they were first seen. However, only three were diagnosed with borderline disorder as adults (two women and one man), while five were diagnosed with antisocial personality disorder as adults (all men). The authors proposed that borderline disorder in childhood, diagnosed with the Bemporad criteria, appears to be a precursor of a broad array of adult personality disorders. The results of this study suggest that the Bemporad criteria do not distinguish clearly children with borderline disorder from those with other personality disorders.

The results of the second attempt to define borderline disorder in children were published in 1986 by Deborah Greenman, John Gunderson, and their co-workers from the McLean Hospital at Harvard University. They studied eighty-six hospitalized children in order to explore the validity of the term *borderline disorder* in children, and its relationship to the disorder in adults. To do so, they developed a modified version of the revised Diagnostic Interview for Borderline for use with children. Of the eighty-six children studied, twenty-seven met these criteria.

A number of findings emerged from this study. Two thirds of the children who met the modified adult criteria for borderline disorder also met the criteria defined by Bemporad. All of the children diagnosed with borderline disorder in this study had disturbances in impulse control, thinking, and interpersonal relationships. Unlike adults, children who met Grunman/Gunderson modified adult criteria for borderline disorder were more likely to be assaultive toward others than to injure themselves. Finally, many of the biological and environmental risk factors for borderline disorder described in adults (see Chapter 4) were found to be present in children with the disorder. The authors concluded that there were enough differences between their criteria for borderline disorder in children and the Bemporad criteria to indicate that a more discriminating set of criteria was needed to identify children with borderline disorder.

At the same time that the Bemporad and Greenman/Gunderson

studies were in progress, a different approach was being used by Donald Cohen and his co-workers at Yale University to determine the proper diagnostic classification of children with "borderline syndrome," as they called it. In 1983, they suggested that borderline disorder should be included in the broad spectrum of childhood mental disorders associated with the abnormalities that resulted from impaired brain development (see Chapter 4). Their proposal was based, in part, on the common occurrence of physiological disturbances of brain function seen in these children, typically evident by age four.

At this time, they defined a pattern of five areas of developmental impairment in these children. As the result of an extensive study of such children, they elaborated on and published a set of diagnostic criteria in 1993 for the disorder and renamed it multiple complex developmental disorder (MCDD).

CHILDREN WITH MCDD have impaired regulation of their emotions, including anxiety, beyond that seen in children of the same mental age, which they demonstrate with two of the following symptoms:

- Intense generalized anxiety, diffuse tension, or irritability
- Unusual fears and phobias
- Recurrent panic episodes, terror, or flooding with anxiety
- Episodes of disorganized behavior lasting from minutes to days with the development of markedly immature, primitive, and/or self-injurious behaviors
- Significant and wide emotional swings with or without environmental causes
- A high frequency of idiosyncratic anxiety reactions such as sustained periods of uncontrollable giggling, giddiness, laughter, or "silly" reactions that are not appropriate in the situation

Children with MCDD demonstrate consistent impairments in their social behavior and sensitivity compared with children of the same mental age. These kids exhibit social disinterest, detachment, avoidance, or withdrawal in spite of being socially competent (at times), particularly with adults. Often their relationships appear friendly and cooperative but really are very superficial, and are based primarily on having their material needs met. MCDD causes them to have difficulty in initiating or maintaining relationships with other children and disturbed relationships with adults. They often display high degrees of ambivalence, particularly toward their parents and caregivers, which causes them to exhibit clinging, overly controlling, needy behavior, or aggressive, oppositional behavior, including rapidly shifting love-hate behavior toward their parents, teachers, or therapists. They have profound limitations in their capacity to empathize with others, or to read or understand others' moods accurately.

Kids with MCDD also have impaired cognitive processing (thinking), which is demonstrated by one of the following:

- Thought disturbances compared with children of the same mental age, including irrationality, sudden interferences of normal thought processes
- Magical thinking
- Making up new words or using nonsense words repeatedly
- Negative thinking
- Blatantly illogical or bizarre ideas
- Confusion between reality and fantasy life
- Perplexity and easy confusability (for example, trouble with understanding social situations and keeping one's thoughts "straight")
- Delusions, including fantasies of personal superiority, paranoid preoccupations, over-engagement with fantasy figures, grandiose fantasies of special powers, and referential ideation

The above symptoms must have been present for longer than six months and the child cannot have the diagnosis of autism.

Adapted with the permission of Lippincott Williams & Wilkins Company, from, Towbin KE, Dykens EM, Pearson GS, Cohen DJ: Conceptualizing "Borderline syndrome of childhood" and "childhood schizophrenia" as a developmental disorder, from the *Journal of the American Academy of Child and Adolescent Psychiatry* 1993; 32:775-782.

You've probably noticed a significant overlap of these criteria and those of Bemporad and of adult borderline disorder, with an emphasis on three of the four dimensions of borderline disorder: (1) poorly regulated emotions; (2) impaired perception and thinking; and (3) markedly disturbed relationships. MCDD is not listed in DSM–IV–TR as a mental disorder.

Cohen and his colleagues noted that the ultimate course of the disorder was unknown. They did indicate, however, that reframing the problems of these children from intentionally willful behaviors to inborn developmental disturbances better enabled their parents to accept their children's condition and to learn how to better deal with the disorder. The authors also suggested the potential benefits of medications in children with MCDD, especially low doses of neuroleptics. As I discussed in Chapter 9, this class of medications has proven to be very useful in treating borderline disorder in adults. Cohen and his colleagues believe that the conservative use of medications enables children with MCDD to learn more readily and relate more effectively.

Other Behavioral Disorders in Children that Resemble Borderline Disorder

There are three other disorders that are listed in DSM–IV–TR that can be confused with the early onset of borderline disorder. They are oppositional defiant disorder, conduct disorder, and attention deficit hyperactivity disorder (ADHD). These are the three childhood disorders most commonly seen by child psychiatrists. A fourth childhood disorder, called the explosive child, though not listed in DSM–IV–TR, also has many of the symptoms of borderline disorder and these other three disorders. It's frequently difficult to distinguish these disorders from one another in children. The correct diagnosis may only become evident in some children as they develop into adolescence. Nonetheless, because the symptoms of these disorders do overlap to some degree with those of borderline disorder, it's important that you have easy access to their diagnostic criteria so you can avoid, when possible, a misdiagnosis and inappropriate treatment.

Oppositional Defiant Disorder

Children with oppositional defiant disorder have a pattern of negative, hostile, and defiant behaviors lasting at least six months that are not commonly observed in children of a similar age and level of development. During this period, four or more of the following symptoms are present:

- Frequent loss of temper
- Often argues with adults
- Often actively defies or refuses to comply with adults' requests or rules
- Frequently deliberately annoys people
- Often blames others for his or her mistakes or misbehavior
- Is often touchy or easily annoyed by others
- Is frequently angry and resentful
- Is often spiteful or vindictive

In order to be diagnosed, the behavior disturbance must cause the child significant problems in social and academic performance, and the child cannot meet the criteria for conduct, mood, or psychotic disorder.

Keep in mind that these children don't demonstrate the disturbances in thinking seen in children with borderline disorder or MCDD, or in attention seen in children with ADHD, nor do they have the impulsive behavior seen in children with these disorders and conduct disorder.

Conduct Disorder

Conduct disorder is a repetitive and persistent pattern of behavior in which the child or adolescent violates the basic rights of others or the norms or rules of society. The diagnosis of this disorder is made by the presence of three or more of the following criteria occurring in the past twelve months, with at least one criterion present in the past six months:

- These children show aggression toward people and animals by bullying, threatening, or intimidating them; by initiating physical fights; by using a weapon that can cause serious physical harm to others; by being physically cruel to people or to animals; by confronting and stealing directly from someone; or by forcing someone into sexual activity.

- Children with conduct disorder frequently destroy property by deliberately setting fires with the intention of causing serious damage, or by deliberately destroying property other than with fire.
- These children are deceitful and steal: they have broken into someone else's house, building, or car; often lie to obtain goods or favors or to avoid obligations, that is, they "con" others; or have stolen items of significant value without confronting the victim, for example, by shoplifting or by forgery.
- Children with conduct disorder commit serious violations of rules: they stay out at night despite parental prohibitions, beginning before age thirteen; run away from home overnight at least twice while living with their parents, or a parental figure, or once without returning for a lengthy period; and are often truant from school, beginning before age thirteen.

Some children who are diagnosed with borderline disorder in childhood are then diagnosed with conduct disorder in adolescence. It appears that this occurs in boys more frequently than in girls, for unknown reasons. The distinction between conduct disorder and borderline disorder is very critical because the methods of treatment are considerably different. For example, medications and psychotherapy don't seem to be especially helpful for children with conduct disorder, while they appear to have some benefit for children with borderline disorder.

Attention Deficit Hyperactivity Disorder (ADHD)

I explored the diagnostic criteria for ADHD in depth in Chapter 7 on page 120, and the criteria are the same for children. Again, it's essential to differentiate between borderline disorder and ADHD, because the treatments known to be effective for each disorder are so different. However, it's not always possible to make this differentiation, because these two disorders may co-occur. When this is the case, treatment for both disorders is necessary.

The Explosive Child

The fourth and final behavioral disorder of childhood, like MCDD, is not listed in DSM-IV. Nonetheless it deserves mention here because of the recent publication of a book, *The Explosive Child**, that has received a lot of attention. The author, Ross Greene, is a psychologist in the Harvard Department of Psychiatry at Massachusetts General Hospital. Based on his clinical experience, he's described a group of children with very low tolerance to frustration, marked inflexibility, and explosive behavior. Greene offers ten characteristics of these inflexible-explosive children, and there appear to be many similarities between these characteristics and the different sets of diagnostic criteria for borderline disorder in children.

1. The child has difficulty managing and controlling the emotions associated with frustration and has difficulty "thinking through" ways of resolving frustrating situations in a rational, mutually satisfactory manner. Thus, frustration (caused by disagreements, changes in plan, demands for "shifting gears") often leads to a point where the child has difficulty remembering how to stay calm and problem-solve, has difficulty recalling the consequences of previous inflexible-explosive episodes, may not be responsive to reasoned attempts to restore coherence, and may deteriorate even further in response to limit-setting and punishment.

2. An extremely low frustration threshold. The child becomes frustrated far more easily and by far more seemingly trivial events than other children of his or her age. Therefore, the child experiences the world as one filled with insurmountable frustration and has little faith in his ability to handle such frustration.

*Greene, R.W. *The Explosive Child*. New York: HarperCollins Publishers, 2001; 16–18

3. An extremely low tolerance for frustration. The child is not only more easily frustrated, but also experiences the emotions associated with frustration more intensely than do other children of the same age. In response to frustration, the child becomes extremely agitated, disorganized, and verbally or physically aggressive.

4. A remarkably limited capacity for flexibility and adaptability. The child often seems unable to shift gears in response to commands or change in plans.

5. The tendency to think in a concrete, rigid, black-and-white manner. The child doesn't recognize the gray in many situations ("Mrs. Robinson is *always* mean! I *hate* her!" rather than "Mrs. Robinson is usually nice, but she was in a really bad mood today"). He or she may apply oversimplified, rigid, inflexible rules to complex situations and may impulsively revert to such rules even when they are obviously inappropriate ("We *always* go out for recess at 10:30. I don't care if there's an assembly today, I'm going out for recess!").

6. The persistence of inflexibility and poor responses to frustration, despite a high level of intrinsic or extrinsic motivation. The child continues to exhibit frequent, intense, and lengthy meltdowns even in the face of salient, potent consequences.

7. Explosive episodes may have an out-of-the-blue quality. The child may seem to be in a good mood, then fall apart unexpectedly in the face of frustrating circumstances, no matter how trivial.

8. The child may have one or several issues about which he or she is especially inflexible—for example, the way clothing looks or feels, the way food tastes or smells, the order or manner in which things must be done.

9. The child's inflexibility and difficulty responding to frustration in an adaptive manner may be fueled by behaviors—moodiness, social impairment—commonly associated with other disorders.

10. While other children are apt to become more irritable when tired or hungry, inflexible-explosive children may completely fall apart under such conditions.

An important contribution Greene makes in his book is that he describes behavioral strategies that parents of children with this disorder may use to help their child better understand and deal more effectively with their behavior problems. He also mentions the importance of the use of medications in order to reduce the symptoms of the disorder, and to enable the child to learn from the new behavioral strategies and experiences.

We don't know to what degree children diagnosed with inflexible-explosive disorder meet current criteria for borderline disorder. The fate of children with this disorder is also unknown. It seems likely that many of these children continue to have difficulties into adulthood, but outcome studies have not been reported that provide us with such information. I suspect that a significant number of children who meet the criteria for this disorder suffer from the early onset of borderline disorder, conduct disorder, or a developmental disorder, and that the most appropriate diagnosis becomes clearer over time.

Should Children Be Diagnosed with Borderline Disorder?

At first, it may seem harmful to "label" children with any mental disorder so early in their lives, especially when we're not certain yet how to validly and consistently diagnose borderline disorder in children. Won't that stigmatize them? To suggest that this won't happen is to deny the reality that negative perceptions about mental disorders do exist. However, you must weigh the consequences of such attitudes against the harmful effects of the disorder on the child and on the rest of the family, now and in the long term.

The Importance of Early Detection of Borderline Disorder in Children

In spite of the small amount of definitive information available to us about borderline disorder in children, it's still crucial to understand what *is* known, for several reasons. First, children with borderline disorder, or those who are at high risk for developing the disorder as teenagers or adults, may be exposed to the environmental traumas I've noted above and in the previous chapter. If they are identified early, steps can be taken to protect these children and to help their parents. Second, if the symptoms of the child are severe enough, appropriate medications may help reduce their severity. This will enable them to benefit from other treatments and decrease the short- and long-term effects of their disorder. A number of experts in the field believe these behaviors should not be left untreated. Finally, the child and their parents can receive therapy and counseling to learn adaptive ways to deal with the symptoms of the disorder.

If you suspect your child has the symptoms of borderline disorder, or any of the disorders I've mentioned, it's crucial that you seek help immediately to determine the nature of the problem and to begin appropriate treatment. Remember, your child may have a problem that has a biological basis. Your child may not just be headstrong and willful and simply require additional discipline. Let's examine, then, the evidence that borderline disorder in children has biological and environmental causes, just as it does in adults.

Biological Risk Factors of Borderline Disorder in Children

The proposal by Cohen and his co-workers that there is a biological basis to borderline disorder/MCDD in children has been supported by research findings at a number of different sites. For example, Joel Paris and his colleagues at McGill University in Montreal recently evaluated the neuropsychological profiles of children with borderline disorder, and observed significant differences in these children from children with conduct disorder. This suggests that there's a biological predisposition for borderline disorder in children. It also suggests that there are fundamental differences in the biological bases of borderline and conduct disorders in children, and that borderline disorder may not evolve from conduct disorder.

In 1998, a different research team led by Alan Lincoln of the Children's Hospital in La Jolla, California, provided additional evidence that children with borderline disorder/MCDD are different in three ways from children with ADHD. First, the borderline/MCDD children were less likely to act out than the ADHD children. Second, as was found in the Paris study noted above, the borderline/MCDD children showed greater impairments in mental performance on neuropsychological tests than did children with ADHD. These impairments were related to difficulty in processing auditory information. Finally, greater electroencephalographic (EEG) disturbances related to auditory attention tasks were also detected in the borderline/MCDD children. In other words, these findings suggest that one of the biological risk factors for borderline disorder in children and in adults is difficulty in the interpretation and use of auditory information. This has significant implications for understanding some of the symptoms of borderline disorder/MCDD, and for its treatment.

Environmental Risk Factors of Borderline Disorder in Children

A small number of research studies of children with borderline disorder have investigated the environmental risk factors of the disorder. The advantage of these studies over those that depend on recollections of adults with borderline disorder is that there is less likelihood of distortions of memory due to time or to the effects of traumatic experiences on memory.

In the first study of this type in children, Jaswant Guzder, Joel Paris, and their co-workers at McGill University reviewed the medical records of ninety-eight children admitted to a day treatment program because of severe behavioral problems. Forty-one of these children met the criteria of Greenman/Gunderson for borderline disorder, and the remaining fifty-seven were used as the comparison group. The findings of this study demonstrated that the environmental risk factors of children with borderline disorder are similar to those of adult borderline disorder. Compared to non-borderline children, those with borderline disorder experienced more sexual abuse, physical abuse, and severe neglect. Evidence of persistent abuse and parental neglect was higher in the borderline children. However, the findings of this study were limited by the fact that medical record reviews were utilized, rather than direct evaluations of patients and their parents.

This problem was addressed in a recent study reported by Phyllis Zelkowitz, Paris, and their colleagues at McGill. They directly evaluated eighty-six children in a day-treatment program, and interviewed at least one of their parents. Thirty-five of the children met Greenman/Gunderson criteria for borderline disorder. The remaining children constituted the control group. Children who had experienced sexual abuse were four times more likely to be diagnosed with borderline disorder than the non-borderline children. Witnessing violence was another factor that placed children at risk for borderline pathology.

Although there's a limited amount of information of this type available, it does support the conclusion that borderline disorder is the result of necessary biological risk factors that interact with environmental risk factors. Although it appears that environmental factors alone do not cause borderline disorder, they certainly seem to increase the likelihood that the disorder will develop.

When Should Your Child Be Evaluated?

Once you've progressed through the difficult task of accepting the possibility that your child may have symptoms of borderline disorder or a related disorder, your next challenge begins. You must now locate a child psychiatrist who's knowledgeable, experienced, and broadly competent in this area of childhood mental disorders. The principles involved in the overall treatment and care of your child are fairly similar to those that apply to adolescents and adults. Of course, there are a number of important age-related variations.

Under certain circumstances, it's not a difficult decision for parents to seek help for their child with a behavior problem. If your child's behaviors are so problematic that they regularly disrupt your normal family routines and special occasions, and seriously interfere with schoolwork and the lives and well-being of the child, other family members, and friends, then it's clearly time for help.

However, under other circumstances, it's not that easy to make such a decision. People have different levels of tolerance for a child's disturbed behavior. Some families will seek help much sooner than others. But is the family's level of tolerance the best guide? Some families may have such a high tolerance level that a child who needs care never receives it.

In other instances, the issue is not so much one of tolerance as it is of accepting the possibility that there is something wrong with your child. This is not a trivial issue. I do understand how difficult it is for parents to consider the possibility that one of their children may have a significant mental impairment. We parents have such high hopes for our children that it can be difficult to accept even their minor shortcomings. It's so much more difficult to consider that they may have a serious problem. To do so clashes with our dreams for them and is extraordinarily heart-wrenching. The main consolation I can offer you is that effective help is available. Also, one of our major tasks as parents is to help our children understand their strengths and limitations, and to figure out how best to help them to build a good life within these boundaries. This is very difficult work, but as my wife and I often have encouraged and reassured one another, this is one of the ways we earn our pay as parents.

So regardless of your level of tolerance and acceptance, I suggest that you consider the following as guidelines for when you should have your child seen for evaluation by a child psychiatrist:

1. There is a significant difference in the behavior of your child from his or her siblings or other children of the same age, or there is a substantial change in behavior. This includes moodiness, anxiety, sadness, anger outbursts, withdrawal from social contacts, and poor school performance.
2. Family members, friends, schoolteachers, church leaders, or others express concern about your child's behavior and performance.
3. You suspect that this may not be just a "phase" the child is going through, but a consistent pattern of behaviors that is emerging and worsening.

4. You determine that your child has several of the symptoms described as characteristics of borderline disorder, or has some of the symptoms listed as characteristics of similar childhood disorders that I discuss in this chapter.

How to Find Professional Help

For most parents, once the decision has been made to seek help, the next two difficult steps are to locate the best help available, and then to make the initial appointment.

In large to mid-size communities, it's easier to find several sources of skilled professionals in child psychiatry than it is in smaller communities. If you are located reasonably close to a university school of medicine, most departments of psychiatry have a division of child and adolescent psychiatry. If you do not live near a university, large to mid-size communities typically have one or more groups of child psychiatrists and other mental health workers.

Child psychiatrists may also be established in solo practices in both small and large communities, usually working closely with other mental health professionals trained and skilled in the care of children.

How to Know If the Mental Health Professional You Contact Is Qualified

Some child psychiatrists and their colleagues have more experience and skills than others in diagnosing and treating children who may be in the early stages of borderline disorder, or another disorder that resembles borderline disorder at this stage of life. It should not take much longer than the initial interview with one of them to determine if the person you have contacted has the level of expertise you are looking for.

First, find out if they evaluate and treat children with the behavioral difficulties demonstrated by your child. Then ask what different diagnoses such children may have, in their experience. If they list a number of the diagnoses discussed in this chapter, ask if they ever see children with borderline disorder. If they haven't, I wouldn't necessarily rule them out, because of the lack of agreement about this issue among health professionals. However, if they tell you that they don't believe in making diagnoses in children, ask them how they develop a treatment plan and what the plan includes. The main purpose for attempting to establish the correct diagnosis, or reasonable diagnostic alternatives, is that the diagnosis provides important guides for further evaluation and in treatment planning. If the child psychiatrist uses the medications listed in Chapter 9, along with psychotherapy and family counseling, you should still consider him or her a viable option. Do be careful if they tell you that they don't believe in using medications for any children, and that they focus on intensive inpatient or outpatient psychotherapy as the primary treatment approach. Also be hesitant if you are told that medications are the primary intervention and that little therapy is required.

Remember that we're not able to determine with a high level of assurance in many children their accurate diagnosis and their course of illness. So it seems to me most reasonable to find a psychiatrist who knows the relevant medical literature, who has an open mind regarding the different diagnostic possibilities and treatment approaches, and who communicates well with you and your child. Given our current level of knowledge about borderline disorder in children, it's likely that such a professional will give your child and you the best help available, now and in the future.

Medications

Many parents are very reluctant to agree that any medication be used to treat their child with borderline disorder or other significant behavioral disorders. I understand their concerns. There are few well-controlled studies of the effectiveness and safety of medications in children with these disorders. However, there are some reports that show certain medications can be very helpful for these children. For example, some children with borderline disorder, MCDD, and the inflexible-explosive syndrome described by Greene do appear to benefit from medications. I urge you to read the medication sections in Chapter 9 carefully and to keep an open mind about this possible method of treatment.

Psychotherapy

There are a number of different psychotherapeutic approaches that are effective for adolescents and adults with borderline disorder. In addition, there are educational experiences for their parents and families. Understandably, these approaches must be greatly modified if they are to be useful for children. For example, the ability to think abstractly does not normally occur in children until about age twelve, a fact reflected in the significant change in the educational information presented to children in school in the sixth and seventh grades. Difficulty in reasoning is a main symptom of borderline disorder, and impaired processing of auditory information has been reported in children with the disorder. Therefore, therapists and parents of affected children must focus on developing ways to make compensations in these and other areas.

Children in general also have difficulty in accurately describing their feelings. This appears to be true of even adolescents and adults with borderline disorder. Child psychiatrists and psychologists are trained and skilled at gently helping children understand their feelings, often through "play" therapy. Play therapy is used by the therapist to communicate with children because of their undeveloped verbal skills compared to adults, and because of their difficulty in abstract thinking. Essentially, it consists of the therapist playing games with the child and asking them to tell stories about these games. Children are usually very creative storytellers, and the stories they tell often reveal the concerns, conflicting thoughts and feelings, and problems that they are not otherwise able to put into words.

In addition, your responses to your child are a very critical part of the treatment process. As part of treatment, you will learn new ways of helping your child understand his or her feelings and behaviors, and channeling these energies in more positive directions. You may also benefit from reading Ross Greene's book, *The Explosive Child*. He provides a number of helpful strategies to guide you in dealing with your situation.

The Bottom Line

The scientific literature suggests that borderline disorder does occur as a distinct entity in children. However, it's extremely difficult to distinguish the disorder from other mental disorders of childhood that result in similar symptoms.

Therefore, one reasonable approach is to enlist the care of a child psychiatrist and treatment team that are knowledgeable about borderline disorder's diagnostic and therapeutic problems. Ideally, these professionals should be highly skilled and experienced, open and flexible in their approaches to medications and psychotherapy, available to you at times of crises, and easy for you and your child to communicate with.

TWELVE

When a Loved One Has Borderline Personality Disorder

IF YOU HAVE a spouse, sibling, parent, child, or friend with borderline disorder, then you know firsthand the difficulties they have with relationships, especially with the people who are closest to them. Episodes of anger outbursts, moodiness, and unreasonable, impulsive, and erratic behaviors, which often appear unprovoked, can cause considerable harm to their important relationships. Any attempt to work out reasonable solutions to problems frequently turns into a highly emotional battle. If effective discussions of differences cannot occur, it's difficult to maintain and improve relationships.

Family and friends usually end up feeling anxious and frustrated. They attempt to placate them, and then become angry when the limits of normal patience have been exceeded. Most families and friends of people with borderline disorder are enormously relieved to learn that effective treatment is available and that there are ways they can help as well. Two of the most significant advances in the area of borderline disorder have been the recent research on the effectiveness of different educational and therapeutic experiences for families, and the development of consumer-led organizations focused on the disorder.

Borderline Disorder from the Inside

In order to be helpful to a family member with borderline disorder, and to minimize the negative effects on the rest of the family, it's important to understand as much as possible about the disorder and how it affects the people who have it. Much of this book is devoted to describing what is currently known about borderline disorder from a clinical perspective. But for the families and others looking at the disorder from the outside, it's also important to understand how your loved one thinks of herself or himself so you can do your best to support them and validate their difficulties.

The Sharon Glick Miller Study

In 1994, Sharon Glick Miller, a psychologist in the Department of Psychiatry at the University of Florida, published a study of ten patients (eight women and two men) with borderline disorder from whom she obtained life-history narratives in a series of ninety-minute interviews over a one-year period. After careful analysis of the data, she concluded that the self-reports of these patients were highly consistent with one another, but they differed in certain respects from typical clinical descriptions.

She found that while clinicians described these patients as having an identity problem, the patients seemed to have a sense of *themselves* as being impaired. They reported that the strategies they used, such as changes in appearance, might seem like a problem with identity, but they were mainly attempts to feel better about themselves. They also indicated that they did not reveal themselves easily to therapists or to others, because they anticipated disapproval and would rather appear to be lacking in identity than have their perceptions of themselves as flawed confirmed.

They did not see themselves as having an illness, but as leading a life in which they constantly struggled against feelings of despair. This was a central theme of how they perceived their fate in the world.

Most of the patients reported feeling alone and inadequate, beginning in some as children, and in others as adolescents, regardless of their achievements. For the most part, they did not know the origins of these feelings, though two identified family problems and another the discrimination she experienced because of obesity. The sense of emotional pain and despair they reported was overwhelming. They all expressed the wish not to be alive.

COPING STRATEGIES

These patients each developed a number of coping strategies to lessen their deep sense of pain and despair, always with the hope that, just once, something would help. The main coping strategy was to block out or dissociate themselves from these feelings as best they could. If that was not successful, many turned to alcohol and drugs.

They viewed their bedrooms or apartments as safe havens, except when they felt depressed and desperate. At these times, some realized that it was dangerous to be alone because of the great impulse to hurt themselves.

Social situations typically provoked anxiety and feelings of inadequacy in them. These feelings resulted in strategies either to push through the event, which exacted a high toll on their energy, or to escape from the situation.

One potential coping strategy that was notably absent was the use of social support. Patients consistently reported that they did not openly share their feelings with family, friends, and even their therapists because of fears of rejection, and of being viewed as a burden. However, not sharing their struggles resulted in the worsening of their sense of isolation.

They also felt conflicted about sharing negative feelings with their therapist. To not do so could be perceived as not working in therapy, but doing so could reveal a lack of progress that might result in increased pressure to perform, or in hospitalization. They viewed hospitalization as a respite from the constant struggles with despair and from the desire not to be in this world. Once the crisis was over, they then wished to be discharged. However, they learned they could not refer often to their constant thoughts of self-harm, as this might result in an undesired hospitalization.

The Importance of Self-Disclosure

An important finding from this study was that patients felt more comfortable revealing information in the research setting than elsewhere, because no challenges were being made to their presentations. This led them to believe that the researchers understood them better than their families, friends, and even some of their therapists. They perceived themselves to be collaborating with the researchers because they were the experts about themselves, which helped reduce their conflicts over dependency issues.

I hope this patients' perspective helps you better understand and deal with the many issues that you confront with your family member with borderline disorder. Of course, there's is no single view of borderline disorder that adequately captures the entirety of their experiences. But it's clear that it's very helpful for you to stay involved with your family member with the disorder. Understanding their perspective is an important early step in the process.

The Family's View

There is growing evidence that family involvement with a family member with borderline disorder is extremely beneficial. However, there is little information available on the perceptions and experiences of the family. In other words, what is it like to have a family member with borderline disorder?

As you now know, I was raised in a family with a sister who suffered from borderline disorder (Chapter 2). I have tried to accurately report some of my perceptions and experiences, and a few of those of my mother and of my other sister without the disorder. However, anecdotal accounts of this type have only limited value. How accurate is my memory? How much of what I recall is colored by my many emotional experiences with my sister over the years? In addition, not all people with borderline disorder suffer from the same symptoms and from symptoms of the same severity. This means that the families of different people with the disorder will have different experiences.

I think it's worthwhile, then, to review some of the few research studies that exist that address the effects and perceptions of borderline disorder in families.

The Gunderson/Lyoo Study

In 1997, John Gunderson and Kyoon Lyoo, at Harvard's McLean Hospital, published a study comparing the perceptions that twenty-one young women with borderline disorder had of their families to the perceptions of their parents. There were two main findings from this study.

First, the women viewed their family environment and their relationships in the family as more negative than their parents did. Specifically, they perceived less cohesiveness, more conflict, less organization, less expressiveness, and less support of independent behavior in the family than did their parents.

The fathers usually perceived their families as healthier, less conflicted, and more supportive of independence than did their daughters. In spite of these perceptions, their daughters were more negative of their fathers than of their mothers, seeing their relationships with their fathers as weak. In addition, daughters felt that their father's values, such as honesty, and their norms, such as dressing neatly for meals, were inconsistent with, and often different from, their behavior.

Both parents viewed their relationship with their daughter with borderline disorder as weak, especially in the areas of expressing emotion, accomplishing tasks, and communication. Parents always agreed with one another more than they did with their daughter. Interestingly, the daughter rated both parents weak on emotional involvement.

Gunderson and Lyoo concluded that when evaluating the quality of parenting of a person with borderline disorder, it's important to get the parents' and siblings' perspectives as well. "We believe that clinicians need to be wary of BPD patients' vilification of their parents and to take active measures to hear and consider parental viewpoints as well."

The Effects on Children of a Mother with Borderline Disorder

The effect that parents with borderline disorder have on their children is another critical aspect of this discussion. Child psychiatrist Margaret Weiss and her colleagues at McGill University in Montreal published a study in 1996 of twenty-one children of mothers with borderline disorder, compared to twenty-three children of mothers with a different personality disorder. Here's some background information: There is a 15 percent risk of mental disorders in the first-degree relatives of people with borderline disorder. Depression and alcoholism are the most common diagnoses in this group. Also, about 10 percent of people with borderline disorder have a mother with the disorder. In this study, only 24 percent of women in the original sample with borderline disorder had children. This is consistent with other studies indicating that fewer women with borderline disorder have children than is the norm.

This study revealed a significantly higher number of mental disorders in the children of mothers with borderline disorder (the borderline group) than children of mothers with a different personality disorder (the control group). The diagnoses found to be more common in the borderline group included borderline disorder, attention deficit hyperactivity disorder (ADHD), and disruptive behavior disorders.

A surprising and important finding was that a higher frequency of trauma did not contribute to the increased occurrence of psychiatric disorders in children of mothers with borderline disorder. However, the borderline families were found to be less stable and less cohesive and organized than the control families.

The authors conclude that the children and mothers in the borderline group have shared biological (genetic) vulnerabilities and a faulty family structure. This is consistent with most other research findings regarding the biological and environmental risk factors of borderline disorder (see Chapter 4).

Unfortunately, there's little hard information on the spectrum of experiences of parents, children, and spouses of people with borderline disorder. Such information is badly needed in order to determine the true toll that borderline disorder takes on all people involved. However, there are a few anecdotal reports on this important topic.

Other Perspectives of the Effects of Borderline Disorder on the Family and Partners

In 1998, Paul Mason and Randi Kreger published *Stop Walking on Eggshells*. Mason is a certified professional counselor who has clinical and teaching experience with borderline disorder and has published a research article on the disorder. Kreger is a professional writer and businesswoman who had a personal relationship with someone with borderline disorder. In their introduction, Kreger notes that "most studies [of the family environment of people with borderline disorder] looked at behavior directed toward the person with BPD rather than the behavior of that person toward others."

Through e-mail, her Web site, and by regular mail, Kreger established contact with numerous people related to someone with borderline disorder. As a result of the information she gathered, Kreger and Mason developed a perception of the most common ways people with borderline disorder affect others. For example, if you are related to someone with borderline disorder, you may suffer a grief reaction, and experience Elisabeth Kübler-Ross's five stages of grief: (1) denial; (2) anger; (3) bargaining; (4) depression; and (5) acceptance.

Other common responses you may have are bewilderment, loss of self-esteem, feeling trapped and helpless, withdrawal, guilt and shame, adapting unhealthy habits, isolation, hypervigilance and physical illness, adoption of borderline-like thoughts and feelings, and co-dependence. Even this long list of problems described by people related to someone with borderline disorder may not capture the true depth of your suffering. People with borderline disorder experience different symptoms and levels of severity, and respond uniquely to their symptoms. Some are more angry and vindictive than others. Some are less willing to seek help for their problems, and blame these problems on their relatives or partners. Therefore, your experiences with a person with borderline disorder could easily be quite different than that of someone else.

The second part of the book offers a number of coping strategies, including those required if the person with borderline disorder does not take appropriate responsibility and seek help, and continues to blame their problems on others.

As one of very few sources of information of this type, it's not surprising that this book has prompted a significant response from people who are affected by someone with borderline disorder. It seems to strike a particularly responsive chord in people related to someone with the disorder who lacks insight into their problem, and who is unwilling to seek help.

Although parents, siblings, and spouses suffer deeply, it's the children of a person with borderline disorder who suffer the most, aside from those with borderline disorder themselves. The only advice I can offer you to reduce this suffering is to try to convince your loved one that he or she needs treatment, to learn as much as you can about the disorder, to find and join an appropriate support group (see Resources), and to be as supportive as possible of everyone involved.

Ten Guidelines for Families

Clearly, it's very difficult and challenging to be related to someone with borderline disorder. Many family members and partners have strong reactions of anger and resentment that conflict with their feelings of empathy and their desire to help. Here are ten specific actions that you can take to help the person in your life with borderline disorder gain better control over her or his life. These actions will also be a big help to you in the process.

1. **Gain Knowledge.** It's essential for you to understand that your loved one with borderline disorder is suffering from an illness that is as real as diabetes, heart disease, or hypertension. Because it's a disorder that affects specific pathways in the brain that control emotions and behavior, you can only see the behavioral symptoms, though physical symptoms may be present as well (see Chapter 1 for more information). For most people, physical symptoms are easier to accept as indications of disease than

behavioral symptoms. But if you think about it, there's no reason to assume that a complex organ such as the brain is less susceptible to diseases that affect behavior than are other bodily organs that result in physical symptoms. Recently developed medical technologies that demonstrate abnormal brain structure and function in people with borderline disorder confirm this conclusion (Chapter 6).

It's also helpful to realize that people with borderline disorder didn't acquire their problem through any actions of their own, nor do they enjoy having the disorder. Imagine what it must be like to feel that you are at the mercy of forces within you, over which you have little control, and that cause you extreme emotional pain and significant life problems.

A critical first step in the process of helping them and yourself is to learn as much as you can about the symptoms and nature of borderline disorder, and the specific causes of severe episodes in your loved one.

2. **Remain Calm.** Try to remain calm, but involved, when episodes do occur. Reacting angrily will usually just add to the problem. Acknowledge that it must be difficult to experience the feelings they express, even if they seem out of proportion to the situation. This doesn't mean that you agree with these feelings, or that you think the actions resulting from them are justified. It's reassuring to them if you listen to their feelings, the pain they are experiencing, and the difficulty they are having in dealing with this pain. Remember that you do not have to defend yourself if attacked, or develop solutions for them yourself, even for their thoughts of self-harm.

Allow and encourage them to try to bring their response levels in line with the situation at hand. You may need to give them a little time alone to collect themselves. Then, it may be possible to more calmly and reasonably discuss the relevant issues.

In addition, don't hesitate to express your feelings freely and openly, but with moderation. Recent research suggests that caring involvement with your family member with borderline disorder is associated with better outcomes than a cool, disinterested approach. Please stay involved.

5. **Get Professional Help.** If your family member has not sought professional help, strongly urge them to do so. You can facilitate the process of finding the best help by using the strategies in Chapter 8. It may be necessary that you do the initial work necessary to set up the first appointment. It's also helpful if you agree to go with them, especially if they say you are a major cause of their problems, but don't insist on it.

Some people with borderline disorder initially refuse to seek professional help. Give them a copy of this book and ask them to read the Introduction and the first two chapters. This may help them understand their potential problems well enough to agree to an initial appointment with a psychiatrist.

Other people with borderline disorder are steadfast in their refusal of help. This, of course, is a major problem. I have asked Dr. Perry Hoffman, the founding president of the National Education Alliance for Borderline Personality Disorder (NEA-BPD) for some advice here. The NEA-BPD is an advocacy group for families of people with borderline disorder, and those with the disorder (see Foreword). She says:

> The best way to approach this problem from my perspective is for one to accept that you cannot get someone into treatment. Timing is important as to when someone might be "open" to hearing the idea. But the bottom line is to free families of feeling guilty, and to understand that they are not so powerful to effect that goal. Along that line, relatives need to get help and support for themselves as they watch their loved one in the throes of the illness.

4. **Stick with the Program**. Once in treatment, encourage your family member to regularly attend therapy sessions, to take

medicine as prescribed, to eat, exercise, and rest appropriately, and to take part in healthful recreational activities. If alcohol or other drugs are a problem, strongly support their efforts to abstain completely from these substances, and encourage regular attendance in treatment programs or self-help groups, such as Alcoholics Anonymous. There is little hope of improvement of the symptoms of borderline disorder if alcohol and drugs are abused. It is very important that you remain persistent in your efforts to do everything possible to help reduce the risk of this behavior, and not enable it.

5. **Plan Ahead for Destructive Behaviors**. Develop a clear understanding (it may even be written) of the realistic consequences of recurring, problematic, destructive behaviors such as episodes of alcohol and drug abuse, physically self-damaging acts, and excessive spending and gambling. Also, agree beforehand on how best to respond to threats of self-harm.

   These behaviors are often triggered by stressful events that need to be identified, and a clear plan needs to be developed for handling these situations more appropriately and effectively in the future. Such a plan is best developed with the help of your family member's therapist. Encourage and support consistent follow-through with the plan.

   Experience has shown that if you respond positively to your loved one's appropriate behaviors, it encourages them to adopt new and more successful ways of handling stressful situations. It also reduces the rate of inappropriate behaviors that then cause additional problems. Issuing ultimatums should be used only when all else fails.

6. **Be Positive and Optimistic**. Remain positive and optimistic about the ultimate results of treatment, especially when your loved one has a setback. The usual course of borderline disorder under treatment is one of increasing periods of time when symptoms are absent or minimal, interrupted by episodes when

the symptoms flare up. As time goes by, the specific causes of these relapses can be identified, for example, separations, family get-togethers, and periods of change. Once these precipitating events are known, they can be anticipated. Then steps can be taken to develop alternative, more adaptive, and effective responses. Occasional family meetings with the therapist may help clarify the causes of relapses and identify new ways of preventing them.

7. **Information Is Your Edge**. If educational experiences about borderline disorder, such as DBT family groups (see Resources for more information), are offered in your community, participate in them. It's very important that you learn as much as possible about borderline disorder and your role in the treatment process. Your participation in such groups will benefit both you and the family member with the disorder.

If an appropriate borderline disorder family support group is active in your community, I encourage you to join it. The problems and challenges of family members of people with borderline disorder are understandably different from those with the disorder itself. Listening to others who have stories and problems similar to yours, learning skills to retain and enhance your own sense of well-being, and developing a support network will be of great help to you. Attending such a group will also validate your own feelings and concerns, and you will discover new approaches to handling your own specific challenges. Working with others who are in similar situations is a very productive way to learn more about borderline disorder, and it may bring you significant relief. Finally, once you become reasonably comfortable in doing so, sharing your thoughts, feelings, and problems with other people who truly understand the situation can be a helpful and strengthening experience.

8. **Join a Lay Advocacy Organization**. If there is a local chapter of a borderline personality lay advocacy organization in

your community, seriously consider joining it. You will then have available to you a large amount of new information about borderline disorder, what you can do to help the member of your family with the disorder and yourself, and compassionate and understanding support in your efforts. If there is not a group in your area, consider starting one with other family members you have met. Also think about joining one of the national advocacy groups for borderline disorder. For information on lay advocacy groups, you can find one or more listed on the Web: for example, the National Education Alliance for Borderline Personality Disorder (NEA-BPD), and the Treatment and Research Advancements National Association for Personality Disorders (TARA). For more information, see the Resources section on page 219.

9. **Encourage Responsibility and Growth**. Remember that it's the responsibility of the person with borderline disorder to take charge of her or his behavior and life. Although difficult at times, it's important for you to provide the opportunity for them to take reasonable risks in order to try new behaviors. It's also important that you help her or him to be accountable for the consequences of old, destructive behaviors.

Excessive dependency on family and friends is not helpful in the long run. Beware of the tendency of people with borderline disorder to act at the extremes. The proper alternative to excessive dependency is not immediate, total independency. During episodes of great stress you may be tempted to propose, or accept the proposal, that he or she separate from the family. Typically, if they do so, at some point they will return for help and the cycle of involvement and no involvement will then just repeat itself without benefit. It's far better for you to remain engaged with your loved one and gradually help them move to a more mature relationship level of mutual interdependency.

10. **Take Good Care of Yourself**. Finally, always remember that you cannot save your loved one with borderline disorder on

your own. Based on my personal experience with my sister Denise (see Chapter 2), I can assure you that to try your best, given the information you have, is all you can do.

Take time for yourself to meet your own needs. Then, when your loved one needs your help the most, you will be best able to provide it.

THIRTEEN

Research:
The Ultimate Reason for Hope

I T'S CLEAR THAT we have a lot more to learn about the prevalence, causes, nature, treatments, and prognosis of borderline disorder, and we won't learn what we need to know without a substantial increase in the amount of high-quality research in the area. I believe that research offers us the best reason to remain hopeful about living with borderline disorder. Here are some of the main current issues in borderline disorder research, the areas of research that hold the most promise, the current sources of funds for research on borderline disorder, and how you can help the overall endeavor.

Where Does Research Information Come From?

There are two main sources of research information. The first source is anecdotal reports, and the second is empirically derived research data. Anecdotal reports arise from the personal experiences of clinicians and researchers as they see patients or perform their research. The information typically does not represent a random sample of patients seen, is not systematically collected, does not include a control group, and is usually more qualitative than it is quantitative. Empirical research employs a more rigorous research design that includes the selection of a random sample of carefully selected patients and a control group, well-controlled interventions, the use of well-defined instruments to measure results, and statistical analysis of the results. Most medical experts consider empirical research to be the "gold standard" in drawing conclusions about the validity of research results, and making decisions on the clinical application of the information. In this book, I have tried to identify the information accordingly, as it has a bearing on the level of credibility you place in the conclusions drawn from the information.

The Value of Anecdotal Information

The value of anecdotal reports should not be trivialized. The clinical observations made and reported in the medical literature often provide influential ideas that become the conceptual basis for rigorous research studies. For example, Adolph Stern's anecdotal observations in 1938 of the clinical symptoms, psychological limitations, and responses to treatment of his "border line group" of patients (see Chapter 3) were very important to later, empirical research endeavors.

Anecdotal reports also give us useful information that helps us do our best to care for patients before empirically derived research findings are published. I wouldn't be able to help my patients as much without these anecdotal reports from other clinicians. I also believe that those anecdotal reports that I have submitted for publication, such as the one with John Brinkley and Bernard Beitman on the use of low-dose neuroleptic therapy for patients with borderline disorder (see Chapter 9), have been of some value to other physicians, patients, and researchers before the ideas were tested by controlled studies.

The Need for Empirical Research

Anecdotal reports alone cannot advance our knowledge to the extent that we need. For this to occur, we must push back the walls of igno-

rance in all areas with empirical research studies. Much of the knowledge we now possess about borderline disorder comes from such
research, and it's crucial for several reasons.

In clinical studies, the most valid research results depend on using
random methods to select research subjects. If subjects are selected
randomly, the results are not subject to the biases of the researchers.
For example, the results of a research study on borderline disorder
would be biased if the researchers selected only patients that they
expected would demonstrate the response they were looking for.

In most empirical studies, in order to minimize further any biases
of researchers or subjects, a control group and the "double-blind"
method are used. The double-blind method means that neither the
subject nor the investigators know if the subject is in the experimental or the control group.

Also, sound research requires the use of instruments that accurately
define the research group used, and that measure validly all critical
information. Careful statistical analysis of the results is obtained, and
this is what doctors base their knowledge on.

Animal studies also enable researchers to better understand the
brain systems associated with the behaviors that are disrupted in borderline disorder. It's not intuitively obvious that animal research could
provide us with important information relevant to a clinical problem
as human and as complex as borderline disorder. However, the brain
mechanisms that control many behaviors of animals have been pre-
served in the human brain. This allows researchers to study the
anatomical, physiological, and biochemical processes of behaviors
related to borderline disorder in ways they otherwise couldn't.

This animal research is critical in determining the fundamental
biological processes that should be evaluated in humans with borderline disorder, using minimally invasive and non-invasive techniques such as brain imaging studies. Animal research also enables
researchers to evaluate the effectiveness and safety of new pharmacological treatments for borderline disorder before they are tested in
humans.

What We Have Learned From Research So Far

Throughout this book, I have relied on, and broken down for you, a considerable amount of information about borderline disorder from both anecdotal and empirical studies. I've also included information about the prevalence of borderline disorder in the general population, the most reliable standards available for diagnosing the disorder, the causes of borderline disorder, the typical course of the illness and its prognosis, and the biological basis for the disorder. In addition, I discussed the best-tested pharmacological and psychotherapeutic treatments for borderline disorder, and the current state of our understanding of the occurrence and treatment of borderline disorder in children.

Very little of this information would be available without research studies conducted by investigators dedicated to better understanding borderline disorder and helping those with the disorder. But, as you have learned, there are many gaps in our knowledge, gaps that need to be filled in. Unfortunately, there are more questions that need answers than there are qualified researchers, and available research funds, to answer them. What we need is a two-pronged strategy to help us move forward. First, we must focus the resources currently available on those questions about borderline disorder that are most pressing and that have the greatest likelihood of significant payoff. Second, we need to increase the number of high-quality researchers in the field of borderline disorder, and the amount of research funds available to them.

The Most Promising Areas of Research

There are at least seven areas of research in the field of borderline disorder that appear to be most promising. They include the epidemiology of the disorder, the development of new diagnostic strategies, the course of the illness, genetic and environmental risk factors, the neurobiological basis of the disorder, and treatment. Following is a short overview of these topics to give you some idea of what the future appears to hold in store.

Epidemiological Issues

The best information currently available suggests that the prevalence of borderline disorder in the general population is about 2 percent, with a 3-to-1 female-to-male ratio. But these estimates are based on a limited number of research studies using methodologies that don't meet current standards. More extensive studies that use current research methods are needed to determine more precisely the prevalence of borderline disorder in the population, and to define gender differences if they do exist.

Epidemiological studies will be greatly beneficial because they'll provide a rationale for allocating an amount of clinical care, training, and research funds to borderline disorder that is warranted by the amount of suffering and the other costs of this disorder to our society. As you'll see later in this chapter, there appears to be a disproportionately small amount of research funds committed to borderline disorder compared to other illnesses of comparable severity and prevalence in the general population.

Diagnostic Strategies

Another important area of research involves developing a new conceptual model for classifying personality disorders. What seems clear is that we are moving toward diagnostic strategies that are based on the genetic, developmental, and environmental causes, and the pathophysiology of these disorders. This diagnostic approach is the same as the one used across all medical disorders. In the area of personality disorders, we need a diagnostic approach that stresses the clear definition and study of the main dimensions (characteristics) of behavior, across the normal and abnormal continuum of personality. In the case of borderline disorder, these behavioral dimensions include emotional control, impulse regulation, perception, and reasoning. Our current categorical diagnostic approach has served us well for almost twenty-five years. However, the new dimensional approach will increase diagnostic sensitivity and accuracy, and stimulate more effective and focused treatment and research. This is generally considered to be one of the most fertile and necessary areas of research on borderline disorder.

The Course of the Illness

Additional studies are needed to determine more precisely the course borderline disorder travels from infancy to old age. The course of illness depends on the specific biological and environmental risk factors operating in each person's life. It will be an arduous task to tease out subpopulations of people with similar risk factors in order to determine the most likely course of illness in each group. However, this work is necessary if we're to offer some concrete answers to the question our patients and their families most frequently ask: "What is my future going to be?"

Genetic Strategies

Genetic approaches to the study of borderline disorder can help identify individual differences in the biological and environmental risk factors of the disorder, and the degree of risk conferred by each of these factors. Separating these individual differences is important if we are to estimate accurately the severity of the specific behavioral dimensions of borderline disorder experienced by an individual, and determine the most specific and effective forms of treatment for you, as opposed to another patient.

You now know that borderline disorder appears to be the result of a number of necessary genetic risk factors. Only some of the genetic risk factors need be present from a larger genetic pool of risk factors for borderline disorder, in order for the disorder to occur. Therefore, we see a wide variation in the type and severity of symptoms from person to person. It's likely that they carry different genetic patterns that place them at risk for the disorder.

We need to identify the total pool of genetic risk factors for borderline disorder. We also need to understand how the different combinations of these factors operate and interact with environmental risk factors, to enhance the risk of developing the behavioral dimensions of the disorder.

Environmental Risk Factors

We know that exposing children with a biological predisposition to borderline disorder to specific environmental factors increases the likelihood that they will develop the disorder (see Chapter 4). However, a number of important questions about the effects of environmental factors on the development of borderline disorder require further study. For example, are some environmental risk factors more serious than others? Also, how do environmental risk factors for borderline disorder interact with genetic and developmental factors to increase the risk of borderline disorder? It's also important to know if there are critical developmental periods when children with genetic predispositions to borderline disorder are most susceptible to negative environmental influences.

The Neurobiological Basis of Borderline Disorder

Defining the specific behaviors in each core dimension of borderline disorder opens up a large new spectrum of research studies. These studies include investigating the anatomical, physiological, and biochemical brain mechanisms and processes that control each behavior associated with the disorder. Recent advances in neuroscience and modern biomedical technology, such as brain imaging techniques, have already resulted in great progress in this area. For example, a variety of brain neuroimaging techniques have shown alterations in structure and function in specific brain regions of people with borderline disorder, and have related these brain changes to specific behaviors, such as impulsivity. We need to know more about the brain circuits that are associated with each specific symptom and behavioral dimension of borderline disorder. Further research utilizing the knowledge and methodological advances already made will greatly facilitate future research in this area.

Treatment

As knowledge expands in the above areas of research, considerably more specific and effective treatments for borderline disorder will be discovered than are now available. For example, we will understand the most accurate indications for the use of medications in the treatment of borderline disorder, and which specific class of medicines is likely to be most effective in each person's case (see Chapter 9). Then we can immediately initiate the most appropriate pharmacological approach. This will require many more controlled studies of the different classes of medications available to us that show promise on the basis of anecdotal reports and controlled trials.

A number of different psychotherapeutic approaches are now being used for people with borderline disorder, but we have little hard data on the specific indications and effectiveness of these techniques (Chapter 10). It's essential that we have this data if we are to develop the most effective and comprehensive treatment plans possible for you and other people with the disorder.

The message that I would like you to take away from this section is that there are a large number of important areas of research on borderline disorder that will yield vital information that will make your life better, if the research is performed. The question is, why isn't all of this research being done?

What Determines How Much Research Is Done for Borderline Disorder?

Understandably, most people don't understand the processes that enable medical research to proceed in this country. Why would they? There's little reason, and few opportunities, for them to be exposed to this information. Those who do understand the system usually suffer from a medical disorder, or are closely related to someone with the disorder.

Actually, the system is fairly straightforward. The amount of medical research performed in any area depends on these factors:

1. **The relative importance of the disease.** There is more research performed on heart disease and cancer than there is on diseases that affect fewer people and are less life-threatening and devastating. However, some medical disorders receive research funding that is greater or less than you would predict based on their prevalence, severity, and importance to society. This means other factors are also important.

2. **The total amount of research funds available in the area from all sources.** No matter how important an area of research is, academic researchers cannot devote their time and talents to an area if there is inadequate funding.

3. **The amount of grassroots support from people and families affected by the disorder, either acting individually or as members of lay advocacy groups.** Advocacy is a constitutional right of every citizen and has proven to be an enormously effective instrument in enhancing research funds and the attention of the academic medical community to areas of need. For example, consider the impact of advocacy groups on the amount of funding for AIDS research in this country.

4. **The perception that the illness has an identifiable biological basis, and therefore is a "real" disease.** It was not until such evidence was available in the areas of schizophrenia and affective disorders that the stigma associated with these illnesses declined and research funding and support services increased. In the area of borderline disorder, the leaders and members of two advocacy groups, NEA–BPD and TARA (see Resources) have been effective in helping secure the funding of a number of research grants on borderline disorder from the National Institute of Mental Health (NIMH) and private sources.

5. **The availability of well-trained researchers at academic institutions.** No university or department of psychiatry is so well funded that it is able to support all areas of academic work. Therefore, the leadership focuses its limited resources on those

areas that match their strengths, and that have the greatest need and greatest potential for research funding. If there are too few high-quality research grant applications in borderline disorder, then one reason is there have been too few funds to attract departmental chairs and bright young investigators to the field.

Current Funding of Research on Borderline Disorder

Funding for research on borderline disorder in this country comes from two major sources. Most funds come from the NIMH, a federal agency that is part of the National Institutes of Health (NIH). The NIMH provides most of the research funds available for clinical and basic research in mental disorders.

Additional funding is provided by private organizations such as the Borderline Personality Disorder Research Foundation (BPDRF) and the National Alliance for Research on Schizophrenia and Affective Disorders (NARSAD).

NIMH

In 2003, the NIMH spent $5.9 million on research for borderline disorder. This was 0.4 percent of the total NIMH research budget, up from 0.3 percent in 2001. Such funds are typically divided between researchers who work at the NIMH in the intramural program, and those who work across the country, usually at academic medical centers, referred to as the extramural program. The decisions on who receives research funds from the NIMH are made by panels of experts in a large number of research areas, such as the ones I discussed earlier. This is called the *peer review system,* and it is designed to fund the best research grant applications. The question that is immediately raised about the current amount of funding for borderline disorder is "Why is there no more money devoted to borderline disorder, given its prevalence and the degree of suffering it causes?"

In 2001, three important review articles describing the future of research on borderline disorder were published in the scientific journal *Biological Psychiatry*. These articles were discussed in an editorial in that issue of the journal titled "A New Beginning for Research on Borderline Personality Disorder" by Stephen Hyman, former Director of the NIMH. In his editorial, Hyman, a psychiatrist and now provost of Harvard University, addressed the issue that in 2001 borderline disorder received only 0.3 percent of the NIMH research budget, in spite of its prevalence and its clinical significance. He stated that these low levels of NIMH funding were not the result of priority-setting by the NIMH, but were due to the small number of high-quality grant applications and well-trained researchers in the field of borderline disorder. In his editorial, Hyman speculated that one reason qualified researchers may avoid the area of borderline disorder is the controversy over the current diagnostic approach to personality disorders in general. He suggested that young researchers might be wary of devoting their academic careers to an area of controversy.

Although this may be one of the problems, it's also well known that researchers will gravitate to those areas that are interesting, challenging, clinically important, ready to yield important results—and that are well-funded. I have had more than thirty years of experience in academic psychiatry, many of them as the chair of departments of psychiatry, with the responsibility for guiding the research careers of young faculty members. It's been my experience that these factors are more important in the selection of a research career pathway than is the lack of controversy in the area. Actually, many of the best researchers are attracted to areas of controversy, because that signals areas of great opportunity. Therefore, I believe that the major determinative factor missing in borderline disorder research is adequate funding.

Private Research Foundations

The Borderline Personality Disorder Research Foundation and the National Alliance for Research on Schizophrenia and Affective Disorders are two private research foundations that provide researchers interested in borderline disorder with access to badly needed additional sources of research funds. The BPDRF is a new organization that supports research on borderline disorder in six core areas: the reliability and validity of the diagnosis of the disorder; investigations on genetics and epidemiology; psychobiology; neuroimaging; animal models; and treatment, including innovative approaches.

NARSAD is a well-established research foundation that has predominantly supported research in the areas of schizophrenia and affective disorders. Recently, its leaders have signaled their interest in also supporting research in the area of borderline disorder.

The acknowledgment that additional federal and private funding for research in borderline disorder is needed is a promising sign, and is the result of three factors. First, it has finally been widely accepted that borderline disorder is a prevalent disease that causes much human suffering, and that it has a clearly demonstrated biological basis. Second, significant advances have been made in the development of specific, effective pharmacological and psychotherapeutic treatments for borderline disorder. Third, the recent emergence of lay advocacy groups has enhanced awareness and knowledge of borderline disorder by the public, and by federal, private-sector, and academic leaders. These are the same factors that came together twenty years ago in the areas of schizophrenia and affective disorders, and that resulted in a tremendous increase in funding of and research on these two groups of illnesses.

How Can You Help Advance Research?

I have noted above the primary determinants of how much of the research on borderline disorder is conducted, and that a disproportionately small amount of funds and qualified researchers are available to the area. You may wonder if there is anything you can do to help increase research on borderline disorder, and thereby help yourself or a loved one. Our experience in the areas of schizophrenia and mood disorders noted above has indicated that you personally have much more influence on the above factors than you probably imagine. I believe in the sentiment that extraordinary achievements are accomplished by ordinary people with an extraordinary passion.

In addition to all of the suggestions that I have made to you in this book, I add the following:

1.   Join a borderline disorder lay advocacy group such as NEA-BPD or TARA. These and others are listed in the Resource section of this book.

2.   If you have the personal funds, make a contribution to these organizations and to private research foundations that solely support research on borderline disorder, such as the BPDRF. If you make a contribution to NARSAD, ask that the money be targeted for research on borderline disorder.

3.   If you have ample personal funds, consider supporting, at a school of medicine, an endowed chair, professorship, or departmental fund directed solely at enhancing clinical care, research, and training in borderline disorder. Departments of psychiatry at these schools need such resources in order to commit faculty time to the care of people with borderline disorder, to more education and training of medical students and residents in the area, and, of course, to research.

4.   Write letters and make visits to your congressman and senators. Letters to the NIMH and to the research office of the American Psychiatric Association (see Resources) are also very appropriate and very effective.

You might think that it would be more effective if these requests for increased support for borderline disorder came from psychiatrists and other mental health professionals, especially those in academic institutions. Having spent most of my professional career at a number of academic medical centers, I have come to understand that advocacy by professionals is only partly successful. While academicians are able to report the latest scientific advances and other relevant information, our pleas for help do not have the heartfelt immediacy of people directly affected by the disorder. Please don't underestimate your capacity to make a difference in this area. It is enormous.

A FINAL WORD

WE'VE MADE A lot of progress in our understanding of the symptoms, course of illness, biological basis, causes, and treatments of borderline disorder. Ignorance and pessimism are being replaced with knowledge and optimism. I find it particularly encouraging that physicians and other mental health professionals are learning more about borderline disorder. Physicians now more often make the proper diagnosis when people with this disorder develop emotional and physical symptoms that are otherwise difficult to diagnose and treat. Once the diagnosis of borderline disorder is determined, referrals are now made more frequently to psychiatrists and other mental health professionals who specialize, and are skilled, in treating this complex disorder. Lay advocacy groups and a resource center that are focused specifically on borderline disorder have been organized recently, and are growing in size, influence, and capacity to offer information and support to people with the disorder and their families.

Not all psychiatrists are equally experienced and proficient in diagnosing and treating people with borderline disorder. However, there are now usually one or more psychiatrists, other physicians, or mental health clinicians in most communities who possess the training, experience, and commitment to be of significant help, and to even serve as the primary clinician, for those with the disorder. It generally doesn't take more than a few phone calls to the offices of local psychiatrists, or a visit to the Web, to figure out the best place to start locating these people.

It's also encouraging that more medical scientists across the world are becoming involved in serious research on the many different aspects of borderline disorder. Studies are being conducted on the prevalence, causes, and natural course of the illness. Advanced research technologies including structural and functional brain imaging, genetic studies, biochemical assays, sophisticated neuropsychological tests, and treatment trials are under way at a number of leading academic medical centers. Although these research efforts are in their preliminary phases, they are already yielding the types of knowledge that I've described in this book.

This takes us back to where we began with my comments in the Introduction. If you have borderline disorder, or if someone in your family or a close friend suffers from this illness, you should feel hopeful about the present and optimistic about the future. We now know enough about borderline disorder to provide quick and significant relief for many of the most disturbing symptoms, and to help bring about continued, incremental improvement in the remaining symptoms and associated problems. Ongoing research will result in additional knowledge and more effective treatments, and someday prevention and cure.

I urge you to continue to make the effort to learn as much as you can about borderline disorder. I promise you won't regret it.

GLOSSARY

ACETYLCHOLINE: a neurotransmitter that stimulates or inhibits the activity of neurons in the brain.

ACTIVATING ANTIDEPRESSANT: an antidepressant that has stimulatory rather than sedating properties, such as bupropion (Wellbutrin).

AMPHETAMINE: a stimulant of the central nervous system used to treat ADHD in children or adults.

AMYGDALA: an almond-shaped cluster of neurons located in the middle portion of the temporal lobes of the brain. It is the central structure in the brain system that processes emotion information.

ANTERIOR CINGULATE CORTEX: a strip of cortex located in the middle portion of the frontal lobes of the brain that monitors and modulates behavior.

ANTIPSYCHOTIC AGENT: a member of a class of drugs used to treat the symptoms of psychotic disorders such as schizophrenia. In low doses, some of these agents also appear to be effective for some patients with borderline disorder.

ANTISOCIAL PERSONALITY DISORDER: Antisocial personality disorder is characterized by a pervasive pattern of disregard and violation of the rights of others present since the age of 15 years, in an individual at least 18 years old.

ATTENTION DEFICIT HYPERACTIVITY DISORDER: a category of mental disorders characterized by developmentally inappropriate short attention span, poor concentration, and frequent hyperactivity and impulsivity.

BEHAVIORAL DIMENSIONS: clusters of behaviors that are grouped according to a common characteristic such as emotional control, impulse control, or thinking and reasoning.

BIPOLAR II DISORDER: a mental disorder characterized by hypomania and associated with depressive episodes.

BORDERLINE PSYCHOTIC: a term previously used to describe people with borderline personality disorder.

BORDERLINE SCHIZOPHRENIA: a term previously used to describe people with borderline personality disorder.

DISSOCIATIVE EPISODE: periods of time when thinking, behavior, and memory occur outside of a person's awareness.

DOPAMINE: a neurotransmitter that stimulates or inhibits the activity of neurons in the brain.

DOPAMINERGIC ACTIVITY: relating to the neurotransmitter activity of dopamine.

DORSOLATERAL PREFRONTAL CORTEX: areas of cortex located on the lateral portion of the frontal lobes of the brain that are involved with the processes of thinking and reasoning.

DORSOLATERAL PREFRONTAL CIRCUIT: the network of nerves that connect the dorsolateral prefrontal cortex to subcortical brain structures.

EGO FUNCTIONS: those psychological processes that regulate our thoughts, feelings, and responses to external reality.

EGO PSYCHOLOGY: that division of psychology that focuses on the mental processes that enables us to deal effectively with our thoughts, feelings, and responses to external reality.

EMOTIONAL LABILITY: unusually rapid fluctuations of mood that are not proportional to the experiences that elicit them.

EMPIRICAL RESEARCH: carefully designed and controlled research studies that lead to quantifiable results.

ETIOLOGY: the causes or origins of a medical disorder.

FACTITIOUS ILLNESS: characterized by physical or psychological symptoms that are intentionally produced or feigned.

GAMMA AMINOBUTYRIC ACID (GABA): the brain's primary inhibitory neurotransmitter.

GLUTAMATE: the brain's primary stimulatory neurotransmitter.

HALLUCINATION: a false sensory experience that has no external stimulus.

HIPPOCAMPAL FORMATION: brain structures that are located on the middle portion of the temporal lobes near the amygdala. They are critically involved with the processes of memory development.

HISTRIONIC PERSONALITY DISORDER: a disorder characterized by a pervasive pattern of emotional and attention-seeking behavior beginning by early adulthood.

HYPERREACTIVE: having or showing abnormally high sensitivity to stimuli.

LATENT SCHIZOPHRENIA: a term previously used to describe people who had some of the symptoms of borderline personality disorder.

LIBIDO: sexual interest and motivation.

MAGICAL THINKING: the conviction that thinking is the equivalent of action. It is present in the dreams of children and in patients with a variety of conditions, and is characterized by an unrealistic relationship between cause and effect.

MAJOR DEPRESSIVE DISORDER: a mental disorder associated with a severe and sustained decrease in mood, decreased ability to experience pleasure, changes in sleep, appetite, weight, inappropriate guilt, impaired thinking, concentration, decision-making, and suicidality.

METHYLPHENIDATE: a stimulant of the central nervous system used to treat narcolepsy and ADHD in children and adults.

MULTIGENIC DISORDERS: disorders that require a number of genetic mutations before the disorder manifests itself.

NARCISSISM: refers to one's capacity to value or "love" oneself.

NARCISSISTIC PERSONALITY DISORDER: a disorder characterized by a pervasive pattern of grandiosity, the need for admiration, and a lack of empathy beginning by early adulthood.

NEURAL: pertaining to one or more nerve cells.

NEUROLEPTIC AGENT: a member of the original class of drugs used to treat patients with psychotic disorders, such as schizophrenia. In low doses, some of these drugs also appear to be useful in some patients with borderline disorder.

NEUROMODULATORS: neurotransmitters that regulate the activity of neural pathways and circuits, e.g., dopamine, serotonin, acetylcholine, and norepinephrine.

NEUROTIC: a term originally used to describe mental disorders that do not have psychotic symptoms.

NEUROTRANSMITTERS: chemical messengers secreted by neurons that stimulate or inhibit other neurons.

NOREPINEPHRINE: a neurotransmitter that stimulates or inhibits the activity of neurons in the brain.

NUCLEUS ACCUMBENS: a cluster of subcortical neurons in the frontal lobes of the brain that are associated with the processes of motivation and reward.

OPEN LABEL TRIALS: research studies in which the medicine used is known to the patient and to the research team.

ORBITOMEDIAL CORTEX: a portion of cortex located on the lower middle part of the prefrontal lobe of the brain, associated with the experience and regulation of feelings.

ORBITOMEDIAL CIRCUIT: the cortical-subcortical pathway of neurons associated with the orbitomedial cortex.

PANIC ATTACKS: discrete episodes of severe anxiety associated with marked symptoms of physiological arousal and a sense of impending death.

PANIC DISORDER: the repeated occurrence of panic attacks.

PARANOID THINKING: the false belief that others are planning harm against one.

PARASUICIDAL ACTS: self-injurious behaviors that are not intended to result in death.

POSTTRAUMATIC STRESS DISORDER: a mental disorder occurring after exposure to a traumatic event of threatened death or serious injury, that is persistently re-experienced and results in avoidance of situations that will recall the trauma, and is associated with symptoms of increased arousal.

PRE-SCHIZOPHRENIA: a term initially used to refer to patients who had symptoms similar to borderline personality disorder.

PRIMARY CLINICIAN: a psychiatrist or other mental health professional skilled in the diagnosis and treatment of a disorder.

PROGNOSIS: expected response to treatment or the natural outcome of a medical disorder.

PROJECTION: the unconscious psychological attempt to deal with anxiety by attributing one's own unacceptable attributes to the outside world.

PSEUDONEUROTIC SCHIZOPHRENIA: the unconscious psychological attempt to deal with anxiety by attributing one's own unacceptable attributes to the outside world. Same as projection.

PSYCHOANALYSIS: a form of psychotherapy based on the psychoanalytic theory of human development and behavior, formulated by Sigmund Freud.

PSYCHODYNAMIC PSYCHOTHERAPY: a form of psychotherapy based on learning and applying a body of knowledge about complex conscious and unconscious thoughts, feelings, and behaviors.

PSYCHOSIS: symptoms of a mental disorder characterized by episodes of significant loss of contact with reality, often accompanied by delusions and hallucinations.

PSYCHOTIC EPISODES: periods of psychosis.

RESIDENT: a physician who is in graduate training to qualify as a specialist in a particular field of medicine, such as psychiatry. The American Board of Psychiatry and Neurology requires four years of postgraduate training in an approved facility to qualify for board examination in psychiatry.

RISK FACTORS: genetic mutations, and developmental and environmental events, that increase the probability of developing a medical illness.

SCHIZOTYPAL PERSONALITY DISORDER: a disorder characterized by difficulty in developing close relationships associated with odd perceptions, distortions, and eccentric behavior beginning in early adulthood.

SEMINAL ARTICLE: an article that significantly influences and stimulates later thinking and research.

SEROTONIN: a neurotransmitter that stimulates or inhibits the activity of neurons in the brain.

SEROTONERGIC ACTIVITY: involving activity of serotonin in the transmission of nerve impulses.

STRESS-DIATHESIS MODEL: a concept of the interaction of a biological (genetic or developmental) predisposition to an illness and environmental factors or stresses that increase the likelihood of developing the illness.

TARDIVE DYSKINESIA: "late-appearing abnormal movements"; spontaneous movements developing in some patients exposed to antipsychotic drugs. Typical movements include tongue writhing or protrusion, chewing, lip puckering, finger movements, toe and ankle movements, leg jiggling, or movements of neck, trunk and pelvis. These movements range from mild to severe, and may occur singly or in many combinations.

THALAMUS: the largest subcortical cluster of neurons, located in the middle of the cerebral hemispheres of the brain, that serves to relay and regulate impulses to and from the cerebral cortex.

RESOURCES

TREATMENT RESOURCES AND REFERRALS

Borderline Personality Disorder Resource
    Center
21 Bloomingdale Road
White Plains, NY 10605
000-094-2273
info@bpdresourcecenter.org
www.bpdresourcecenter.org

American Psychiatric Association
1000 Wilson Boulevard
Suite 1825
Arlington, VA 22209-3901
Toll-free: 888-357-7924
703-907-7300
apa@psych.org
www.psych.org

American Academy of Child and Adoles-
    cent Psychiatry, AACAP
3615 Wisconsin Avenue N.W.
Washington, DC 20016-3007
Office: 202-966-7300
Fax: 202-966-2891
www.aacap.org

GENERAL MENTAL HEALTH INFORMATION

The Carter Center Mental Health
    Program
One Copenhill
453 Freedom Parkway
Atlanta, GA 30307
carterweb@emory.edu
www.cartercenter.org

National Institute of Mental Health, NIMH
6001 Executive Blvd.
Room 8184
MSC 9663
Bethesda, MD 20892-9663
Office: 301-443-4513
Fax: 301-443-4279
nimhinfo@nih.gov
www.nimh.nih.gov

ADVOCACY ORGANIZATIONS

National Education Alliance for Borderline
    Personality Disorder, NEA-BPD
P.O. Box 974
Rye, NY 10580
Office: 914-835-9011
NEABPD@aol.com
www.borderlinepersonalitydisorder.com

Treatment and Research Advancements
National Association for Personality
Disorder, TARA NAPD
23 Greene Street
New York, NY 10013
Office: 212-966-6514
TARA4BPD.org

National Alliance for the Mentally Ill,
NAMI
Colonial Place Three
2107 Wilson Blvd.
Suite 300
Arlington, VA 22201-3042
Toll-free: 1-800-950-6264
Office: 703-524-7600
Fax: 703-524-9094
www.nami.org

National Mental Health Association,
NMHA
2001 N. Beauregard Street
12th Floor
Alexandria, VA 22311
Toll-free: 800-969-6642
Office: 703-684-7722
Fax: 703-684-5968
infoctr@nmha.org
www.nmha.org

FEDERAL RESEARCH

National Institute of Mental Health,
NIMH
6001 Executive Blvd.
Room 8184
MSC 9663
Bethesda, MD 20892-9663
Toll-free: 866-615-6464
Office: 301-443-4513
Fax: 301-443-4279
nimhinfo@nih.gov
www.nimh.nih.gov

PRIVATE RESEARCH FOUNDATIONS

Borderline Personality Disorder Research
Foundation
650 Madison Avenue
18th Floor
New York, NY 10022
Office: 212-421-5244
Fax: 212-421-5243
bpdrf.usa@verizon.net

www.borderlineresearch.org

National Alliance for Research of Schizo-
phrenia and Depression, NARSAD
60 Cutter Mill Road
Suite 404
Great Neck, NY 11021
Toll-free: 800-829-8289 (voice mail)
Office: 516-829-0091
Fax: 516-487-6930
info@narsad.org
www.narsad.org

ADDITIONAL INFORMATION SOURCES

BPD Central
P.O. Box 070106
Milwaukee, WI 53207-0106
Toll-free: 888-357-4355 and 800-431-
1579
BPDCentral@aol.com
www.bpdcentral.com

Internet Mental Health, Borderline Personality Disorder
www.mentalhealth.com

MayoClinic
www.mayoclinic.com

MEDLINEplus Health Information
c/o U.S. National Library of Medicine
8600 Rockville Pike
Bethesda, MD 20894
888-346-3656
custserv@nlm.nih.gov
www.medlineplus.gov

Medscape
WebMD Medscape Health Network
224 W. 30th Street
New York, NY 10001-5399
Office: 888-506-6098
www.medscape.com

PubMed
National Library of Medicine
www.ncbi.nih.gov/entrez/query.fcgi?db=
PubMed
custserv@nlm.nih.gov
American Psychiatric Foundation
www.psychfoundation.org

National Survey of Substance Abuse
Treatment Services
www.samhsa.gov/oas/dasis/htm#nssats2

Self-Injury, Abuse & Trauma Resource
Directory
www.self-injury-abuse-trauma-
directory.info

DISABILITY
ASSISTANCE

Americans with Disabilities Act, ADA
U.S. Department of Justice
950 N.W. Pennsylvania Avenue
Civil Rights Division
Disability Rights Section—NYAVE
Washington, DC 20530
Toll-free: 1-800-514-0301
www.usdoj.gov/crt/ada/adahom1.htm

FINANCIAL SUPPORT

Social Security Administration
Office of Public Inquiries
6401 Security Blvd.
Windsor Park Bldg.
Baltimore, MD 21235
Toll-free: 800-772-1213
www.ssa.gov

INFORMATION ON
MEDICATIONS

U.S. Food and Drug Administration
5600 Fishers Lane
Rockville, MD 20857
Toll-free: 888-463-6332
www.fda.gov

LEGAL INFORMATION

Bazelon Center for Mental Health Law
1101 15th Street N.W.
Suite 1212
Washington, DC 20005-5002
Office: 202-467-5730
Fax: 202-223-0409
webmaster@bazelon.org
www.bazelon.org

RESEARCH AND
TREATMENT PROGRAMS

Gerald Adler, MD
Mass. General Hospital
Westend House
16 Lawson Street
Boston, MA 02114
Office: 617-726-2983

Emil F. Coccaro, MD
Dept. of Psychiatry
Eastern Penn. Psychiatric Institute
Medical College of Pennsylvania
3200 Henry Avenue
Philadelphia, PA 19129
Office: 215-842-4192

Karen Conterio
Wendy Lader, PhD
S.A.F.E. Alternatives
MacNeal Hospital
3249 S. Oak Park Avenue
Berwen, IL 60402
Toll-free: 800-366-8288

Rex W. Cowdry, MD
NIMH
Neuroscience Center at St. Elizabeth's
Washington, DC 20032
Office: 202-373-6068

Wayne Fenton, MD
Research Institute
Chestnut Lodge
50 West Montogmery Avenue
Rockville, MD 20850
Office: 301-424-8300

Robert O. Friedel, MD
Department of Psychiatry
Medical College of Virginia, VCU
Nelson Clinic, Suite 200
401 North 11th Street
P.O. Box 980253
Richmond, VA 23298-0253
Office: 804-828-9452
Fax: 804-828-5058
rofriedel@aol.com

Brian Greenfield, MD
Dept. of Psychiatry
Montreal Children's Hospital
2300 Tupper Street
McGill University

Montreal, Quebec H3H 1P3
Canada
Office: 514-412-4400

John Gunderson, MD
McLean Hospital
115 Mill Street
Belmont, MA 02178
Office: 617-855-2293

Warren Jackson, PhD
Borderline Personality Disorder Program
Department of Psychiatry
University of Alabama
1700 7th Avenue South
Birmingham, AL 35294
205-934-4301

Otto Kernberg, MD
New York Hospital
Westchester Division
21 Bloomingdale Road
White Plains, NY 10605
Office: 914-949-8384

Jerold Kriesman, MD
St. John's Mercy Medical Center
Comprehensive Treatment Unit
615 S. New Ballas
St. Louis, MO 63141
Office: 314-997-3443

Marsha M. Linehan, PhD
Dept. of Psychology, NI
University of Washington
Seattle, WA 98195
Office: 206-543-9886

Paul Links, MD
Dept. of Psychiatry
Hamilton General Hospital
327 Barton Street East
Hamilton, ON L8L 2X2
Canada
Office: 416-527-0271

Thomas H. McGlashan, MD
Yale Psychiatric Institute
P.O. Box 12A Yale Station
New Haven, CT 06520
Office: 203-785-7210

John C. Markowitz, MD
Department of Psychiatry

Weill Medical College of Cornell
    University
525 E. 68th Street
New York, NY 10021
Office: 212-543-6283, 212-746-3774

James Masterson, MD
60 Sutton Place South
New York, NY 10022
Office: 212-751-4992

Department of Psychiatry
Mt. Sinai School of Medicine
One Gustave L. Levy Place
New York, NY 10029
www.mssm.edu/psychiatry/mpdp/index.
    shtml

Joel Paris, MD
Dept. of Psychiatry
Research and Training Building
1033 Pine Avenue West
McGill University
Montreal, Quebec H3A 1A1
Canada
Office: 514-398-7293

J. Christopher Perry, MD
The Cambridge Hospital
1493 Cambridge Street
Cambridge, MA 02139
Office: 617-492-8142

Charles P. Peters, MD
Personality Disorder Program
Sheppard & Enoch Pratt Hospital
Towson, MD 21204
Office: 301-823-8200

S. Charles Schulz, MD
Department of Psychiatry
University of Minnesota, Medical School
F282/2A West
2450 Riverside Avenue
Minneapolis, MN 55454
Office: 612-273-9820
Fax: 612-273-9817

Larry J. Siever, MD
Department of Psychiatry
Bronx VA Medical Center
130 W. Knightsbridge Road
Bronx, NY 10468
Office: 212-584-1825

Kenneth R. Silk, MD
Department of Psychiatry
University of Michigan 0120
1500 E. Medical Center Drive
UH 9150 9C
Ann Arbor, MI 48109
Office: 313-936-4944

Paul Soloff, MD
Western Psychiatric Institute and Clinic
3811 O'Hara Street
Room 868
Pittsburgh, PA 15213
Office: 412-624-2046

SUBSTANCE ABUSE

National Clearinghouse for Alcohol and
    Drug Information, NCADI
P.O. Box 2345
Rockville, MD 20847-2345
Toll-free: 800-729-6686
Office: 301-468-2600
Fax: 301-468-6433
infor@health.org
www.health.org

Substance Abuse and Mental Health
    Information Center, SAMHSA
National Mental Health Information Cen-
    ter, CMHS
P.O. Box 42490
Washington, DC 20015
Toll-free: 800-789-2647
ken@mentalhealth.org
www.mentalhealth.org

REFERENCES

INTRODUCTION

American Psychiatric Association: Practice guideline for the treatment of patients with borderline personality disorder. *Am J Psychiatry* 2001; 158 (October supplement).

Gunderson JG. *Borderline Personality Disorder: A Clinical Guide.* Washington, DC: American Psychiatric Publishing 2001.

Hyman SE. A new beginning for research on borderline personality disorder. *Biol Psychiatry* 2002; 51:933–935.

CHAPTER 1: WHAT IS BORDERLINE PERSONALITY DISORDER AND HOW IS IT DIAGNOSED?

Group 1: Emotional Dysregulation

Akiskal HS. The temperamental borders of affective disorders. *Acta Psychiatr Scand* 1994; 379 (supplement):32–37.

Deltito J, Martin L, Riefkohl J, Austria B, Kissilenko A, Corless C, Morse P. Do patients with borderline personality disorder belong to the bipolar spectrum? *J Affect Disord* 2001; 67:221–228.

Herpertz SC. Emotional processing in personality disorder. *Curr Psychiatry Rep* 2003; 5:23–27.

Pukrop R. Dimensional personality profiles of borderline personality disorder in comparison with other personality disorders and healthy controls. *J Personal Disord* 2002; 16:135–147.

Sanislow CA, Grilo CM, McGlashan TH. Factor analysis of the DSM-III-R borderline personality disorder criteria in psychiatric inpatients. *Am J Psychiatry* 2000; 157:1629–1633.

Shearin EN, Linehan NM. Dialectical behavior therapy for borderline personality disorder: theoretical and empirical foundations. *Acta Psychiatr Scand* 1994; 379 (supplement):61–68.

Skodol AE, Gunderson JG, Pfohl B, Widiger TA, Livesley WJ, Siever LJ. The borderline diagnosis I: psychopathology, comorbidity, and personality structure. *Biol Psychiatry* 2002; 51:936–950.

Zanarini MC, Frankenburg FR, LeLuca CJ, Hennese J, Khera GS, Gunderson JG. The pain of being borderline: dysphoric states specific to borderline personality disorder. *Harv Rev Psychiatry* 1998; 6:201–207.

Group 2: Impulsivity

Goodman M, New A. Impulsive aggression in borderline personality disorder. *Curr Psychiatry Rep* 2000; 2:56–61

Henry C, Mitropoulou V, New AS, Koenigsberg HW, Silverman J, Siever LJ. Affective instability and impulsivity in borderline personality and bipolar II disorders: similarities and differences. *J Psychiatr Res* 2001; 35:307–312.

Links PS, Heslegrave R, van Reekum R. Impulsivity: core aspect of borderline personality disorder. *J Personal Disord* 1999; 13:1-9.

Paris J. Chronic suicidality among patients with borderline personality disorder. *Psychiatric Services* 2002; 53:738–742.

Sanislow CA, Grilo CM, Morey LC, Bender DS, Skodol AE, Gunderson JG, Shea T, Stout RL, Zanarini MC, McGlashan TH. Confirmatory factor analysis of DSM-IV criteria for borderline personality disorder: findings from the collaborative longitudinal personality disorders study. *Am J Psychiatry* 2002; 159:284–290.

Group 3: Cognitive Dysfunction

Arntz A, Appels C, Sierwerda S. Hypervigilence in borderline disorder: a test with the emotional Stroop paradigm. *J Personal Disord* 2000; 14:366–373.

O'Leary KM. Borderline personality disorder; neuropsychological testing results. *Psychiatric Clin North Am* 2000; 23:41–60.

O'Leary KM, Cowdry RW. Neuropsychological testing results in borderline personality disorder. In Silk KR, ed., *Biological and Behavioral Studies of Borderline Personality Disorder.* Washington, DC: American Psychiatric Press 1994; 127–157.

Group 4: Impaired Relationships

Gunderson, JG. *Borderline Personality Disorder: A Clinical Guide.* Washington, DC: American Psychiatric Publishing 2001.

Judd PH, McGlashan TH. *A Developmental Model of Borderline Personality Disorder: Understanding Variations in Course and Outcome.* Washington, DC: American Psychiatric Publishing 2003.

Koenigsberg HW, Harvey PD, Mitropoulou V, New AS, Goodman M, Silverman J, Serby M, Schopick F, Siever LJ. Are the interpersonal and identity disturbances in the borderline personality disorder criteria linked to the traits of affective instability and impulsivity? *J Personal Disord* 2001; 15:358–370.

Skodol AE, Siever LJ, Livesley WJ, Gunderson JG, Pfohl B, Widiger TA. The borderline diagnosis II: biology, genetics, and clinical course. *Biol Psychiatry* 2002; 51:951–963.

CHAPTER 3: THE HISTORY OF BORDERLINE PERSONALITY DISORDER

American Psychiatric Association: *Diagnostic and Statistical Manual of Mental Disorders*, 3rd Edition. Washington, DC, American Psychiatric Publishing 1980.

Grinker R, Werble B, Drye R: *The Borderline Syndrome: A Behavioral Study of Ego Functions.* New York, Basic Books 1968.

Gunderson J. *Borderline Personality Disorder: A Clinical Guide*. Washington, DC: American Psychiatric Publishing 2001.

Gunderson J, Singer M: Defining borderline patients: an overview. *Am J Psychiatry* 1975; 132:1–10.

Kernberg OF: Borderline personality organization. *J Am Psychoanal Assoc* 1967; 15:641–685.

Knight RP: Borderline states. *Bulletin of the Menninger Clinic* 1953; 17:1–12.

Millon T: The borderline construct: introductory notes on its history, theory, and empirical grounding. In: Clarkin JF, Marziali E, Munroe-Blum H, ed., *Borderline Personality Disorder, Clinical and Empirical Perspectives.* The Guilford Press: New York 1992.

Skodol AE, Gunderson JG, Pfohl, B, Wideger TA, Livesley WJ, Siever LJ: The borderline diagnosis I: psychopathology comorbidity, and personality structure. *Biol Psychiatry* 2002; 51:936–950.

Spitzer RL, Endicott J, Gibbon M: Crossing the border into borderline personality and borderline schizophrenia. The development of criteria. *Arch Gen Psychiatry* 1979; 36:17–24.

Stern A: Psychoanalytic investigation of and therapy in the borderline group of neuroses. *Psychoanal Q* 7:467–489, 1938.

CHAPTER 4: WHAT ARE THE CAUSES?

Gunderson, JG. *Borderline personality disorder: a clinical guide.* Washington, DC: American Psychiatric Publishing 2001.

Judd PH, McGlashan TH. *A Developmental Model of Borderline Personality Disorder: Understanding Variations in Course and Outcome.* Washington, DC: American Psychiatric Publishing 2003.

Millon T: Sociocultural conceptions of the borderline personality. In: Paris J., ed., *The Psychiatric Clinics of North America* 2000; 23:123–136.

Paris J: Childhood precursors of borderline personality disorder. *Psychiatric Clin North Am* 2000; 23:77–88.

Reich DB, Zanarini MC. Developmental aspects of borderline personality disorder. *Harv Rev Psychiatry* 2001; 9:294–301.

Skodol AE, Siever LJ, Livesley WJ, Gunderson JG, Pfohl B, Widiger TA. The borderline diagnosis II: biology, genetics, and clinical course. *Biol Psychiatry* 2002; 51:951–963.

Soloff PH, Lynch KG, Kelly TM. Childhood abuse as a risk factor for suicidal behavior in borderline personality disorder. *J Personal Disord* 2002; 16:201–214.

Torgersen S, Lygren S, Oien, PA, Skre I, Onstad S, Edvardsen J, Tambs K, Kringlen E: A twin study of personality disorders. *Compr Psychiatry* 2000; 41:416–425.

Trull TJ. Structural relations between borderline personality disorder features and putative etiological correlates. *J Abnorm Psychol* 2001; 110:471–481.

Zanarini MC, Frankenburg FR, Reich DB, Marino MF, Lewis RE, Williams AA, Khera GS. Biparental failure in the childhood experiences of borderline patients. *J Personal Disord* 2000; 14:264–273.

Zanarini MC. Childhood experiences associated with the development of borderline personality disorder. *Psychiatric Clin North Am* 2000; 23:89–101.

CHAPTER 5: TRACING THE COURSE OF THE DISORDER

Becker DF, Grilo CM, Edel WS, McGlashan TH. Diagnostic efficiency of borderline personality disorder criteria in hospitalized adolescents: comparison with hospitalized adults. *Am J Psychiatr* 2002; 159:2042–2047.

Garnet KE, Levy KN, Mattanah JJF, Edell WS, McGlashan TH. Borderline personality disorder in adolescents: ubiquitous or specific? *Am J Psychiatry* 1994; 151:1380–1382.

Gunderson JG, Bender D, Sanislow C, Yen S, Rettew JB, Dolan-Sewell R, Dyck I, Morey LC, McGlashan TH, Shea MT, Skodol AE. Plausibility and possible determinants of sudden "remissions" in borderline patients. *Psychiatry* 2003; 66:11–119.

Judd PH, McGlashan TH. *A Developmental Model of Borderline Personality Disorder: Understanding Variations in Course and Outcome.* Washington, DC: American Psychiatric Publishing 2003.

Links PS, Heslegrave RJ. Prospective studies of outcome; understanding mechanisms of change in patients with borderline personality disorder. In Paris J., ed., *The Psychiatric Clinics of North America* 2000; 23:137–150.

Ludolph PS, Westen D, Misle B, Jackson A, Wixom J, Wiss FC. The borderline diagnosis in adolescents: symptoms and developmental history. *Am J Psychiatry* 1990; 147:470–476.

Paris J, Brown R, Nowlis D. Long-term follow-up of borderline patients in a general hospital. *Compr Psychiatry* 1987; 28:530–536.

Seivewright H, Tyrer P, Johnson T. Change in personality status in neurotic disorders. *Lancet* 2002; 359:2253–2254.

Stevenson J, Meares R, Comerford A. Diminished impulsivity in older patients with borderline personality disorder. *Am J Psychiatry* 2003; 160:165–166.

Zanarini MC, Frankenburg FR, Hennen J, Silk KR. The longitudinal course of borderline psychopathology: 6-year prospective follow-up of the phenomenology of borderline personality disorder. *Am J Psychiatry* 2003; 160:274–283.

CHAPTER 6: BORDERLINE PERSONALITY DISORDER AND THE BRAIN

American Psychiatric Association: Practice Guideline for the Treatment of Patients with Borderline Personality Disorder. *Am J Psychiatry* 2001; 158 (October supplement).

Bohus M, Schmahl C, Lieb K: New developments in the neurobiology of borderline personality disorder. *Curr Psych Reports* 2004; 6:43–50.

De la Fuente JM, Goldman S, Stanus E, Vizuete C, Morlan I, Bobes J, Mendlewicz J: Brain glucose metabolism in borderline personality disorder. *J Psychiatr Res* 1997; 31:531–541.

Donegan NH, Sanislow CA, Blumberg HP, Fulbright RK, Lacadie C, Skudlarski P, Gore JC, Olson IR, McGlashan TH, Wexler BE: Amygdala hyperreactivity in borderline personality disorder: implications for emotional dysregulation. *Biol Psychiatry* 2003 54:1284–1293.

Friedel RO: Dopamine dysfunction in borderline personality disorder: a hypothesis. *Neuropsychopharmacology*. 2004; 29: 1029–1039.

Gurvits IG, Koenigsberg HW, Siever LJ. Neurotransmitter dysfunction in patients with borderline personality disorder. *Psychiatric Clin North Am* 2000; 23:27–40.

Herpertz SC, Dietrich TM, Wenning B, Krings T, Erberich SG, Willmes K, Thron A, Sass H. Evidence of abnormal amygdala functioning in borderline personality disorder: a functional MRI study. *Biol Psychiatry* 2001; 50:292–298.

LeDoux J. *The Emotional Brain*. New York: Touchstone 1996.

LeDoux J. *Synaptic Self: How Our Brains Become Who We Are*. New York: Viking Penguin 2002.

Leyton M, Okazawa H, Diksic M, Paris J, Ross P, Mzengeza S, Young SN, Blier P, Benkelfat C. Brain regional alpha-(11C)methyl-L-tryptophan trapping in impulsive subjects with borderline personality disorder. *Am J Psychiatry* 2001; 158:775-782.

O'Leary KM. Borderline personality disorder; neuropsychological testing results. *Psychiatric Clin North Am* 2000; 23:41–60.

Paris J, ed. *Borderline Personality Disorder: Etiology and Treatment*. Washington, DC: American Psychiatric Press 1993.

Silk KR: Borderline personality disorder: overview of biological factors. *Psychiatric Clin North Am* 2000; 23:61–76.

Skodol AE, Siever LJ, Livesley WJ, Gunderson JG, Pfohl B, Widiger TA: The borderline diagnosis II: biology, genetics, and clinical course. *Biol Psychiatry* 2002; 51:951–963.

Soloff PH, Meltzer CC, Greer PJ, Constantine D, Kelly TM: A fenfluramine-activated FDG-PET study of borderline personality disorder. *Biol Psychiatry* 2000; 47:540–547.

Tebartz van Elst L, Theil T, Hesslinger B, Lieb K, Bohus M, Henning J, Ebert D. Subtle prefrontal neuropathology in a pilot magnetic resonance spectroscopy study in patients with borderline personality disorder. *J Neuropsychiatry Clin Neurosci* 2001; 13:511-514.

CHAPTER 7: COMMON CO-OCCURRING DISORDERS

Aldenkamp AP, De Krom M, Reijs R. Newer antiepileptic drugs and cognitive issues. *Epilepsia* 2003; 44 Suppl 4:21–29.

Becker DF, Grilo CM, Edell WS, McGlashan TH. Comorbidity of borderline personality disorder with other personality disorders in hospitalized adolescents and adults. *Am J Psychiatry* 2000; 157(12):2011–2016.

Deltito J, Martin L, Riefkohl J, Austria B, Kissilenko A, Corless C, Morse P. Do patients with borderline personality disorder belong to the bipolar spectrum? *J Affect Disord* 2001; 67:221–228.

Golier JA, Yehuda R, Bierer LM, Mitropoulou V, New AS, Schmeidler J, Silverman JM, Siever LJ. The relationship of borderline personality disorder to posttraumatic stress disorder and traumatic events. *Am J Psychiatry* 2003; 160:2018–2024.

Johnson BA, Ait-Daoud N, Bowden CL, DiClemente CC, Roache JD, Lawson K, Javors MA, Ma JZ. Oral topiramate for treatment of alcohol dependence: a randomized controlled trial. *Lancet* 2003; 361:1677–1685.

Oldham JM, Skodol AE, Kellman HD, Hyler SE, Doidge N, Rosnick L, Gallaher PE. Comorbidity of axis I and axis II disorders. *Am J Psychiatry* 1995; 152:571–578.

Skodol AE, Oldham JM, Gallaher PE. Axis II comorbidity of substance use disorders among patients referred for treatment of personality disorders. *Am J Psychiatry* 1999; 156:733–738.

Zanarini MC, Frankenburg FR, Dubo ED, Sickel AE, Trikha A, Levin A, Reynolds V. Axis I comorbidity of borderline personality disorder. *Am J Psychiatry* 1998; 155:1733–1739.

Zanarini MC, Frankenburg FR, Dubo ED, Sickel AE, Trikha A, Levi A, Reynolds V. Axis II comorbidity of borderline personality disorder. *Compr Psychiatry* 1998; 39(5):296–302.

Zimmerman M, Mattia JI. Axis I diagnostic comorbidity and border-line personality disorder. *Compr Psychiatry* 1999; 40(4):245–52.

CHAPTER 8: THE KEY ELEMENTS OF TREATMENT

American Psychiatric Association: Practice Guideline for the Treatment of Patients with borderline Personality Disorder. *Am J Psychiatry* 2001; 158 (October supplement).

Fossati A, Novella L, Donati D, Donini M, Maffei C. History of child-hood attention deficit/hyperactivity disorder symptoms and border-line personality disorder: a controlled study. *Compr Psychiatry* 2002; 43(5): 369–377.

Gunderson, JG. *Borderline Personality Disorder: A Clinical Guide*. Wash-ington, DC: American Psychiatric Publishing 2001.

Judd PH, McGlashan TH. *A Developmental Model of Borderline Personal-ity Disorder: Understanding Variations in Course and Outcome*. Washing-ton, DC: American Psychiatric Publishing 2003.

CHAPTER 9: MEDICATIONS

American Psychiatric Association: Practice Guideline for the Treatment of Patients with Borderline Personality Disorder. *Am J Psychiatry* 2001; 158 (October supplement).

Brinkley JR, Beltman BD, Friedel RO. Low-dose neuroleptic regimens in the treatment of borderline patients. *Arch Gen Pschiatry* 1979; 36:319–326.

Soloff PH. Psychopharmacology of borderline personality disorder. *Psy-chiatric Clin North Am* 2000; 23:169–192.

Zanarini M: Update on pharmacotherapy of borderline personality dis-order. *Curr Psych Reports* 2004; 6:66–70.

American Psychiatric Association: Practice Guideline for the Treatment of Patients With Borderline Personality Disorder. *Am J Psychiatry* 2001; 158 (October supplement).

Bateman A, Fonagy P. Treatment of borderline personality disorder with psychoanalytically oriented partial hospitalization: an 18-month follow-up. *Am J Psychiatry* 2001; 158:36–42.

Beck AT, Freeman A, Davis DD and Associates. *Cognitive Therapy of Personality Disorders*; Second Edition. New York: Guilford Press 2003.

Blum N, Pfohl B, John DS, Monahan P, Black DW. STEPPS: a cognitive-behavioral systems-based group treatment for outpatients with borderline personality disorder—a preliminary report. *Compr Psychiatry* 2002; 43:301–310.

Gunderson, JG. *Borderline Personality Disorder: A Clinical Guide*. Washington, DC: American Psychiatric Publishing 2001.

Hoffman PD, Fruzzetti AE, Swenson CR. Dialectical behavior therapy—family skills training. *Fam Process* 1999; 38:399–414.

Hooley JM, Hoffman PD. Expressed emotions and clinical outcome in borderline personality disorder. *Am J Psychiatry* 1999; 156:1557–1562.

Koerner K, Linehan MM. Research on dialectical behavior therapy for patients with borderline personality disorder. *Psychiatric Clin North Am* 2000; 23:151–167.

Linehan MM. *Cognitive Behavioral Treatment of Borderline Personality Disorder*. New York: Guilford Press 1993.

Livesley WJ. A practical approach to the treatment of patients with borderline personality disorder. *Psychiatric Clin North Am* 2000; 23:211–232.

Miller BC. Characteristics of effective day treatment programming for persons with borderline personality disorder. *Psychiatric Services* 1995; 46:605–608.

Robins CJ, Chapman AL. Dialectical behavior therapy: current status, recent developments and future directions. *J Personal Disord* 2004; 18:73–89.

Roller B, Nelson V. Group psychotherapy treatment of borderline personalities. *Int J Group Psychother* 1999; 49:369–385.

Stone MH. Clinical guidelines for psychotherapy for patients with borderline personality disorder. *Psychiatric Clin North Am* 2000; 23:193–210.

CHAPTER 11: BORDERLINE PERSONALITY DISORDER IN CHILDREN

Bemporad JR, Smith HF, Hanson G, Cicchetti D: Borderline syndromes in childhood: criteria for diagnosis. *Am J Psychiatry* 1982; 139:596–602.

Cohen DJ, Paul R, Volmar FR: Issues in the classification of pervasive and other developmental disorders: toward DSM-IV. *J Am Acad Child Psychiatry* 1986; 25:213–220.

Green RW. *The Explosive Child.* New York: HarperCollins Publishers 2001.

Greenman DA, Gunderson JG, Cane M, Saltzman PR: An examination of the borderline diagnosis in children. *Am J Psychiatry* 1986; 143:998–1003.

Guzder J, Paris J, Zelkowitz P, Marchessault K: Risk factors for borderline pathology in children. *J Am Acad Child Adolesc Psychiatry* 1996; 35:26–33.

Lincoln AJ, Bloom D, Katz M, Boksenbaum N: Neuropsychological and neurophysiological indices of auditory processing impairment in children with multiple complex developmental disorder. *J Am Acad Child Adolesc Psychiatry* 1998 37:100–112.

Lofgren DP, Bemporad J, King J, Lindem K, O'Driscoll G: A prospective follow-up study of so-called borderline children. *Am J Psychiatry* 1991; 148:1541–1547.

Paris J: Childhood precursors of borderline personality disorder. *Psychiatr Clin North Am* 2000; 23:77–88.

Paris J, Zelkowitz P, Guzder J, Joseph S, Feldman R: Neurophyshological factors associated with borderline pathology in children. *J Am Acad Child Adolesc Psychiatry* 1999; 38:770–774.

Zanarini MC: Childhood experiences associated with the development of borderline personality disorder. *Psychiatr Clin North Am* 2000; 23:89–101.

Zelkowitz P, Paris J, Guzder J, Feldman R: Diatheses and stressors in borderline pathology of childhood: the role of neuropsychological risk and trauma. *J Am Acad Child Adolesc Psychiatry* 2001 40:100–105.

CHAPTER 12: WHEN A LOVED ONE HAS BORDERLINE PERSONALITY DISORDER

Gunderson, JG. *Borderline Personality Disorder: A Clinical Guide.* Washington, DC: American Psychiatric Publishing 2001.

Gunderson JG, Berkowitz C, Ruiz-Sancho A. Families of borderline patients: a psychoeducational approach. *Bull Menninger Clin* 1997; 61:446–457.

Gunderson JG, Lyoo IK. Family problems and relationships for adults with borderline personality disorder. *Harv Rev Psychiatry* 1997; 4:272–278.

Hoffman PD, Fruzzetti AE, Swenson CR. Dialectical behavior therapy—family skills training. *Fam Process* 1999; 38:399–414.

Hooley JM, Hoffman PD. Expressed emotion and clinical outcome in borderline personality disorder. *Am J Psychiatry* 1999; 156:1557–1562.

Judd PH, McGlashan TH. *A Developmental Model of Borderline Personality Disorder: Understanding Variations in Course and Outcome.* Washington, DC: American Psychiatric Publishing 2003.

Mason PT, Kreger R. *Stop Walking on Eggshells.* Oakland, CA: New Harbinger Publications, Inc. 1998.

Weiss M, Zelkowitz P, Feldman RB, Vogel J, Heyman M, Paris J. Psychopathology in offspring of mothers with borderline personality disorder: a pilot study. *Can J Psychiatry* 1996; 41:285–290.

Zweig-Frank H, Paris J. Predictors of outcome in a 27-year follow-up of patients with borderline personality disorder. *Compr Psychiatry* 2002; 43:103–107.

Chapter 13: Research:
The Ultimate Reason for Hope

Hyman SE. A new beginning for research on borderline personality disorder. *Biol Psychiatry* 2002; 51:933–935.

Siever LJ, Torgersen JG, Gunderson W, Livesley W, Kendler, KS. The borderline diagnosis III: identifying endophenotypes for genetic studies. *Biol Psychiatry* 2002; 51:964–968.

Skodol AE, Gunderson JG, Pfohl, B, Wideger TA, Livesley WJ, Siever LJ: The borderline diagnosis I: psychopathology comorbidity, and personality structure. *Biol Psychiatry* 2002; 51:936–950.

Skodol AE, Siever LJ, Livesley WJ, Gunderson JG, Pfohl B, Widiger TA. The borderline diagnosis II: biology, genetics, and clinical course. *Biol Psychiatry* 2002; 51:951–963.

ACKNOWLEDGMENTS

I AM VERY grateful to Perry Hoffman, Dixianne Penney, and Patricia Woodward at the National Education Alliance for Borderline Personality Disorder. Their encouragement to expand my handout to my patients with borderline disorder to book length initiated work on this book. They also reviewed a number of versions of the manuscript and provided many helpful suggestions. I also thank them for writing the Foreword.

My daughter, Karin Bunting, prepared most of the manuscript. She made numerous contributions to many of the central ideas and concepts in the book. She also read the material carefully for consistencies of content, style, and grammatical accuracy, and overlooked the idiosyncrasies of my writing habits. I cannot overstate her contributions or thank her adequately.

My wife, Sue, and another daughter, Linda Cox, read over chapters that were especially challenging, and helped me to think them through more clearly. Their knowledge and insights were of great help.

Dr. Bernard Beitman read a very early version of the manuscript and pointed out areas where much additional work was needed.

I am very appreciative of the advice from many of my patients with borderline disorder, and their families, on how the original handouts could be improved to be of more help to them. Without the trust of my patients, and the candid accounts of their symptoms and their lives, I would not have had the inspiration to either begin or complete this project.

Although I have written articles and books for the medical literature during my career, this was my first venture into publishing for a wider audience. I thought it would be a long and arduous task to locate a publisher. However, my agent, Katherine Boyle, who probably creates miracles on a routine basis, located Sue McCloskey at Marlowe & Company in what seemed like days. Katie believed in the book from the beginning.

It has been a great pleasure to work with a professional editor. Sue McCloskey provided me with a tremendous amount of guidance on the inclusion of relevant topics, on structuring the book properly, and in using phrasing that is understandable.

I thank my sister Beatrice for reading my account of some details of our sister Denise's life and experiences with borderline disorder, and for writing some of her own memories and perceptions.

Finally, I am continually grateful to my deceased father and mother, August and Denise. Their boundless love, high values, and tireless efforts provided my sisters, brothers, and me with the encouragement and means to achieve the most we could. There are no greater gifts that parents can give to their children.

INDEX

childhood separations, 68
child psychiatrists, 179–80
children
    ADHD in, 171–72
    affect of risk factors on brains of,
        71–72
    biological risk factors in, 175–76
    borderline disorder in, 161–82
        defining, 164–69
        diagnosis of, 174
        evaluating, 177–79
        importance of early detection
            of, 174–75
        research on, 164–69
    conduct disorder in, 170–71
    effects on, of mother with
        borderline disorder, 187–88
    environmental risk factors in,
        176–77
    explosive child, 172–74
    finding professional help for,
        179–80
    medications for, 169, 180
    multiple complex developmental
        disorder (MCDD) in, 167–69
    oppositional defiant disorder in,
        169–70
    psychotherapy for, 181
    symptoms in, 161–62, 165
cognitive behavioral therapy (CBT),
    109, 116, 154–55, 159
Cohen, Donald, 166–67, 169
Collaborative Longitudinal
    Personality Disorder Study
    (CLPS), 83–84
conditioned fear responses, 97
conduct disorder, 170–71
co-occurring disorders, 105–28
    anxiety and panic disorders,
        115–18
    attention deficit hyperactivity
        disorder (ADHD), 120–23,
        171–72, 214
    eating disorders, 119–20
    importance of, 127–28

mood disorders, 106–12
personality disorders, 123–27
substance-related disorders,
    112–15
coping strategies, 185

D
DBT (Dialectical Behavior
    Therapy), 155–56, 159
delusions, 214
dependent personality disorder, 126
depersonalization, 14
depression. See major depressive
    disorder
developmental risk factors, 67–68
diabetes, 65
diagnosis
    in children, 164–69, 174
    dimensional approach to, 58–60
    strategies for, 201–2
Diagnostic and Statistical Manual of
    Mental Disorders (APA), 19–20,
    56, 106
diagnostic criteria, 19–20, 48, 55–60
Diagnostic Interview for Borderline
    Patients (DIB), 56
Dialectical Behavior Therapy
    (DBT), 155–56, 159
dissociative episodes, 14, 90, 214
dopamine, 93, 98, 138, 141, 214
dopamine modulatory pathways, 103
dopaminergic activity, 103, 214
dorsolateral prefrontal
    cortex/circuits, 101–2, 104, 214
drug use. See substance-related
    disorders
dysthymic disorder, 106, 108–9

E
eating disorders, 119–20, 144
ego functions, 53, 214
ego psychology, 53, 214
electroconvulsive therapy (ECT),
    27–28
emotional abuse, 69

emotional lability, 3, 89, 214

emotional responses, disproportional, 88–89

emotions
anger, 5
anxiety, 4
conditioned fear responses, 97
delayed return of, to normal state, 89
feelings of emptiness, 5–6
hyperreactive, 3
memory and, 92, 98–99
mood swings, 3–4, 89
motivation/reward pathways and, 97–98
neural systems of, 94–99
poorly regulated, 2–6, 76, 88–89
unstable, 3–4

empirical research, 55, 197–99, 214

emptiness, feelings of, 5–6

endocrines, 97

environmental risk factors
affect of, on brain, 71–72
in children, 176–77
early separations/loss, 68
ineffective parenting, 69
interaction of, with biological risk factors, 72–74
research on, 203
social-cultural, 69–71
trauma, 69

epidemiological issues, 201

etiology, 59, 215

explosive child disorder, 172–74

F

factitious illness, 9–10, 215

families
advice for, 183–96
effects of borderline disorder on, 187–90
guidelines for, 190–96
view of, of borderline disorder, 186–87

family programs, 157–58, 160

Fatal Attraction (film), 8–9

fear responses, conditioned, 97

feelings. *See* emotions

Freud, Sigmund, 47

G

gamma aminobutyric acid (GABA), 93, 143–44, 146, 215

genetic risk factors, 66–67, 202–3

glutamate, 93, 143–44, 146, 215

Greene, Ross, 172, 181

Greenman, Deborah, 166

grief, stages of, 189

Grinker, Roy, 55

group therapy, 130, 156–57

Gunderson, John, 55, 131–32, 166, 187

Gunderson/Lyoo study, 187

H

hallucinations, 14, 215

Heslegrave, Ronald, 84

hippocampal formation, 98, 215

histrionic personality disorder, 57, 125, 215

Hoffman, Perry, 192

Hyman, Stephen, 207

hyperactivity, 122

hyperreactive, 3, 215

hypersensitivity, 51

hypomanic episodes, 110, 111

I

illegal drug use, 112–15, 144

illness, factitious, 9–10, 215

impaired perception/reasoning, 12–16, 90
in adolescents, 77
depersonalization, 14
dissociative episodes, 14
magical thinking, 14
paranoid thinking, 13–14
unstable self-image, 15–16

impulse control, neural systems of, 99–100

impulsive behavior, 6–12, 89–90